ENDYMION PORTER

ENDYMION PORTER

THE LIFE OF A COURTIER
1587 – 1649

GERVAS HUXLEY

'Tho' obscure, yet he was a great man
and beloved of two Kings, James I for
his admirable wit and Charles I (to
whom he was a servant) for his general
learning, brave stile, sweet temper,
great experience, travels and modern
languages.'
ANTHONY WOOD

1959
CHATTO & WINDUS
LONDON

Published by
Chatto and Windus Ltd
42 William IV Street
London WC2

*

Clarke Irwin & Co. Ltd.
Toronto

Printed in Great Britain by
Ebenezer Baylis & Son Ltd
Worcester and London

For
ELSPETH & CHARLES
Endymion's descendants

Contents

Illustrations

Author's Note

IN January 1642, Endymion Porter rode hurriedly away from London with the King, leaving his house in the Strand, which he was not to see again for seven years. Since he was an object of Parliament's deep suspicion, his house was entered and all the papers found there removed to be searched for anything which might be considered treasonable in Parliament's eyes. The search must have been fruitless, since the papers were mostly of the kind that any devoted family man, in any age, might have hoarded as reminders of his past life. There were early letters to his wife, letters about the children, his eldest son's first Latin essay, his second son's last letter before his tragic death and so on. There was, too, recent business correspondence with his steward, and the steward's own letters and some household bills and laundry lists—the sort of oddments that accumulate in all our desks. Nevertheless, the confiscated papers were not returned to the family, but were deposited in the State Paper Office which had been founded in Queen Elizabeth's day. The papers are now among the Domestic State Papers in the Public Records Office. They have provided the foundation for this book, although there are also to be found many other contemporary references and letters to and from Endymion Porter in other historical manuscripts and records.

The references at the end of the book give the sources from which the biographical and background material has been directly taken. Where such material has been calendared the references, for ease and uniformity, are to the calendar, although the full documents have been frequently used and quoted. In the case of books, the full name and date of publication have been given for the first citing;

thereafter an abbreviated title has been used. Many other works have, of course, been consulted and no student of the period can fail to acknowledge his debt to S. R. Gardiner's volumes on the reigns of James I and Charles I and on the Civil War.

In the seventeenth century the calendar year started on March 25th, but I have adopted the modern system of starting the calendar year on January 1st. A further complication in the seventeenth century was that, in most of the countries of Europe, the calendar had already been reformed, so that dates were ten days ahead of England. I have used the English dates. The spelling in letters and quotations has been modernized.

I am greatly indebted to many friends for help and guidance, especially to Miss C. V. Wedgwood, Dr. David Mathew, Mr. Gerald Aylmer and Mr. John P. Feil for their good advice and suggestions; to Mr. Noel Blakiston and his staff at the Public Records Office for much invaluable assistance; above all, to Mr. Oliver Millar both for his generosity in placing his expert knowledge of the art of the period unreservedly at my disposal and also for reading my manuscript. I am also indebted to the Earl of Harrowby, Miss Hamilton and Miss Calley for very kindly allowing me to see and use documents in their possession. Finally, I wish to record my thanks to the staff of the London Library, to Miss Eileen Stiff, Librarian of the Athenaeum Club, for her patient help in finding so many of the books consulted, and to Mrs. Phillips-Birt for her indefatigable labour in deciphering and typing my MSS.

CHAPTER I

(i)

A MILE or so west of the little Cotswold town of Chipping Campden in the north-west corner of Gloucestershire, the land falls sharply down to the Vale of Evesham and the wide midland plain. At the foot of the escarpment, among fields and orchards, lie the adjacent villages of Mickleton and Aston-sub-Edge. Here, in the gabled grey stone Manor House of Mickleton, Endymion Porter was born some time in 1587.[1]

The Porters had originally come from Warwickshire, but a Richard Porter was settled at Mickleton at the end of the fifteenth century and owned land in Campden. The Charity he established in 1513 still survives. It gave lands for the repair of Mickleton Church, for the salary of a schoolmaster and for the relief of the poor.[2] Richard Porter's son, Sir William, was Serjeant at Arms to Henry VII and accompanied Henry VIII to the French Wars in 1513.[3] Apart from this Sir William, the Porter family had no claim to distinction, though locally they were people of some consequence, owning the Manor of Aston-sub-Edge, land and houses at Campden and elsewhere in the neighbourhood, and occupying, on long leases, the Manor of Mickleton, which had belonged to the Abbey of Eynsham.

At the time of Endymion's birth, Sir William's great-grandson, Nicholas, was the head of the family. He seems to have restored some of the family fortunes which had been so crippled by the payment of his grandfather Antony's debts and by law-suits that his father, William, had 'died in misery'.[4] William had even been forced, in 1568, to sell the Manor of Aston-sub-Edge,[5] but Nicholas bought it back twenty years later,[6] and lived there with his wife and children. Nicholas had also inherited the Mickleton leaseholds of the manor, parsonage and lands.[7] Edmund—his younger brother and Endymion's father—occupied Mickleton Manor house, with the wife he had recently married. She was Angela, one of the two daughters of his father's first cousin, Giles Porter.

The career and connections of Giles Porter were to exercise an all-important influence on his grandson Endymion's life. Somewhere about 1560, Giles had gone to Spain, probably as a member of an English embassy, and had married a Spanish wife. She was Dona Juana de Figueroa y Mont Salve, a member of a noble and distinguished family. Giles seems to have made his home in Spain, though sometimes visiting England. In 1583, Mendoza, the Spanish Ambassador in London, wrote to King Philip that he had managed to get an English gentleman named Giles Porter on board an English ship bound for Syria. Mendoza added that Porter 'is married in Seville and is a good Catholic and a faithful adherent of Your Majesty'. Giles had made a vow, which he fulfilled, to visit Jerusalem and had apparently accepted Mendoza's suggestion that he should report on English doings in the Levant.[8] Giles's children were brought up in Spain and his son, Luis, entered the Spanish diplomatic service, adding his mother's surname to his own and calling himself Porter de Figueroy. He came to England in 1610, with the new Spanish Ambassador, Velasco, and the English Embassy in Madrid thought that he might be used to help uncover a red-headed young Jesuit who had secretly entered England.[9] Early in 1612, Luis was living in Brussels, apparently in the Archduke's service. From there he wrote to his brother-in-law Edmund Porter to announce that he would shortly be paying a visit to Mickleton, bringing with him a hawk from one of the Archduke's falconers and hoping, in exchange, to take back a good water dog, for the lack of which he was losing half the game he killed.[10]

His father Giles, had, however, come back about 1585 to

live in England. He rented a house in Mickleton[11] and brought home his wife and two daughters, one of whom, Angela, soon married her cousin Edmund.

There are no records to suggest why Edmund and Angela should have named their first-born child after the young shepherd loved by the Goddess of the Moon. Perhaps the name came from their Canning relations who had an Endymion in their family. Edmund and Angela's other children had no such fanciful names—Thomas, Edmund, Giles, Eleanor, Mary, Jane and Margaret.

Endymion's childhood was spent at Mickleton and Aston, where the Porters lived the normal life of the small country gentry, occupied with farming, with country sports and with local affairs. Giles was exceptional in his Catholic affiliations. The rest of the Porter family belonged to the Anglican faith and young Endymion would have been taken to worship in the church at Mickleton on one of whose walls a tablet recorded his ancestor's Charity. But the Porters' Anglican background was clearly of the kind that viewed Catholicism with friendly tolerance and had no share in the bitter Puritan hatred of Rome.

Endymion's first schooling was probably under the Mickleton schoolmaster whom the Porter charity supported. Later, he may well have attended the Grammar School at Chipping Campden which had been founded in 1487. But, in one important respect, his education differed from that of other English children of his class. He learned Spanish at his mother's knee. Many years later, the letters she wrote to him were still in Spanish. His mother's upbringing and background, with much travelled grandfather Giles living at Mickleton, would also have given Endymion's home a wider culture than would normally have been found in a small Cotswold manor. There was certainly music there, for Angela's brother, Luis, wrote expressing his delight at being told of the good music they had at Mickleton.

Meantime, the Porter fortunes seem to have been on the decline. In 1595, Nicholas was involved in a lawsuit with the Vicar of Mickleton over tithes and lost his case.[12] In the same year he gave up his lease of Mickleton Manor and, the next year, his other Mickleton leaseholds,[13] while Edmund and his family seem to have moved to a smaller house in the village. Nicholas's wife died in 1600 and in the succeeding years there are records of further disposals of leases and sales of lands.[14] At some point the manor at Aston was sold to a cousin, Richard Catesby. Nicholas himself seems to have gone to Beaconsfield where he died in 1613 with his affairs in disorder.[15] It was, therefore, to his father-in-law, Giles, that Edmund Porter looked for help with the careers of his two elder sons, Endymion and Thomas, when, in 1605, the opportunity arose.

Late in 1604, King James had finally concluded peace negotiations with Spain. In the spring of 1605 he sent out a mission to witness and accept King Philip III's ratification of the treaty. It was a splendid embassy, headed by the Earl of Nottingham, who had commanded the naval forces against the Armada, and including four other peers and twenty-five knights, as well as Sir Charles Cornwallis who was to remain in Spain as Ambassador. Giles Porter was appointed to the important post of the Mission's interpreter.[16]

Through their grandfather's appointment, the chance had come of giving Endymion and Tom a better opening than Mickleton could ever afford. In Spain, there were their grandmother's influential relations, while Giles had old connections which could be happily re-established under the prestige of his new post. Giles, therefore, must have taken his two grandsons with him, Endymion being eighteen and Tom a year or so younger.[17]

(ii)

The journey would, of course, have been an immense adventure to the two brothers who had probably never been more than a few miles from their midland home and had never seen the sea. To land in Spain also held the excite-

ment of the unknown for most of the members of the
Mission. For a quarter of a century, intercourse between
England and Spain had been cut off by war. Diplomatic
and commercial relations had both to be started anew; and,
to ignorance of Spain, there had been added patriotic prejudice, inflamed by tales of the Inquisition, of the cruelties
of Spanish misrule in the Indies and of the sufferings of
English prisoners of war in the galleys or the mines.

Nottingham's party was a very large one, 650 people in
all.[18] They assembled in London and left on March 26th,
going down the river to Queenborough where the ships
awaited them. These included the *Bear*, the *Due-Repulse*
and the *Waste-Spight* of the Royal Navy, which were to
carry Nottingham and his principal followers, among them
his indispensable interpreter. Owing to adverse winds it was
not until April 6th that they left Dover, but fair weather
brought them to Corunna on April 15th. Here, a magnificent welcome awaited them, the guns from the Castle
and the forts firing salvoes, which the ships' broadsides
answered. The next day the English went ashore to the
strains of 'sweet and delectable melody', and were received
by the Governor with all ceremony and hospitality. The
banquets, fireworks and sports were only marred by the
behaviour of one of the English sailors who got drunk and
struck a priest. Nottingham promptly had him tried. He
was ordered to be hanged, but the Spanish Governor inter-
ceded so powerfully on his behalf that he was pardoned.

On May 3rd the English, accompanied by a large number
of Spanish, set off on their arduous journey through moun-
tainous Galicia into Castile: 800 mules and 300 muleteers
were provided by the Spanish authorities, together with all
provisions needed for the journey.

The English were struck by the 'exceeding bareness' of
the country and the extreme poverty of the inhabitants.[19]
There were 'neither beds, nor inns nor meals' on the roads
and travelling was 'more painful and uncomfortable than
in any other deserted land in Europe'.[20] Great as was still

the renown of the Spanish Empire, it had, in fact, passed its zenith. At sea, the Armada had marked the turning point. On land, Rocroy and the eclipse of the legendary Spanish infantry was less than thirty years ahead. But it was in her economy that Spain's strength was being most rapidly sapped. The arrival each year of the fabulous Treasure fleets only disguised the truth of the report to the King that 'every year more than twelve millions of gold and silver go out of Spain and even though ten millions come in, we have to mint bad money to live'.[21] Economic measures designed to check rising prices by forbidding exports and encouraging imports had almost ruined Spanish industry. Trade had dwindled and passed into foreign hands. 'Treasury exhausted,' reported Cornwallis, 'rents and customs mortgaged for payment of debts, nobility poor and much indebted, merchants wasted, people in all extremity of necessity, credit decayed, oversea possessions held by force and fear.'[22]

A fortnight after their departure from Corunna, the English party reached Valladolid, where the Court was residing. Their ceremonial entry into the city was spoiled by torrential rain which soaked the visitors and the welcoming crowds, amongst which were 800 coaches filled with ladies. The next day Nottingham was visited by the great Duke of Lerma, who had acquired complete domination over the King, Philip III, and was the real ruler of Spain. The day after, Nottingham had his first audience with the King, delivering his oration 'by the mouth of Mr. Giles Porter'.

The festivities continued for three weeks. There was first the christening of the King's son. Then, on May 30th, the Corpus Christi procession, which offended English eyes by its curious mixture of 'things sacred with profane', giants, Morris dancers, dragons with fireworks, wild men and so on intermingling with the priests, the holy relics, the images and the crosses. The same day King Philip formally and publicly ratified the peace treaty. The day after, the English were treated to a great bull fight in the market place which had been surrounded by strong scaffolding, the ground being thickly covered with sand. All the English party were given seats. They saw the bulls being maddened by 'sticks with pins and pricks'; and 'he seemed to be the most valiant that dared affray the bull in the face and escape untouched, but some escaped not well, for it cost them their lives'. Then, well mounted 'Lords and gentlemen' struck the bull with spears 'very cunningly and manly', though some of their horses lost their lives in the process. Finally, the bull was despatched by two riders with spears 'that struck him in his head'. Fourteen bulls were killed, but four men lost their lives and a number were hurt. 'A sport raising more pity than pleasure,' Cornwallis called it.[23]

The Duke of Lerma gave a great banquet, where two Marquises and two Earls waited at the table and one of the Marquises carved. The feast was followed by a play, 'but of more length than pleasure', Cornwallis remarked. [24]

Finally, after receiving rich presents from the King— amongst the gifts to Nottingham was a diamond ring worth £3,000—Nottingham and his party, with Giles amongst them, left for Santander and home.

Giles's conduct had earned high praise both from Nottingham and from Cornwallis. 'I must think myself happy,' wrote Nottingham to the Earl of Salisbury, 'by having Mr. Porter my interpreter, whom I find so sufficient in the language and experienced in the fashions of the country, as, through England or Spain, I could not have found a man more necessary for me, or of better discretion';[25] and Cornwallis reported that 'Mr. Giles Porter hath here behaved himself very well and with good allowance of all in his employment'.[26] If Giles's loyalty and religion might seem to have been more Spanish than English in the past, this was no longer the case. Cornwallis wrote of how Giles had kept a watch on Creswell, the Rector of the English Jesuits, who had been haunting Nottingham's house, and how Giles had reported that Lerma, after cross-questioning him about

Creswell, had advised him to tell Nottingham not to have any dealings with such a 'busy fellow'.[27]

In the course of his official duties Giles had met Count Olivares—'a man of many years and an ancient councillor of this Kingdom'—who had called on Nottingham to discuss the procedure for ratifying the treaties.[28] Olivares had visited England in the time of Queen Mary and Giles had probably known him in his earlier years in Spain. At any rate, it was now arranged that Endymion should enter the Olivares' household as a page. It was still a common practice in England for great noblemen to give opportunities to young men of good family by taking them into the service of their households. In 1606, for instance, a correspondent wrote recommending his son to the Earl of Salisbury 'to serve either about his person or at the table or in other employment'.[29] Service with the Olivares family was certainly a good opportunity for Endymion. At the same time, Thomas was placed with his grandmother's kinsman, the Bishop at Segorbe, near Valencia.[30]

(iii)

It was for service with old Count Olivares's heir, Don Gaspar, that Endymion was engaged. They were of the same age. Don Gaspar, his parents' second son, had been born in Rome, where his father was Spanish Ambassador, and had spent his youth in Italy. When the family returned to Spain in 1601, Don Gaspar, aged 14, who was intended for the Church, had been sent to the University of Salamanca. There he had acquired a love and knowledge of the arts. In 1604, Don Gaspar's elder brother had died. As the new heir, Don Gaspar gave up any idea of a career in the Church and returned to join his father at the Court at Valladolid. The state he kept was princely. Even when, as a younger son, he had gone as a student to Salamanca, he had been accompanied by two tutors, eight pages, three valets, four footmen and many other servants.

It was to such a household that the young Englishman was added in 1605. Two years later, the old Count died. He was buried with most elaborate ceremonial and Endymion's master succeeded to the family honours. The year after, the new Count married his cousin, a lady in waiting to the Queen, and it was probably about this time that Endymion left his service.[31]

Endymion's close association with the man who, before long, was to become the ruler of Spain, was of great importance to his future life. A friendship grew up between them which was to last throughout their careers and was to survive the severe strain that events were to impose on it. In a letter to Endymion, as late as 1630, Cottington, the English Ambassador in Spain, was to write 'I delivered your letters to the Conde and to his lady, who were both very glad to hear from you and asked me 1,000 questions concerning you, all expressing their love and loving care towards you.'[32]

Culturally, Endymion's years in Spain were of special value to him. If Spain had begun to decay materially, she was leading Europe in culture and in the graces of polite society. Universities such as Salamanca and Alcala were world-famous and Spanish books were in world demand. Cervantes' *Don Quixote* was published the year of Endymion's arrival, and Lope de Vega, the creator of Spanish drama, was bringing out his comedies. In painting, El Greco was at the height of his powers, while Rubens, in 1603, had visited Spain and painted an equestrian portrait of the Duke of Lerma. Spain, too, was rich in fine examples of Renaissance painting and sculpture, notably the truly superb collection that Philip II had made.

There was, however, one aspect of Endymion's years in Spain that was ever after to make him an object of suspicion in Puritan circles. There seems to be no doubt that Endymion, like many visitors to Spain other than deeply convinced Protestants, chose to follow the custom of the country and, when in Spain, conformed to the Catholic faith. Indeed, he would have had little other choice as a member of the Olivares household in the isolation of a country where the only Anglican services, grudgingly permitted, were those in the English Embassy for its few members. Fifteen or so years later a Jesuit writer, referring to Endymion's service 'in the Chamber of the Count of Olivares', alleged that his advance in Olivares' favour was 'in proportion to the zeal which he displayed for the Catholic religion'.[33] But this is not to say that Endymion abandoned the Anglican faith to become a convinced Catholic. In another contemporary instance, William Calley, the merchant whose service Endymion was soon to enter and whom Cottington, then serving in the Embassy, found 'much gone in papistry', announced that he intended 'to go again to church in England at his coming home'.[34]

Whatever religious conformity Endymion may have displayed in Catholic countries and however friendly he always was to Catholics, at home he seems to have remained an outward and, in all probability, a genuine adherent of the Church of England, even when, in later years, his wife became a proselytising convert of Rome.

Two years after his arrival in Spain, Endymion was welcoming his grandfather back to Madrid. Giles left England again for Spain in July 1607.[35] He came to pursue a lawsuit concerning some of his wife's property. In a long letter to Endymion's father at Mickleton, Giles told him how he had been busy on his suit for two months with the help of one of his wife's relations who had just gone to Segorbe to get the help of the Bishop, to whom his wife had given her power of attorney. Giles was hopeful of success, as the lawyers told him he had justice on his side. The old gentleman ended his letter with a message to a Mickleton neighbour referring in indelicate if somewhat obscure terms to the morals of Spanish women.[36]

Giles's suit followed the customary Spanish pattern of interminable delays. As Giles wrote 'suits here are so endless that a man may wear out his life before he shall end them'.[37]

Two years later, in January 1610, Francis Cottington, who had taken charge of the English Embassy when Cornwallis returned to England in 1609, was writing home that Giles was still pursuing his suit with good hopes of a settlement.[38] But Giles's hopes were not fulfilled, for when the new Ambassador, Sir John Digby, arrived in Madrid more than a year later, Giles was reported as being daily at the Embassy asking for the Ambassador's help.[39] Digby must have found Giles's long experience of Spain useful, as he took him to live in his house, 'the pleasantest house in Madrid with garden and other conveniences,' he called it.[40] Finally, early in 1612, when all that could be obtained was a judgement giving Giles the right to a trial, but still withholding possession of the property, the old man made up his mind to go home.[41]

Meantime, Endymion had left the Olivares household to take service with William Calley, a friend of his grandfather who was similarly pursuing a suit in Madrid.[42] Calley's story affords a good example of what Cornwallis called 'the intolerable delays' in obtaining restitution for merchants, when everything had to be referred to the Duke of Lerma 'through whose hands all generations of papers of what worth soever must have the passage'.[43] 'What a misery it is,' wrote a member of the Embassy, 'to be at the mercy of Spain.'[44]

Calley belonged to a merchant family, citizens and drapers of London, and members of the Drapers Company for over one hundred years. In partnership with Colford, his agent in Brussels, he had supplied a large contract for cloth for the Spanish forces in the Netherlands. The quality had been so good and the price so reasonable that the Spanish Regent had written specially to the King of Spain urging prompt payment.[45] In spite of this, no money had been forthcoming and, early in 1607, Calley had conducted his own negotiations through the English Jesuits.[46] After six months, having got nowhere through these channels, he sought Ambassador Cornwallis's help. The Ambassador was, at first, suspicious of Calley's Catholic connections, but after Calley had 'shown himself no feather of the Jesuit wings' by joining Cornwallis in prayers at the Embassy, the Ambassador took his case up. The debt was a huge one—£100,000 including interest—and, as Cornwallis wrote home to the Earl of Salisbury, 'the body of the Commonwealth of our country is interested in so great a sum if any of the particular members of the same should lose it.'[47]

After Cornwallis went home, Cottington pressed Calley's case with so little success that, a year later, all he had obtained was a promise of 5,000 ducats.[48] This was all that Calley had been paid by the summer of 1611, but Digby's arrival renewed his hopes and he joined Giles Porter in their daily attendance at the Embassy.[49] By then, Endymion seems to have entered Calley's service, and to have helped in the negotiations.

Calley's affairs were now complicated by claims on anything he might recover made by his agent Colford and by Lionel Wake, the Antwerp merchant, to whom Calley owed money. Wake's brother had come to Madrid and, though Digby's sympathies were with Calley, the wranglings of the various claimants so exasperated him that he threatened to give up the case.[50] In March, 1612, however, he succeeded in getting an offer from the Spanish Government to pay the debt 'in 4 fleets'.[51] So dependent was the Spanish economy on gold from the Americas, that it was only by the safe arrival of the annual treasure fleet that merchants could get their claims paid. As an Embassy correspondent wrote 'The Indian fleet brings the golden fleece and the *aurum potabile* that will quench their thirst'.[52] Calley pressed for payment in three fleets (that is in three years) and, in April, Digby at last secured a promise to this effect with interest at ten per cent added to the principal.[53]

It would seem that it was at this happy moment that Endymion left Spain. We know that Giles had gone home by the end of May, and, in all likelihood, he took his two grandsons back to England with him.[54]

To conclude Calley's story, the 1612 treasure fleet duly arrived in Spanish ports in November. Though Calley's business was still further complicated by Colford's arrival in Madrid, which caused fresh wranglings, they settled their differences and Calley seems to have received the first year's instalment of his debt.[55]

CHAPTER II

(i)

ALTHOUGH Nicholas Porter had gone from Aston, Edmund was still living at Mickleton when his twenty-five-year-old son came home from Spain. Endymion's apprenticeship had given him a number of advantages. In the first place, his knowledge of Spain was shared by few young Englishmen. In spite of the peace, Spain had not become a fashionable touring ground like Italy and France. The bad roads and worse accommodation on them and the harshness of the climate discouraged travellers, while Spain did not offer such obvious cultural attractions as did Italy. Fear of the Inquisition persisted, combined with suspicions of the loyalty of those who wished to visit England's late enemy. The result was that, apart from Catholic exiles, English travellers mostly went to Spain either on business or as members of an embassy.

Moreover, Endymion's Spanish contacts were of a most useful kind. In the Olivares circle and through his grandfather and his relations he would have met all the important figures in Spanish affairs, from Lerma downwards and including the future Gondomar; while his master, the young Olivares, was, before long, to dominate Philip IV as completely as Lerma dominated Philip III. The English Embassy, where his grandfather had lived, was also familiar ground to him, with Digby—the future Earl of Bristol—and Cottington no strangers. In Spain, too, he had met such future English friends as Tobie Matthew and George Gage who, in 1610, had lodged with Calley in Madrid.[1] Another advantage of his service in a noble Spanish household was the training in the courtly manners and etiquette for which Spain was renowned. It was in Spain that Endymion would have acquired that 'brave stile' of which Antony Wood was to write. Nor had Endymion's employment with Calley been wasted. It had given him commercial experience which would prove useful when handling the finances of future employers. It had, too, brought its contacts, notably with the Wakes, with whom Endymion was later to have many dealings over pictures.

But perhaps the most important result of Endymion's sojourn in Spain was that, in his most impressionable years, the full sun of European culture had warmed his mind and had awoken in him that love of the arts which, as much as his knowledge of Spain, was to commend him to his future royal master.

It was not long before Endymion obtained an appointment at home, 'to be Edward Villiers' servant in Fleet street'.[2] Edward and George Villiers were half brothers, Edward being one of the two sons of Sir George Villiers by his first marriage and George the second surviving son of his second marriage. While not of the great nobility, the Villiers family claimed Norman descent and had been seated at Brooksby in Leicestershire for over 400 years.

Endymion probably owed his appointment to his Uncle Nicholas, since Edward Villiers's sister Elizabeth, the wife of Sir Henry Boteler and Endymion's future mother-in-law, was godmother to one of Nicholas's children. It was not long before he caught the eye of Edward's half-brother. As Endymion was gratefully to acknowledge, it was from George Villiers, the future Duke of Buckingham, that all his fortunes were to stem.

All contemporary writers pay tribute to George Villiers's charm and good looks. 'One of the handsomest men in the whole world,' Sir John Oglander called him,[3] and Bishop Goodman wrote of him as 'the handsomest bodied man of England, his limbs so well compacted and his conversation so pleasing and of so sweet a disposition'.[4]

George Villiers was twenty-two when King James first saw him at Apethorpe in the course of the summer progress of 1614. Almost at once he was installed as the King's cupbearer. There can be no doubt that the attraction was primarily a physical one. As Sir John Oglander wrote, James loved young men better than women, and he went on to say that 'I never yet saw any fond husband make so much or so great dalliance over his beautiful spouse as I have seen King James over his favourites, especially the Duke of Buckingham'.[5] Yet the ageing James's enslaving passion for Buckingham, with all its foolish, doting manifestations, may well have been largely paternal. Buckingham was 'his sweet and dear child', and the King was Buckingham's 'dear Dad and Gossip'. Both the Queen and the Archbishop of Canterbury gave Buckingham their friendship and their backing, while Prince Charles, whose rigidly strict moral code was never in question, was soon to come fully as much under Buckingham's romantic spell as ever James had been.

At the same time, the King was becoming increasingly disillusioned in regard to the reigning favourite, Robert Ker, Earl of Somerset, who had been made Lord Chamberlain in 1614. Success had gone to his head and James' indulgence only fed his arrogance and his disrespect to his master. His downfall came with dramatic suddenness at the end of 1615, when he and his wife were arrested and subsequently convicted for their part in the poisoning, over two years earlier, of his erstwhile friend Sir Thomas Overbury, who had opposed his wife's divorce from her first husband.

Somerset's fall did not only clear the way for a new royal favourite. The sordid circumstances of the trial furnished a background of goodwill towards Somerset's supplanter, who was, moreover, an Englishman and not, as Somerset had been, a Scot; and Villiers' own rise also meant new prospects for the Villiers family and for those in their service such as Endymion.

In April 1615, George Villiers had been knighted and made Gentleman of the Bedchamber with a pension of £1,000. Next year, after Somerset's disgrace, honours poured on him in a stream—Master of the Horse, Knight of the Garter, Viscount Villiers, as well as a number of highly profitable posts. In 1617 he was made Earl of Buckingham and a Privy Counsellor. At the beginning of 1618 he was created Marquis of Buckingham, and, a year later, Lord High Admiral. 'A prodigious ascent' Clarendon called it.[6]

Villiers, still pliant and impressionable, bore his new fortunes with modesty and friendliness. The King resolved 'to make him a masterpiece and to mould him, as it were, platonically to his own idea',[7] and Villiers played his part with wit and affection, becoming the King's constant companion and lending himself cheerfully to his foibles. Abbot the Archbishop of Canterbury, who was his chief sponsor, gave him sage advice. So did Sir Francis Bacon, who had become Attorney General in 1613. But there was still one formidable obstacle to Villiers' future prospects.

The young Prince Charles, now in his middle teens, proud, reserved but deeply loving his father, was not unnaturally jealous and resentful at the open preference shown by the King to a young man only eight years older than himself. There were a number of scenes and quarrels in which the King took Buckingham's side. Finally, in the summer of 1618, after a violent quarrel between the two young men over a game of tennis, the King called them before him and insisted on a reconciliation. Buckingham made this the occasion of a great outdoor feast at his new estate at Wanstead in Essex. To the King's great joy, Charles forgot his jealousy and allowed himself to succumb to Buckingham's charm and friendliness. From then on, the friendship that was to colour all the rest of Charles' life began to grow closer.

At the Wanstead feast the King had drunk a toast to the house of Villiers, declaring that he desired himself and his posterity to advance it above all others.[8] In fact, the royal favour had already begun to reward Buckingham's relatives. Endymion's master, Edward Villiers, had been knighted in

1616. The next year he was made Master of the Mint and secured a profitable patent for gold and silver thread. In 1618 he was appointed Comptroller of the Court of Wards.

(ii)

It was probably late in 1617 or early in 1618 that Buckingham took Endymion from his brother's service into his own. He made him Master of his Horse and put him in charge of his Spanish correspondence.

Endymion found Balthasar Gerbier already installed in Buckingham's service. This cosmopolitan character came from a Huguenot family who had fled to Holland. Finding his way to England in 1616, when he was twenty-five years old, Gerbier had almost immediately been given employment by Buckingham. According to his own account, Buckingham engaged him because of his 'several languages' (he knew French, Dutch and Spanish), 'good hand in writing, skill in sciences as mathematics, architecture, drawing, painting, contriving of scenes, masques, shows and entertainments for great Princes.'[9]

Gerbier's own artistic efforts were amateur and were mainly confined to portraits, mostly miniatures. But he had a very considerable knowledge of works of art, combined with good taste and discernment, and it was he who was the principal agent in amassing Buckingham's great collection of pictures and statuary and in providing the furnishings for Buckingham's palatial residences. His letters to Buckingham show that he possessed the enthusiasm of a true art lover. Writing in 1624, for instance, from France where he was scouting for art treasures for his patron, he tells how he has come across 'a most beautiful piece of Tintoret, of a Danae, a naked figure the most beautiful that flint as cold as ice might fall in love with it'. Of a crucifixion by Michael Angelo, he writes that it 'should be seen kneeling . . . I have been such an idolater as to kiss it three times, for there is nothing that can be more perfect'. When he finds a Raphael that has been restored, he describes it as 'repainted by some devil who I trust was hanged'.[10] Endymion shared such tastes and must have found many interests in common with his fellow member of the household. He was to have much to do with this mercurial adventurer in later years, mainly in connection with pictures and painters, but also in the diplomatic field, where Gerbier's talents for intrigue and self-advancement found scope, culminating in his nine years as English resident in Brussels.

The three years or so that Endymion spent in Buckingham's service were those in which the new Marquis became all powerful. At the beginning of 1618, the influence of the Howard group had still been paramount. The Earl of Suffolk was Lord Treasurer, the Earl of Nottingham was Lord High Admiral. A Howard supporter, Sir Thomas Lake, was Secretary of State. The Howards owed nothing to Buckingham, whom they regarded as an upstart. They foolishly thought to oust him by the simple device of introducing another handsome youth to the King's attention in the person of John Monson, a connection of the Nottingham Howards. Although they took 'great pains in tricking and pranking him up, besides washing his face every day with possett curd',[11] the attempt only angered James whose devotion to Buckingham was unshakeable.

Suffolk's extremely lax conduct of the Lord Treasurership had resulted in a chronic shortage of money. James now resolved on retrenchment and financial reform, and it soon became apparent that Suffolk was guilty at least of conniving at wholesale bribery. At the same time, Lake became involved in a domestic scandal and lost the Secretaryship. Suffolk and his wife were tried for embezzlement of funds, were found guilty, and retired from public life to the lovely house of Audley End which they had built in Essex. Nottingham was also dismissed for his gross mismanagement of the Navy. In spite of heavy expenditure, nearly half of the King's forty-three ships were found to be utterly unserviceable.

In January 1619 Buckingham succeeded Nottingham in the great office of Lord High Admiral, while still retaining the Mastership of the Horse. He was now supreme, 'conferring all the honours and all the offices of the three Kingdoms without a rival.'[12] The new régime introduced some badly needed reforms and some capable administrators were brought in, such as Cranfield, a former city merchant.

Buckingham's own energies were largely devoted to James's pleasures. The King was now in his fifties. He was beginning to age and suffered from gout and arthritis. In spite of a severe illness early in 1619, his love for the chase was undiminished, though he now followed his hounds more slowly. Under Buckingham's régime, he found that he 'never was master of such horses and hounds',[13] though Buckingham never produced such a novelty as the cheetah presented to James ten years before by the Ambassador of Savoy, which followed the king like a dog, would 'catch a hare at 2 or 3 leaps' and kill any deer that the King pointed out to it.[14] The feasts, masques and dancing that James loved also took on a new zest with Buckingham to play his part in them. Endymion, as Buckingham's Master of the Horse, was, of course, closely concerned with all these pursuits. Amongst other duties, he was responsible for some of his master's finances. Records of payments made by Endymion to Sackville Crowe, Buckingham's major domo, include receipts for close on £10,000 for one period of five months. Other payments made by Endymion on Buckingham's behalf ranged from £1,400 for a diamond ring to £30 10s. 0d. for a pearl, £30 for boots and shoes, £10 to 'a musician that presented a set of books' and £200 each to Lanier the musician and Ben Jonson the poet.[15]

The Queen had died in the spring of 1619. James and Anne had not lived together for many years and, for female society, the King had turned happily to Buckingham's relations. There was only one other major influence at Court. It was that of the Spanish Ambassador, Count Gondomar, who had subtly worked his way into virtual dominance over the King. His influence over Buckingham was equally strong and was not to be broken until the rude awakening given by the visit to Madrid in 1623. It was Gondomar who, in 1618, forced the execution of Raleigh after his return from the pitiful fiasco of his last voyage and, although most of England looked upon Raleigh's death as a national disgrace, Buckingham supported Gondomar's demands. Endymion, as might be expected from his youthful Spanish associations, followed Buckingham's lead in his relations with Gondomar, whom he had in all likelihood known in Madrid. The Venetian Ambassador indeed reported that Endymion challenged to a duel someone he heard speaking ill of Gondomar.[16] Was it, perhaps, the remembrance of these days that, eighteen years later, caused Raleigh's son Carew to challenge Endymion, when, to prevent their fighting, both were confined to their quarters in Whitehall?[17]

(iii)

Endymion's own fortunes rose, of course, with those of his master. At the end of 1618 he had acquired, jointly with a friend, a grant for seven years of all fines for non-payment of customs on the importation and exportation of prohibited goods. The fact that a rent of £800 a year had to be paid for this privilege shows how lucrative it could be. In September 1619 he and his co-beneficiary were granted permission to assign debts over to the King to enable them to pay this rent.[18] Again, in 1619, the State Papers record the lease to Endymion of the Rectory of Exminster in Devon, 'he having found out the King's right to the same', on condition of his repairing the premises and paying £50 a year to a curate.[19]

Another important source of income came directly from the confidential status which he had acquired in Buckingham's affairs. This was described by the Venetian Ambassador Lando in the 'Relation of England' which he sent to the Doge on his retirement in 1622. Writing of Buckingham in this report, Lando stated that 'the means to his favour is one Porter, an Englishman, now become gentleman to the Prince, and the gateway to all favours, with whom nothing but money prevails and who has become most rich'. Lando went on to give the entirely false information that Endymion had been brought up by Buckingham, mostly in Spain, and to repeat a most unlikely rumour that, while Endymion lived very quietly and frugally, he changed the torrents of wealth that flowed to him on every hand into coin which he kept in Spain under other names.[20]

Lando's inaccuracies do not, however, make it less certain that Endymion used his position to accept money from those seeking Buckingham's favour. It would, indeed, have been a departure from contemporary practice had he not done so, at least within limits. In contemporary eyes there was a line drawn, however fine it may now seem to us, between gratuities and bribes; and while Endymion, throughout his life, was an eager beneficiary of every fruit obtainable from the tree of office, no doubt was ever raised of his honesty and integrity in the positions of trust which he filled.

Throughout Government, the old administrative system still prevailed. Officers were still paid less by salary than by fees, perquisites and gratuities, which were regarded as the natural and proper emoluments of office. Nor was there any pensions system, and a prudent man was expected to provide for his old age through securing patents or reversions to offices.

Endymion, without any inherited lands or money and nearly thirty years old when his opportunity came, had his way to make in the world. Very soon he had the responsibility of a wife from a much richer background than his own, and a growing family to provide for. Even with the advantages of free lodging and allowances, the actual salaries of most court officials were small and the standards a courtier had to keep up were extravagant. No doubt, too, Endymion's own tastes were opulent, formed as they had been in so wealthy an atmosphere as that of the household of a Spanish Grandee, and, as soon as he was able to do so, he began to gratify his love of works of art with modest purchases.

It is clear, at any rate, that Endymion was not slow to take advantage of the opportunities that were now open to him of bettering his finances. By 1619, he had already so far succeeded as to be able to buy back, from his cousin Richard Catesby, the Porter manor house and lands at Aston, which his Uncle Nicholas had sold and which Endymion now made his own country home.[21]

In the same year, Endymion was admitted to Gray's Inn. While it was common for those who had been at Oxford and Cambridge to proceed to an Inn, admission was not confined to such people, and the Inns not only afforded a useful acquaintance with the law but were also an important source of personal and social contacts. Endymion's admission to Gray's Inn was a sign of his rising in the world.

By 1619, too, Endymion was sufficiently well-known in court circles to make his marriage a matter of public interest. In May of that year, the Reverend Thomas Lorkyn wrote from London to a friend living in the country that 'Endymion Porter, that waits upon my Lord Buckingham shall (if general voice deceive not) set my Lady Roos at liberty, and enjoy her for his wife. I heard of it above a fortnight since, but gave no credit to it, but now it is confidently assured'.[22] Other letters from London told the same story.[23]

Lady Roos, with whom Endymion's name was thus linked, was the chief protagonist in one of the most unsavoury scandals of the day. She was Anne, daughter of Sir Thomas Lake, the Secretary of State, 'a man of weak, thin body, overawed by his wife and if he did not do what she wanted, she would beat him.'[24] Anne, 'a very pert lady,'[25] had married Lord Roos, 'a worthless weak man, low in morals and disgusting in manners',[26] but wealthy, and the grandson of the Earl of Exeter. Before long, Roos and the Lakes became involved in a dispute about his money. Threatened by Anne with divorce on the grounds of impotence if he did not give way, Roos, fled the country, turned Catholic and shortly afterwards died in Naples. Lady Exeter, the young second wife of Roos's grandfather, had taken Roos's side in the quarrel with the Lakes. They now turned on her. Encouraged by Lady Lake, Anne accused her of incest with her step-grandson and of trying to poison the Lakes. Lady Exeter's reply was to appeal to King James for a trial.

The King was fascinated by this spicy case. Sending for Lady Roos, he demanded that she should swear to the truth of her accusations. When she declined to do so, James decided to preside at the trial in person. In his opening speech, he compared himself to Solomon and throughout the five days of the trial he took an active part in the proceedings. The Lakes miserably failed to prove their case, and the King was able to show that they had persuaded their chief witness, one of their maidservants, to commit perjury. James himself delivered judgement in open court. He related how Lady Roos had started back when he had asked her to take her oath on the Bible. Comparing Sir Thomas Lake to Adam, his daughter to Eve and Lady Lake to the serpent, he pronounced all three guilty of bringing false accusations. They were sent to the Tower and very heavily fined, while their maidservant was ordered to be whipped through the streets, to be branded with the letters F.A. (false accuser) one on each cheek, and to be sent to the Bridewell for the rest of her life. It was while Anne Roos was in prison that her marriage to Endymion was rumoured. Shortly afterwards she made a full written confession to the King and was set free.[27]

There was no truth in this rumour of Endymion's betrothal. His affections were already centred elsewhere. Service with the Villiers had brought him into contact with their ladies. There was Buckingham's ambitious and unscrupulous mother, old Lady Compton, whom the King created Countess of Buckingham in 1619, there was Buckingham's full sister, Susan, married to Sir William Feilding who was made Earl of Denbigh, and there was Elizabeth, Buckingham's half-sister by his father's first marriage, with her six daughters, of whom the two eldest were already married and the others of marriageable age.

Elizabèth, who was Buckingham's favourite sister, was the wife of Sir John Boteler, the head of an old Hertfordshire family who had long held the manor of Walton Woodhall near Hatfield. Sir John had been knighted by King James in 1607, and, two years later at the age of forty-three, had succeeded to the family estates, making his home in the family house of Woodhall. The house was close to the royal palace of Hatfield, which the King gave to the Earl of Salisbury in 1607 in exchange for Theobalds.[28]*

It was on Olivia—called Olive in her home—the fourth Boteler daughter, that Endymion's hopes were set. An alliance by marriage, as well as by occupation, with the ever-growing power of Buckingham would, of course, be of great advantage to Endymion's career. But it is clear that Endymion's feelings for Olive were by no means mainly mercenary. He had, in fact, fallen deeply and passionately in love with her. Olive seems never to have fully responded to his ardour. High-spirited and self-willed, she was, however, attracted by Endymion's handsome face and the charm of his manners, and she respected his learning and experience.

Only one of Endymion's letters written during his courtship has survived. It is full of hurt pride at Olive's apparent coldness. The letter is headed 'Endymion Porter to his mistress Olive'.

'Dear Heart,' it runs, 'I assure you that nothing could have prevented my writing to you but want of health, which hath been the cause I have not troubled you all this while with my letters. I make no doubt that your careless disposition will not let you perish with any want of my lines,

---

* In 1690, the Salisburys bought Woodhall and demolished the house.

for I think that my presence affords you no more joy than my love obliges you to, nor my absence no more sorrow than you not caring whether you ever see me again or no, however you profess otherwise: and this I gather by the salutation I had in the park from you when I was last there, which strikes in my mind, but cannot any whit diminish that resolution I have so constantly settled in my thoughts to love you, for now I find that neither scorns from you, nor favours from any other creature can alter

Your servant
Endymion Porter.'[29]

(iv)

Endymion and Olive were married some time in the second half of 1619. As part of Olive's jointure, Endymion settled on her his Aston estate for her life after his death, with remainder to their first begotten son.[30] It is probable that Lord Boteler gave Olive £2,000 as her marriage portion, as this was the sum given to another daughter on her marriage.[31] Thanks to Buckingham, Endymion's new relations formed or were to form an influential group. His father-in-law was made a baronet in 1620 and, eight years later, was raised to the peerage as Lord Boteler of Brantfield. Sir John's only distinction, however, lay in his having married Buckingham's sister. Nor was he fortunate in his sons. Henry, the eldest, had already died unmarried. He had been knighted in 1616, but the next year was sent to Spain with a tutor 'to cure him of the disease of drinking, which, young as he was, he was already much given to'.[32] The cure must have failed, as he died soon afterwards. William, the only surviving son, was an idiot from birth. But all Endymion's sisters-in-law made good alliances with husbands who were helped by the Buckingham connection to rise to importance. Through them, indeed, the Villiers blood was to descend to some of the most famous names in English history.

Audrey, the eldest, had early lost her first husband and was married to Sir Francis Leigh. He was made Lord Dunsmore in 1628 and finally Earl of Chichester when he was with the King at Oxford in 1644. They had two daughters. One married the Earl of Southampton. The other married her Villiers cousin Lord Grandison. Her granddaughter was the mother of William Pitt, the great Earl of Chatham.

Helen, the second Boteler daughter, married Sir John Drake of Ashe in Devon. Her daughter, marrying Sir Winston Churchill, became the mother of John Churchill, Duke of Marlborough and the ancestor of our Sir Winston Churchill.

When Endymion married Olive, her three other sisters were still unmarried, but their weddings soon added to the list of Endymion's influential relations. Jane, the third daughter, married old Sir James Ley, Chief Justice of England. He was created Baron Ley in 1624, when he became Lord High Treasurer, and, two years later, was made Earl of Marlborough. He died childless in 1629, aged 77. Soon after, Jane married William Ashburnham, cofferer to Charles I and Charles II, living happily with him till her death in 1672.

Mary, the fifth daughter, married in 1623 Sir Edward Howard of Escrick, the youngest son of the Earl of Suffolk. Once more, Buckingham's influence was responsible for the advancement of another niece's husband, and Howard was made a Baron in 1628. Mary died in 1634. Lord Howard, no longer able to look to the Buckingham influence for further advancement, 'delivered himself up body and soul' to Parliament.[33] He was one of the three Peers who became members of the House of Commons in 1649, but two years later he was found guilty of bribery, was imprisoned and removed from his seat and sank into contempt and insignificance.

The youngest of Endymion's sisters-in-law, Anne, was married in 1627 to Mountjoy Blount, Lord Mountjoy of Ireland, who, the year after, was made Earl of Newport.

He was a faithful follower of both Charles I and Charles II.

Another relation, who was to be a Porter family friend, came with Buckingham's own marriage which took place not long after Endymion's. The bride was Lady Katharine Manners, the only surviving child of the Earl of Rutland. She was seventeen, attractive and a great heiress. Buckingham certainly loved her and she worshipped him. Unfortunately, she was a Roman Catholic. This difficulty was, however, overcome by Dr. Williams, the worldly Dean of Salisbury, who persuaded the simple, love-torn girl to join the Church of England. King James took her to his heart at once. She was equally beloved by Endymion and Olive, to whom she used to write as her 'sweet cousin', signing herself 'your most constant friend'.[34]

Despite Endymion's rising fortunes, the start of his married life was by no means an easy one. Both Buckingham (of whom the Venetian Ambassador wrote that 'the King will not eat, sup or remain an hour without him'[35]) and Prince Charles were tied to King James's peripatetic court with its endless round of travel from one house to another. Endymion's attendance on Buckingham or on the Prince, into whose own service he was taken a year later, meant therefore that he and Olive could enjoy no settled home life and could only see each other at moments snatched from court duties.

The Court was based on Whitehall, an irregular mass of buildings covering several acres with the highway from London to Westminster running through the centre. But James had always disliked London. He took every opportunity of leaving it and of escaping from affairs of state and the importunity of suitors by staying in one or other of his many country residences, where, with his chosen companions, he could lead the careless, informal life that he loved, with its days devoted to hunting the stag and the hare. Besides this endless circulation from one royal house to another, every summer saw a Progress further afield, when the King was entertained by the nobility in their country seats or by the civic heads in the towns. Whitehall, Hampton Court, Windsor, Greenwich and Richmond were the most important palaces. All five were situated on the Thames. The smaller country residences which the King most favoured for his hunting were Oatlands in Surrey, Havering in Essex, Eltham in Kent, Woodstock in Oxfordshire, Theobalds and Royston in Hertfordshire and Newmarket in Cambridgeshire.

In 1620,[36] for instance, the first year of Endymion's marriage, the court saw the New Year in at Whitehall where the King had, as usual, spent Christmas. There were plays and revels and a great feast given by the French Ambassador to Buckingham and other courtiers. In the middle of January the court moved to Newmarket, stopping at Theobalds and Royston on the way. The court stayed at Newmarket until Lent, 'passing the time merrily'[37] with entertainments that included a masque presented by the three beautiful daughters of Sir John Crofts of Saxham near Bury. The King was back in Whitehall for Ash Wednesday, but then went to Theobalds before returning to London at the end of February.

The months of April and May were divided between Whitehall, Hampton Court and Greenwich, and in the middle of May Buckingham was married at Lumley House near Tower Hill. At the end of the month the King moved to Theobalds, but was back at Greenwich for Whitsun. In June, James celebrated his birthday at Windsor, but soon after went to Wanstead in Essex. Early in July the court was at Oatlands, then at Windsor again, then back to Whitehall and Theobalds.

In the middle of July, the King started his summer Progress. This year it was to the West. His journey first took him to Andover, then to Lord Hertford's seat of Tottenham Park, and on to Charlton Park, Sir Thomas Howard's new mansion near Malmesbury, where his 'entertainment was much commended and well accepted'.[38] From Charlton the King went on to Wilton, the Earl of Pem-

broke's seat. A visit to Stonehenge aroused his curiosity, so
Pembroke sent for Inigo Jones to make a report. After
meticulously measuring all the stones and examining their
foundations, Inigo Jones informed the King that Stone-
henge was undoubtedly a Roman Temple dating from the
Roman occupation of Britain![39] The next stop was at
Salisbury, where the King lodged in a house in the Close.
The progress then continued to Beaulieu and to Farnham
Castle, where the King's entertainment cost the Bishop of
Winchester £1,000.[40]

In September, after one day in London, the court moved
to Wanstead, then to Havering and on to Theobalds and
Hampton Court, circling back to Royston about Michaelmas. October saw the King at Theobalds and Royston, with
a visit to Whitehall to inspect the progress made by Inigo
Jones in the building of the new Banqueting House to
replace the one destroyed by fire the year before. Early in
November, the court was on the move once more, to
Theobalds, Royston and Newmarket, where the King
stayed until returning to London for Christmas and for
the reception of the French Ambassador Extraordinary.
There was a banquet given by James and a display of tilting
at which Prince Charles excelled. On Twelfth Night, the
King and the French Ambassador were entertained by Ben
Jonson's new masque 'News from the Moon'.

The letters that Endymion wrote to Olive during this,
their first married year, show how bitterly he felt the separation imposed by his duties. For most of the time, Olive
lived with her parents at Woodhall. Here she at least had
the company of her family, and Woodhall, within reach of
Theobalds and Royston, was conveniently placed for visits
from Endymion. Occasionally Olive visited Aston, where
Endymion's parents were living with his younger brothers
and sister. Before long, however, Endymion also had a
house in London, where Olive could stay when the court
was at Whitehall.

'My dear Olive,' one letter ran, 'everytime I part with

thee I discover in myself more love than I have patience to live without thee; and am sorry for nothing but that I cannot be always with thee, but that God out of His divine wisdom thought it too great a happiness to give me thee and thy company, lest I should forget there were any other glory. Sweet Olive, I thank you for your kind letter and I protest to God I love you so as this last absence seems to me more than any I have thitherto endured, therefore believe that Friday shall be the festival day of the greatest joy this world can afford me, till when and ever I will be

Thy true loving husband
Endymion Porter.'[41]

Having to leave Olive unwell at Woodhall, Endymion sent her a note as soon as he got to Royston.

'My dear Heart.—I cannot go farther and farther from you but with an infinite desire to hear of your amendment, although the sergeant told me that he left you much better, which was more welcome news to me than any other worldly happiness I could have heard of. Mend apace, my sweet love, and send me word of it, that you may keep me alive with that cordial.

Your husband
Endymion Porter.

Royston, this Saturday.'[42]

The letters showed, too, how deeply he was in love. 'Whenever I go to sleep,' he wrote, 'I send my soul to watch with thee, and whatsoever waking I can see with mine eyes, I look on it through thee; for if it be a beauty it is none to me, my thoughts do so prefer thine, that I see nothing but thy goodness and love, which makes me happier in thee than the world can with all the rest of the pleasures it can afford.'[43] Another letter ended, 'you know that neither fortune can make me rich without you, nor misery make me poor, so long as I enjoy you and give myself the title of your husband'.[44]

Olive was jealous of the women that Endymion would meet on the summer Progress. Answering her letter, 'My dearest love,' he replied, 'Thy care in sending to me shows how truly thou lovest me, and thy fear of my inconstancy argues no want of affection, but of faith, which if any good works of mine may strengthen, I will come on my knees to see thee and put out my eyes, rather than look with an unchaste desire upon any creature whilst I breathe, and to be more secure of me, I would have thee enquire if ever I was false to any friend, and then consider what a traitor I should be if to a wife, such a wife, so virtuous and good, I should prove false and not to my friends. . . . But what can I say or what in the least little I can do? Love you. That I do and ever shall, as he that vows never to be anybody's but

Your husband

Endymion Porter.'[45]

When the Progress reached Salisbury, Endymion wrote, 'This place, Salisbury, which the King has made choice of for his pleasure, can afford me none, because I have resolved to make myself happy only within the limits of thy sight.' But a letter from Olive brought him 'a great deal more of joy than I ever expected to have had in Salisbury', and he sent her 'a nag which I think is the best in England'.[46]

At some point during the Progress, Endymion had stolen a night with Olive at Woodhall, but it got him into trouble, for he wrote, 'my stay with you last night hath so incensed the King and my Lord against me that I was forced to excuse it with saying that I went to take my leave of you and by that means I am now prevented of the happiness to see you till the end of the Progress'.[47]

Towards the end of 1620, Endymion's and Olive's first child was born at Woodhall. Endymion could not get leave from Buckingham to visit Olive even for such an occasion and he wrote to her in great distress, 'God in Heaven bless thee and send thee a very safe delivery. My lord will by no means consent that I should come unto you, which grieves me extremely, and for God's sake believe it there never happened a thing that doth so much trouble me. Good sweetheart, show thy love to me now in excusing to thyself the wrong I do thee to thyself in not leaving the commands of a master to see so good a wife at such a time. I protest to God I am distracted with discontent and know not what to say more than that I love thee as my life and will ever be thine both friend and your husband

Endymion Porter.'[48]

As soon as he could, Endymion hurried to Woodhall to see Olive and the baby. It was a boy and was christened George, after Buckingham. 'My only love,' Endymion wrote, 'This night will divide me from the happiness of seeing thee, but tomorrow I shall enjoy that company of thine which indeed I must confess I do not deserve; for my man tells me you say I might have lost a wife; I do confess I might and such a one as the world hath not the like. But since God hath preserved you as a greater blessing for me, I give Him thanks and acknowledge my unworthiness, praying to the Almighty to bestow on thee as many graces as He can, that thou mayst be blessed and thy posterity and that I may never forget to be

Thy loving husband

Endymion Porter.

On Wednesday your young gentleman will be Georgified; pray God bless it.'[49]

Endymion's letters were now full of pride and anxiety about his baby son. One letter is a reminder of how the very high rate of infant mortality forced seventeenth century parents to resign themselves to the death of their children. 'My sweet love,' it ran, 'Although it be very ill news to hear of George his being not well, yet the good news they bring me of thy health makes amends for that or any misfortune that can come to me; and, dear Olive, believe me that I love George for having such a Mother as well as for being my own flesh and blood. I hope it is nothing but breeding of teeth, and when they come forth he will be well. In the meantime, if you love me, be not overmuch discontented with anything that may happen, for God, who is the giver of all good things can take them away when He pleaseth, and His divine will be done.'[50] But little George flourished. 'God bless thy child and make him a Saint George' wrote Endymion, and ended another letter, 'The Lord bless little George and give him grace to be good and virtuous. I will never forget to be thy true loving husband, that will not go to Saxum.'[51] The reference to 'Saxum' was a teasing one; it was to Saxham, the house not far from Newmarket that contained Sir John Croft's beautiful daughters of whom Olive must have expressed her jealousy!

(v)

The closing months of 1620 also recorded Endymion's first official connection with the sphere of pictures, which was to occupy much of his life in Charles' service.

The English Court's interest in the arts had begun with Charles's elder brother Henry, who in the last few years of his brief life had gathered together a collection of pictures and objects of art. Still only a youth, Henry was not only a splendid horseman, devoted to every kind of sport, filled with martial enthusiasm and especially with a love for ships and the sea; he was also 'known to value none but extraordinary persons',[52] and one of his closest friends was Thomas Howard, Earl of Arundel, whose love of pictures was even then well known, although he was not yet in a position to collect for himself on a large scale.

Their original inspiration may well have come to some extent from Inigo Jones. Born in 1573, he had begun life as a painter, but during an early visit to Italy his interest in architecture had been roused by the works of Palladio. Returning to England, he had made his name with his superb stage designs and costumes for the fashionable masques. He had designed the dresses and staging of a masque, 'Oberon, the Fairy Prince,' which Prince Henry presented to the King on New Year's Day, 1611.[53] A few weeks later, when Prince Henry was given his own establishment, he made Inigo Jones his Surveyor of the Works and commissioned him to build a room in Whitehall to house his collection of pictures.[54] No other Englishman was, at the time, so familiar with the great works of the Italian Renaissance and so likely to have inspired the first enthusiasm for pictures in the minds not only of Prince Henry but also of Arundel, whose adviser he later became.

When, in 1612, Prince Henry's splendid promise was cut short at the age of 18 by his death from typhoid, his art collection passed to his brother Charles. The collection was a valuable one. A contemporary letter stated that 'The Prince's debts are but £9,000 and his moveables amount to much more, especially his horses and pictures, which are many and rare; and his medals, or ancient coins of gold, will yield above £3,000.'[55] Charles was only 12 when his brother died. Early as his taste for the arts developed, he was still too young to follow Henry's footsteps as a collector. The torch, in the meantime, was carried forward by Arundel, whose knowledge, enthusiasm and taste were deeply influenced by the journey he and his wife Aletheia made to Italy in 1613 and 1614, accompanied by Inigo Jones. Two years later, Arundel's collection was enlarged by King James' presenting to him the valuable pictures that, inspired by Arundel's example, the disgraced Earl of Somerset had purchased. Arundel's father-in-law, the Earl of Shrewsbury, died about the same time, and the great Talbot inheritance devolved upon Lady Arundel and her two sisters. Now possessed of ample means to gratify his collecting zeal, one of Arundel's first steps was to arrange, through Ambassador Carleton and his agent in Venice, Daniel Nys, for the purchase of more pictures from Italy to be shared with Lord Pembroke.

The Arundel collection was already a celebrated one by 1618, when the Earl and his Countess were painted, probably by Mytens, whom Arundel had brought over from Holland. Their portraits show them sitting respectively in the sculpture and picture galleries of Arundel House in the

Strand. The nucleus of Arundel's collection was the
Venetian School, though Holbein was the painter whom
Arundel most admired.[56] By 1620, Prince Charles was also
becoming recognized as a leader in Court circles in matters
of art. In a letter, dated the next year, Rubens, long established as the foremost painter of the day, wrote to say how
pleased he would be to be represented 'in a place as eminent
as the gallery of his Royal Highness, the Prince of Wales';[57]
and a year later the Venetian Ambassador remarked on
Charles's love of old paintings, especially those of the
Venetian school.[58]

Buckingham too, by 1620, was beginning to devote some
of his newly acquired wealth to lavish buying of works of
art. A year later, in 1621, Gerbier was in Italy on Buckingham's behalf, buying, through Daniel Nys, pictures which
included Titian's great 'Ecce Homo', the gem of Buckingham's collection,* for which £225 was paid;[59] and at the
beginning of 1625 Gerbier was to write to his master 'Of all
the amateurs and Princes and Kings, there is not one who
has collected in forty years as many pictures as your
Excellency has collected in five'.[60]

But it was probably Arundel who, towards the end of
1620, was instrumental in bringing to England Rubens'
most esteemed pupil, the young Van Dyck, then aged 21.
Although he was given a pension of £100 a year by the
King 'for special service by him performed for his Majesty',
this first visit was only a very short one and he went
back to Antwerp early in 1621, thus losing his pension.[61]
It seems, however, that he was also patronized by Buckingham, for in an account of payments made by Endymion
on Buckingham's behalf at the end of 1620 there occurs the
item 'given to Van Dyke the picture drawer' (unfortunately
the paper is torn and no other particulars are given).[62]
There is no known portrait of Buckingham by Van Dyck
and it is possible that this payment was for the picture
'Continence of Scipio', now at Christ Church, Oxford. It is

* Now in Vienna.

an early work of Van Dyck's and a picture on the subject by Van Dyck was listed in the inventory of Buckingham's pictures at York House in 1635.[63] What is certain is that it was at this time that Endymion first met Van Dyck, who was later to become one of his close friends.

Nor was painting the only one of the arts with which Endymion was already concerned. By 1620 his interest in literature was sufficiently well known for Thomas Dekker, the ageing dramatist and poet, to dedicate a poem 'To the truly accomplished gentleman, and worthy deserver of all Men's loves, Master Endymion Porter'. The poem was 'Dekker his Dreame, in which, being rapt with a Poeticall enthusiasme, the great Volumes of Heaven and Hell to him were opened, in which he read many Wonderful Things'. Expectations roused by this portentous title are doomed to disappointment. The poem is a turgid account of Christ's second coming, largely consisting of a description of the horrors of Hell, 'which being truly interpreted is able to comfort the Good and terrifie the Bad'.[64]

(vi)

Some time in 1621, Endymion entered Prince Charles's own service. The Prince was twenty-one—thirteen years younger than the new member of his household. This is how, a year later, an impartial but experienced observer, the Venetian Ambassador in London, saw Endymion's new master. 'The Prince,' he reported to the Doge, 'has developed with his years, has a truly royal presence, a grave brow, and much grace in his eyes and in the movements of his body, showing a prudent temperance. Such qualities make him more than a Prince, just as his qualities and mind surpass his age. His admirable opinions and customs earn him the universal goodwill and affection of the people. . . . He, as one born to command, seems to scorn obedience to lust and the vices, his self control at his age causing amazement. He shows no immoderate or vast appetites, but stands fast to virtue, either subduing or not feeling the sensual promptings. So far as one knows, he has not tasted certain youthful pleasures and apparently has not felt love except for some show of poetry; he even blushes like a modest maiden if he hears any scandalous conversation, so the women do not tempt him as they did his brother. . . . In all corporal exercises he is admirable. He excels at tilting and indulges in every other kind of horsemanship. . . . His only defect some impediment through the size and length of his tongue which prevents him expressing himself freely.'[65]

Charles's household presented a great contrast to the disorderly confusion and lavish extravagance of that of his father. He was, the Venetian Ambassador wrote, 'methodical and most regular in his affairs, and, in the conduct of his household, wishes to manage everything economically. He wishes his servants to be paid justly and at the proper times, but not bother him with their demands. Of his own accord he gladly procures for them advantages and honours.'[66]

Although Endymion's general conduct in Buckingham's service must have been such as to attract the King's and the Prince's favourable notice, his knowledge of Spain was probably the major factor in securing his employment with the Prince. Gondomar's influence at the court was at its height and the possibilities of a Spanish alliance were ever present in James' mind. The King, too, was making Charles learn Spanish[67] and Endymion may well have been one of his teachers. But to have taken Endymion into the small circle of his personal associates, Charles must also have seen in him some of the qualities and character that appealed to his own dignified, sober and cultured tastes. While Endymion never forgot his debt to Buckingham, his loyalty and devotion were now to be given unreservedly to Charles, who, in turn, rewarded him with his affection and trust.

The chief event of 1621 was the opening at the end of January of James's third Parliament. The King and the Prince rode in state the short distance between Whitehall and Westminster, the King calling 'God Bless Ye' to the loyal crowds that lined the way. He spoke to Buckingham's wife and mother who were in a window along the route and bowed to Gondomar; but seeing another window full of ladies in yellow cuffs and ruffs, a colour which he associated with Mrs. Turner, the Overbury poisoner, James shouted 'A Pox take ye' at them, causing their hasty withdrawal.[68]

The attention which the Commons focused on the gross abuses connected with patents and monopolies involved Buckingham's family and friends, Endymion's old master Sir Edward Villiers being deeply implicated. Nor can Endymion himself have felt free from anxiety. The King and Buckingham were not prepared to stand by the monopolists. Edward Villiers had fortunately just been sent to Bohemia as Ambassador, but the two most notorious offenders, Sir Giles Mompesson and Sir Francis Mitchell, whose exactions upon wine and ale-house keepers had touched so many people, were brought to trial. Mompesson fled the country, but they were both degraded from knighthood and heavily fined, while Mitchell was sent to prison after being made to ride through the city with his face to his horse's tail.[69]

This spring of 1621 also saw the fall of a much greater man. Lord Chancellor Bacon, just created Viscount St. Albans, was involved in the Commons' exposures. Charged with bribery, his trial was left by James to the Lords and ended in his disgrace.

When the King adjourned Parliament in May, Endymion left Whitehall with the rest of the court and the usual peripatetic round was resumed. This summer, the Progress took the court to the Midlands. From Royston, they went to Ampthill, Bletsoe, Castle Ashby and on to Buckingham's newly acquired mansion at Burley-on-the-Hill* in Rutland. There, the visitors, Endymion amongst them, were entertained by a masque which Buckingham had commissioned Ben Jonson to write for the occasion. It was called 'The

* It was burned to the ground by the Parliamentary forces in 1645.

Metamorphosed Gypsies' and the masked actors were all lords and gentlemen, with Buckingham himself disguised as the Gypsy Captain. After songs, dances and verses full of topical and personal allusions, the Gypsies proceeded, in flattering terms, to tell the fortunes of the King, the Prince and the ladies of the court. They then entered 'metamorphosed' by being dressed in rich clothes, and, after a dance, invoked blessings on the King by listing, in Gilbertian verses, all the unpleasant things which the King's various senses might be spared. James' well-known antipathies were brought into the lists. His dislike of high-handed women, for instance, was to free his 'Seeing' from

> 'A smock rampant and the itches
> To be putting on the breeches.'

His 'Smelling' was, of course, to be free from tobacco as well as from such contacts as

> 'A lady that doth breathe
> Worse above than underneath.'

While the verses of blessing on his 'Tasting' listed his dislikes in the way of food

> 'From an oyster and fried fish
> A sow's baby in a dish
> From any portion of a swine
> From bad venison and worse wine.'

The masque ended with further songs in adulation of the King, Buckingham as the Gypsy Captain speaking the last lines.

> 'Love, love, his fortunes then and virtues known,
> Who is the top of men, but makes the happiness our
>   own;
> Since where the Prince for goodness is renowned
> The Subject with felicity is crowned.'[70]

The King was so delighted with the Masque that it had to be repeated five days later when the court had moved to Belvoir, where Buckingham's father-in-law, the Earl of Rutland, was the host. After enjoying hunting in Sherwood Forest, the Progress moved to Nottingham. On the way, a stop was made at Rufford, Sir George Savile's seat. Endymion wrote from there to Olive at Woodhall. He was still unreconciled to absence from her.

'All the pleasure I can take now is in thinking of thee, and the best way to vent these thoughts in absence is by writing. Sweet love, I entertain myself with the prettiest delusions my fancies can afford, for I make a thousand means to represent thee unto me. . . . At Woodstock I have commanded Charles* to meet me, that I may hear of thy good health, which I pray for on my knees. . . . Farewell, my soul's joy, and assure thyself I will live and die

Thy ever-loving husband
Endymion Porter.

From Rufford, this 12 August 1621.'[71]

At Woodstock the King was met by the Vice-Chancellor of Oxford. Scholars of the University entertained James with a play, but he was with great difficulty persuaded to sit the performance out. Not only was the play dull and the actors fuddled with drink, but the author was foolish enough to introduce a song in praise of James' pet abomination, tobacco.

It was probably from Woodstock that Endymion rode over to Aston, since he wrote to Olive, 'I was at Aston where I had the happiness to see thy picture and that did somewhat please me, but when I found it wanted that pretty discourse which thy sweet company doth afford, I kissed it with a great deal of devotion, and, with many wishes for the original, there I left it. Now I am coming nearer towards you, but cannot as yet have so great a blessing as these lines shall have, to be seen by you, but when the King comes to Windsor I will hazard the

* Endymion's servant.

loss of all my friends, rather than be a day longer from thee.'[72]

The King and the Prince reached Windsor early in September, when Endymion was no doubt able to get to Woodhall to see Olive again. After a short time in London, the court moved to Newmarket.

CHAPTER III

(i)

NEGOTIATIONS for a Spanish bride for Prince Charles, in which Endymion was soon to play a prominent part, were reaching a critical stage. The idea of a matrimonial alliance between England and Spain was no new one. As soon, indeed, as peace had been made with Spain in 1604, the possibility of a match between Prince Henry and a Spanish princess had been discussed.

To King James, such an alliance had considerable attractions. Most important, perhaps, was that of a dowry of Spanish gold. James's treasury was generally empty and it was repugnant to his ideas of kingship to have to beg Parliament for financial assistance to which strings were likely to be attached. The Gunpowder plot, too, was ever present in his memory, and allying his son to a Catholic princess would give him greater security against assassination at Catholic hands. His whole concept of statesmanship was also essentially pacific, and he believed that an alliance with Spain might help him to fulfil his dream of going down to history as Europe's great peacemaker. His views on a Spanish match were not, however, shared by his people. Spain was still 'the enemy', and, except for the Catholics, English public opinion regarded the prospect of a Spanish marriage with dislike and fear.

On the Spanish side, the attractions were not so great. Spain's chief consideration was to prevent England joining her enemies and, in a naval war, striking at the sources of her wealth. The marriage was regarded as a last expedient which might have to be used to keep peace with England, but, knowing James's dislike of war, the Spaniards hoped that it was a sacrifice that need never be made. Political expediency governed their attitude. While they professed to desire the marriage, their real purpose was to procrastinate so that Spain might remain free to do whatever would profit her most.

There was also a third party—Rome. The Pope cherished the belief that the marriage might be used to bring about the conversion of England. The Spanish game of procrastination was also favoured by Rome as the method which would secure the best possible terms.

The negotiations which were to reach their climax in 1623 had begun almost ten years before with the arrival in London of the Spanish Ambassador, Sarmiento, shortly to become Count Gondomar. He was a consistent protagonist of the marriage, believing that it would infallibly lead to the conversion of the English royal house and that, once this was accomplished, the conversion of the whole of England would quickly follow and Spain's interests would be secure. Gondomar's opportunity came when the Parliament summoned in 1614 to vote James urgently needed funds insisted on putting grievances before supply and was summarily dismissed. It was at this point that Gondomar persuaded the Spanish Government to draw up marriage articles. When they arrived, they proved to be onerous: the Pope must grant a dispensation; the penalties on English Catholics must not be enforced; the Infanta's household must be Spanish and must be allowed to worship publicly.

For the time being, negotiations were dropped; but, as the months went by, James' financial needs grew more pressing. Threats of assassination had been heard and the King was equally alarmed at manifestations of popular martial spirit, demanding war with Spain. In 1616, James accordingly reopened negotiations, but a new and long delay was imposed by the Spanish decision to refer the whole matter to a junta of theologians. When, nearly a year later, the theologians gave their answer, they advised stiffer terms. The English penal laws must be entirely repealed, and the Prince must fetch his bride from Spain. Since the penal laws could not be repealed except by Parliament and since James knew that Parliament would never agree to repeal them, the negotiations came to a standstill.

A new factor, however, arose to increase James' desire for Spanish aid. The Protestant nobles of Bohemia revolted against the aged Emperor Mathias's imposition of his Catholic cousin Ferdinand as their King. In May 1618 they broke into the Palace at Prague and threw the Emperor's regents out of the window. In a short time they held the whole of Bohemia. The future of the Austrian Hapsburgs depended on crushing the rebellion. The Bohemians begged James for help, but his vanity, abetted by Spanish promptings, impelled him to assume the role of peacemaker. Unfortunately, neither side wanted his mediation.

In March 1619 the old Emperor died, and in August Ferdinand was elected as his successor. The Bohemians at once formally deposed him as their King and invited Frederick, the Elector Palatine and the husband of James' daughter Elizabeth, to take his place. Frederick rashly accepted and went to Prague in October.

English public opinion, united in anti-Catholic and anti-Spanish sentiments, hotly supported Frederick. But James was torn by doubts. In his view, Frederick's acceptance of the Bohemian crown was a usurpation and a rebellion against the Emperor. Besides, all his instincts were opposed to war and he had no money and no army. On the other hand, Frederick's wife was his own daughter, and his little grandson had written in his childish hand asking for help. In his uncertainty, he fell back on his favourite policy of drift.

In the meantime, Ferdinand had enlisted the aid of Maximilian of Bavaria, the leader of the Catholic League, by promising him Frederick's electoral dignity and a large part of his lands. Spain had also agreed to join in by attacking the Palatinate from the Netherlands. In August 1620, the Emperor moved on Prague, while a Spanish army invaded the Palatinate.

Whatever might be the rights of the case in Bohemia, the Spanish aggression against his son-in-law's own hereditary possessions roused even James's anger. In a short time Frederick, routed at Prague, was flying for his life. James had no alternative but to summon the Parliament that met in January 1621. Before its adjournment in May it had granted the King some money, but less than he had asked for, and far less than he needed if Frederick was to be given effective armed support. James, however, continued his futile efforts to mediate in the struggle which Frederick refused to abandon and in which his General, Mansfeld, was proving little better than a bandit.

When Parliament reassembled in November, it turned at once to foreign affairs. One member after another attacked Spain abroad and the Catholics at home. The debate ended in the framing of a petition to the King asking for war with Spain, the enforcement of the anti-Catholic laws and a Protestant bride for Prince Charles.

James had remained obstinately at Newmarket and the twelve members of the Commons deputed to present the petition had a cold journey there. Concealing his anger, the King received them graciously, but firmly refused to allow any interference in affairs which he considered to be within his own prerogative. Back in Whitehall for Christmas, James was urged by Gondomar and Buckingham to get rid of a body so obstinate in the assertion of its rights. At the end of December the King made up his mind. Tearing out of the Commons' journal the page that contained the protestation of their privileges, he dissolved Parliament. It was, wrote Gondomar to the King of Spain, 'the best thing that has happened in the interests of Spain and of the Catholic religion since Luther began preaching.'[1]

With his finances at their lowest ebb, with affairs in the Palatinate going from bad to worse—even Frederick's capital of Heidelberg fell in September 1622—James had to turn again to Spain and the marriage alliance as the only way to restore both his own finances and his son-in-law's inheritance.

Little progress had, meantime, been made with the marriage articles. The Spanish had sent them to the Pope, who, in turn, had remitted them to a committee of cardinals. They recommended that the articles must be stiffened and, in August 1622, the new terms reached James. Not only must the penal laws be repealed, but the Infanta's Church must be open to all, her priests must be headed by a Bishop and all must be outside the law of England, and the education of any children must be in the Infanta's hands, boys till fourteen and girls till twelve.

James was greatly distressed by these enhanced terms. He wrote to Digby, his Ambassador in Spain—whom he now made Earl of Bristol—to say that he could not do more than promise that the penal laws would not, in practice, be invoked. Buckingham at the same time wrote to Gondomar, who had left England for Spain in May 1622, telling him that James had gone as far as he possibly could to satisfy Spain, and begging him to use his good offices to obtain concessions so that the match might be concluded. Before leaving England, Gondomar had suggested to Charles the possibility of his visiting Madrid, if Gondomar, when he got back to Spain, should think it advisable.

Ever since entering Buckingham's service, Endymion had, of course, been closely concerned with these events, as he had charge of the Spanish correspondence, first of Buckingham and then of Charles, and he had acted as interpreter in their discussions with Gondomar.[2] Throughout 1622, during the normal court round, Spanish affairs must have taken up much of Endymion's time. On September 18th, at Buckingham's request, Endymion wrote to Gondomar to tell him that a fleet was ready and that Buckingham, as Lord High Admiral, intended to take his friend with him in secret, to bring back the Infanta.[3]

Under pressure from Buckingham and Charles, James

was forced to agree that he could no longer wait in uncertainty as to Spain's intentions. He called the Council together at Hampton Court at the end of September and it was decided that a direct summons must be addressed to the King of Spain. Philip must obtain the restitution of Heidelberg from the Emperor within seventy days; if the Emperor refused to consent, Philip must order a Spanish army to take the field against him, or, at least, allow an English force to march through the Netherlands to the Palatinate; if Philip failed to give a favourable answer within ten days, Bristol was to break off the marriage negotiations and leave Madrid. A special envoy was to carry the despatch containing these demands.

James thought that this would be a good opportunity to send someone to Madrid on whose ability and integrity he could rely to bring him back a faithful report of the attitude of the Spanish ministers, while Buckingham and Charles wished the envoy to be someone close enough in their confidence to discuss with Gondomar the possibilities of the Prince visiting Spain. The man chosen was Endymion.

The King, Philip IV, was only seventeen years old and almost wholly absorbed in his own amusements. Devoting his time to boar and stag hunting and to displays of tilting, he was glad to hand over the cares of business to Endymion's former master, Count Olivares, now the virtual ruler of Spain, through whom passed all the political communications between the King and the various Councils responsible for the government.

Olivares cared little for pleasure or amusement. His interest lay in the conduct of State affairs. Able and vigorous, he was narrow and ignorant of other countries and other ways of thought. He saw that the great need of Spain's shaky economy was peace, and especially peace with England. Like James, however, he believed that the fruits of victory could be secured without the danger of war.

The third important figure on the Spanish side in the business of the marriage was the Infanta Maria herself. In

1622 she was sixteen, a year younger than her brother the King. Her face was too heavy and her lips too full for beauty, but she had a very sweet expression, and her blonde hair and pink and white complexion made her stand out among the olive-skinned ladies of the Court. Her courage was notable. She was unafraid of thunder and lightning and once, when the scaffolding suddenly burst into flames at an entertainment and panic seized the spectators, the Infanta quietly asked Olivares to protect her from the press of the crowd and left, at her usual pace, without the slightest sign of fear.

She was of a silent disposition, very sensitive, and renowned for her hatred of gossip and for never speaking ill of anyone. Philip was very fond of her and visited her every day. She, on her side, was careful never to meddle in his business, nor to ask, for other people, favours that he might be unwilling to grant. 'It is not reason,' she said, 'that because he desires to give me gust, I should suffer myself to be persuaded to give him disgust.'

But her outstanding characteristic was the depth of her religious fervour. She spent two or three hours a day in prayer, confessed and partook of Holy Communion every Wednesday and Saturday, and was 'especially devoted to the Blessed Sacrament and to Our Lady's Immaculate Conception'. Her religion was equally conspicuous in works. Most of the money given her by the King was bestowed on the poor, and she spent much of her time in making, with her own hands, comforts for the sick and wounded.[4]

(ii)

On October 3rd, Endymion was given the despatch which he was to carry to Madrid. He was to have left Hampton Court the next day. But just as he was about to start, Francis Cottington arrived from Madrid, having been recalled from the Embassy staff there to become Charles's secretary. Such news as he brought was encouraging. The

Spanish had expressed to Bristol their disapproval of Rome's additions to the articles and Gondomar had given him an optimistic letter to James.

The Council, however, saw no reason any longer to postpone Endymion's departure, and with it the summons to Philip. Buckingham and Charles warmly agreed, but James compromised by directing Endymion to tell Bristol that, if necessary, he might consent to the extension to nine years of the age up to which children of the marriage were to be in the Infanta's charge. Nor was Bristol to come home if the Spanish proved obdurate; he was merely to report back. Endymion took, too, secret instructions from Charles and Buckingham to find out Gondomar's views on their projected visit to Spain.[5]

The Court in the meantime had moved to Theobalds and it was from there, on October 7th, 1622, that Endymion finally left on the journey which, it was confidently believed, would settle, one way or the other, the negotiations which had been drawn out over so many years.

It was, unfortunately, to take much more than Endymion's mission to shatter the illusions on which the whole edifice of the match was based—James's illusion that the Catholic King of Spain could be induced to take up arms against the Catholic Emperor in order to restore the Palatinate to James's Protestant son-in-law; Olivares's illusion that the match could be indefinitely postponed or even broken off without a rupture with James; Gondomar's illusion that Charles had only to visit Madrid to be converted to the Catholic faith; the Pope's illusion that just as Henry VIII had turned England away from the true faith, so a Catholic King, converted by his consort, would now restore England to the fold.

At Dover, Endymion was joined by his younger brother, Tom. After his return from Spain, Tom had chosen the sea as his profession and had become a Captain in the Navy. His knowledge of Spain had proved useful to him and he had commanded a ship in Sir Robert Mansell's expedition against the pirates of Algiers in 1620–1 when the English ships were based on Spanish ports.[6] The Channel crossing was made in a ship under Tom's command. It ended disastrously. Nearing Calais in a stormy sea, their ship fell foul of a larger vessel and was in danger of sinking. As the two ships collided, Endymion, jumping onto the larger ship, fell heavily and broke his shoulder. His servant, following him, only just managed to clutch the larger ship's side where he hung until the two ships crashed together again, crushing the unfortunate man who fell dead into the sea. Tom escaped injury. As a report of the event stated, 'the Roman Augurs would have taken this for an ominous sign of the success of the business'.[7]

Endymion was forced to stay in Calais until he was fit to travel. He had Tom for company and as soon as the news reached England, Charles sent his surgeon over to him.[8] Endymion at once wrote to Olive. His first letter was only a message of affection. In order to spare her any anxiety, he made no mention of his accident until, in his second letter, he was able to say that he had recovered.

'My sweetest Olive,' his first letter ran, 'I am on my journey and Tom will acquaint you how I do. . . . All I can say is that I love thee better than my life and nothing shall alter your true loving husband.'[9]

His second letter was written after he had been nearly a week in Calais. 'Although I writ you in my last that I was well, it was not being so, for I had my share of the hurt and all the misfortune. My shoulder was broken, which now is as well as ever it was in my life, and Tom and I are very merry, and do heartily drink your health, wishing it were possible to have you here with us.

On Wednesday, if it please God, I propose to go to Spain, till when I have entreated my brother to stay with me, and then I will write you more at large. My sweet and kind Olive, I protest unto God I am now merry, well and joyed to think how thy good prayers did preserve me; when I return I will thank thee with as many kisses as thou canst

let me take, wherein I know thy bounty will afford an
equality to my desires.

God in Heaven bless little George and make him a
dutiful child to thee and his grandmother, to whom I desire
to be remembered, for I love her dearly, and I pray you
forget me not to Sir John and my Lady and to Mall,* and
all the rest of our worthy friends.

Farewell, dearest love,

> Your true loving husband
> Endymion Porter.

Calais, this Monday morning,
the 14 October, 1622.'

Brother Tom added a postscript to this letter.

'As I hope to be saved, my brother is very well, I thank
God for it and I am

> Your true loving brother
> Thomas Porter.'[10]

In spite of his and Tom's protestations to Olive, Endymion's shoulder was by no means fully recovered when,
after only a week's delay, he set off down the long autumn-
leaf-strewn road to Madrid. On November 1st, after a fortnight's hard riding, he reached his destination. The news
of his arrival was well received by the Spanish. 'Mr. Porter
is highly favoured in this Court,' it was reported.[11] Bristol,
however, was far from pleased at this intervention in his
conduct of the negotiations by someone so inferior to him
in rank and experience, whom he had known as a youth ten
years before in Madrid. Besides, he had recently been given
further assurances by Olivares and the King of their desire
for the marriage and of their goodwill in trying to bring
about an end to the fighting in the Palatinate.[12]

Endymion's right shoulder was still much bruised from
his mishap at Calais and a member of Bristol's household
wrote that there was even a fear that he might lose the use
of his right arm.[13] In spite of this disability, he was most
anxious to fulfil his instructions to complete his mission in

* The Duchess of Buckingham and her little daughter Lady Mary Villiers.

fifteen days, but Bristol showed no disposition to help him bring matters to an issue.

Three years later when Bristol was impeached for his part in the negotiations for the match, Endymion was examined by the House of Lords. The evidence that he then gave tells the story of his efforts to wring a definite answer from the unwilling Olivares.[14] The King was away hunting and the Ambassador advised him to wait till he returned before doing anything. When the King got back a week later, Bristol promised to arrange an early interview but declared that an attempt to force an immediate answer out of the Spanish was 'a threatening way to which they were not used, and said and bound it with an oath that were the way to destroy all'. Smallpox, too, had attacked Bristol's household.[15] His daughter and niece were dangerously ill and two of his wife's maids had died. This provided a further excuse for not approaching the King in person.

The days passed with no sign of Endymion's interview being arranged, although Bristol held frequent conferences with the Spanish ministers, from which Endymion was excluded. Much more than the fifteen days allowed by Endymion's instructions had elapsed. In this difficult position, Endymion now took the courageous decision to ignore Bristol and, trading on his past service and friendship with Olivares, to go straight to the great man. His welcome was most cordial, Olivares calling him 'child' and promising, for old times' sake, that he would give him whatever he wanted. But when Endymion asked for an assurance that the King of Spain would use his armed forces to help restore the Palatinate, if the Emperor refused its restitution, Olivares started as if Endymion 'had shot him', saying 'however wilt thou demand such an unreasonable request, unless thou wouldst have the King of Spain declare himself against the Catholic League, against the Emperor, against the house of Austria? I am ashamed thou shouldst ask such a thing'. On Endymion's replying that his demands were no more than what, according to Bristol, the Spanish

Government had agreed to, Olivares answered that if Bristol said this he 'lied a thousand times'. In respect of the marriage, all that Endymion could get out of Olivares was that he knew nothing about it. 'Let the Pope and them shift that amongst them,' he said.

Startled at hearing sentiments so much at variance with what Bristol had told him, Endymion went straight back to the Ambassador, gave him a full account of the interview and told him that 'all was knavery'. Bristol was furious. 'Olivares should know,' he exclaimed, 'that an Earl of England is as good as a Conde of Spain.' He promised to take Endymion with him immediately to see Olivares and to justify, to Olivares's face, the reports that he had made about Spanish assurances of help over the Palatinate.

Next morning, however, Bristol had second thoughts. It was better, he said, not to vex so great a minister, since to do so might injure the prospects for the marriage. Two days later, Bristol told Endymion that he had solved the mystery of why Olivares had spoken as he did. It was because he had not liked to discuss such a matter with someone who was not a public minister.

In spite of this snub, Endymion went back to Olivares, to ask why he was so angry with him. Olivares repudiated Bristol's story, but said that the cause of his anger was that Endymion, 'his child', had revealed what Olivares had told him in secret. 'I will never abide you more,' he declared. His fury, indeed, at having been betrayed into speaking the truth by someone who had once been his servant was so great that, when Buckingham reached Madrid four months later, Olivares told him that he hated the very ground Porter stood on.[16] Meantime, Endymion could only reply that what Olivares had told him directly concerned the business of his mission and that he could not betray his King and country.

Olivares had, in fact, a new and very good reason for equivocation, apart from his natural Spanish dislike of any pressure to give a direct reply to a direct question. The

Infanta herself had suddenly taken a hand in the game. Now that the Pope's opposition seemed to be weakening, the prospect loomed nearer of a marriage to a heretic, against which her every instinct revolted. Her Confessor only confirmed her apprehensions when he reminded her of what a comfortable bed-fellow she would have when 'he who lies by your side and who will be the father of your children, is certain to go to hell!' Finally she sent for Olivares and told him that rather than marry Prince Charles she would take refuge in a nunnery.[17]

When Philip was told of this on his return from hunting, he ordered Olivares to find a way out of the marriage.

In face of the dilemma, Olivares and Philip secretly fell back on a plan that the former had long had up his sleeve— Charles should marry the Emperor's daughter and the Elector Frederick's eldest son should be given a Catholic education in Vienna. In public, however, it was to appear that the marriage between Charles and the Infanta was still the object. Not only were James and Bristol to be hoodwinked. Even Gondomar and the other Spanish ministers were to be allowed to continue, in good faith, their efforts for the conclusion of the match.

After Endymion's rebuff, Bristol had brought himself to present a formal written demand for the restitution of the towns in the Palatinate within seventy days. He wrote home that the Spanish ministers were in great confusion how to answer this, but that he believed that they still wished to please James. Endymion, who had had a bout of sickness, was to wait in Madrid till he could take back the Spanish reply.[18]

Early in December, Bristol was given what he supposed to be the final decision of the Spanish Government. Concessions were to be made to James' views in respect of the marriage articles. While the Infanta's priests must not be subject to the laws of England, only her household would have the right of public worship in her Church. The children could leave their mother's hands at the age of nine and it would be acceptable if James merely promised in general terms not to persecute his Catholic subjects so long as they worshipped in private. In regard to the Palatinate, everything was to be done to satisfy James, but it would be unseemly to ask the Emperor to give up the towns at seventy days' notice.

Bristol was well satisfied with these answers. In face of all the evidence before him, it would have been hardly possible for him to see through a deception in which Philip's own ministers were themselves unwitting tools. Nevertheless a neutral observer, the Venetian Ambassador in London, was writing to the Doge that all that Porter would bring back would be a narcotic to make James sleep more soundly this winter.[19]

On December 13th Endymion at last started for home. He carried with him a despatch from Bristol, the amended articles and a secret message from Gondomar warmly welcoming the offer of a visit from the Prince. He also took back with him the conviction that Bristol's cautious diplomacy was not likely to cut through the web of Spanish procrastination and deceit.

(iii)

Endymion reached London, without mishap, on January 2nd, 1623.[20] He had been away nearly three months. The Court, as usual, had come to Whitehall for Christmas. Olive, too, was in London. The preceding June, Endymion had taken a seven-year lease of a London house from the widow of Sir George Coppin. It was on the north side of the Strand, opposite the gate of Durham House and also facing the New Exchange which had been built in 1608 between Durham and York Houses. The property had originally belonged to the Bishops of Durham as part of their Durham House estate. Henry VIII had taken possession of it and sold it to the Fortescues, from whom it had later been bought by Sir George Coppin's father. The situation in

the Parish of St. Martin-in-the-Fields and at the west
end of the Strand only some two hundred yards east of
Charing Cross, was fashionable and conveniently close to
Whitehall. The house faced onto the street, but the back
looked north over the open space of Covent Garden. The
property consisted of the house, a yard with pump and
cistern, stables and a coach-house. There was, too, a small
garden on the west side, 124 feet long by 30 feet broad, with
a little brick building in it. The garden was held on lease
from the Earl of Bedford.

The house was a substantial one. On the ground floor
there was a hall with benches round the walls, a panelled
parlour and a panelled dining-room. The best bedroom was
also on the ground floor, with a door through to the dining-
room. It had four cupboards. On the ground floor, too, were
the kitchen, the larder, the buttery with a cupboard for
glass and a bench for pressing linen, the wash-house with a
cistern and water pipes leading to the kitchen, and the coal
house. The cellar below had three divisions, one for beer
casks and the other two fitted with racks for wine bottles.
The main staircase led up from the dining-room to a panelled study at the top of the stairs. On the first floor there
were also four bedrooms, a closet, a maids' chamber and a
wardrobe leading to the back stairs which went down to the
kitchen. Above, on the top floor, there was a garret.

The lease, a repairing one, was initially for seven years
and cost £80 a year, a large sum in terms of the contemporary value of money. The house in the Strand was to
be Endymion's and Olive's main home for the next twenty
years and it was here that he found his wife awaiting the
birth of their second child.[21]

Endymion's reception at Court was, at first, a cool one.
Someone—possibly Bristol—had reported home that he
'had dealt so meddlingly in Spain, that he deserved to be
turned out of his place'; and it was some time before he was
allowed to give Charles and Buckingham his full story of
what had happened and what he had discovered. It was, of

course, disappointing news, 'fraught with generalities,' as Buckingham later declared, 'without any one particular or certainty at all.'[22]

James and Charles had no hesitation in signing and sending to Bristol the amended marriage articles or in promising that the English Catholics should no longer be persecuted. But James' hopes of an immediate settlement of Palatinate and marriage were no nearer fruition.

Buckingham and Charles were, however, stirred to action. Delay, they felt, was worse than a denial, and a desperate disease must have a desperate remedy.[23] Desperate, indeed, was the remedy they now proposed.

Although Gondomar had once suggested that Charles should visit Madrid incognito, the recent plan had been for the Prince, accompanied by Buckingham as Admiral of the Fleet, to fetch the Infanta home by sea in May, when the dispensation from Rome would have arrived and all the marriage conditions would have been finally settled. Now, they determined to cut through all further delays and obstacles by an immediate visit to Madrid, travelling over-land incognito. It was for this astonishing idea that they sought the King's approval, urging that the risks were negligible, since they would, for greater secrecy, only take two attendants with them and would ride so fast that they would be in Spain before it was known that they had left England.

James was unable to resist the combined appeal of his son and his favourite. He gave his consent with less than his normal hesitation. But as soon as he had time for reflection, the appalling rashness of the young men's proposal came home to him and robbed him of all peace of mind. His only son and the heir to the throne would be exposed to great personal dangers; public opinion in England would be outraged; and to present Philip and Olivares with such a hostage would be to play straight into their hands and to invite them to put up their terms for the marriage.

When Charles and Buckingham came next day to discuss

the detailed plans, James burst into tears and told them
that it would break his heart if they pursued their plan.
But Charles and Buckingham were ruthless. They reminded
James of his yesterday's promise and accused him of having
confided the secret to someone who had inflamed him
against the journey. Brushing aside his protestations, they
suggested Francis Cottington and Endymion Porter as
their two attendants. James approved their choice but
asked to see Cottington who was waiting outside the room.
Pledging him to secrecy, 'Cottington,' said James, 'here is
Baby Charles and Steenie, who have a great mind to go by
post into Spain, to fetch home the Infanta, and will have
but two more in their company, and have chosen you for
one. What think you of the journey?' Cottington was so
astonished that he could hardly speak, but made the
trembling reply that he could not think well of it and that
it would make all previous negotiations fruitless, since,
once they had the Prince in their hands, the Spanish would
make new overtures, especially in regard to matters of
religion. Hearing his own fears thus confirmed, James flung
himself on his bed. 'I told you this before,' he shrieked, 'I
am undone. I shall lose Baby Charles.' The Prince and
Buckingham were furious at this setback. Turning on Cottington, they told him that the only reason he was objecting
was because he had not been consulted first. No one had
asked his opinion on matters of state, they said. All that the
King wanted was his views on which was the best road to
Madrid. James tried to stand up for Cottington, but, in the
end, he was forced to yield and give his final consent to the
journey.[24]

Once he had agreed to the plan, James's better judgement
seems to have been lost in the rosy haze of romance which
surrounded the project, the whole idea taking on the
colour of some great exploit of knight-errantry. James's
thoughts went back to his own Leander-like dash across the
sea to fetch home his fair bride from Denmark.[25] He was
soon writing to the two travellers as his 'dear venturous

Knights, worthy to be put in a new romance';[26] and when ultimately Charles and Buckingham had safely reached Madrid he was glorying in what the Venetian Ambassador tactfully called a master-stroke.[27]

Charles himself had hitherto regarded marriage with the Infanta solely as a matter of state. Indeed, he had been overheard to say that 'was it not for sin, it would be as well if princes could have two wives; one for reasons of state, the other to please themselves'.[28] He was not yet in love with the Infanta, but he was in love with the idea of being in love, and it was in the spirit of a romantic escapade, with all the trappings of a gay and brilliant adventure, that Charles and Buckingham made their hasty preparations for the journey.

On February 16th, Cottington and Endymion were sent off from Theobalds to Dover with orders to procure a vessel for the party's crossing and to get the ports closed for all other shipping. So secret was their departure that Endymion was not even allowed to tell Olive that he was leaving or to see his newly born second son, who had been christened in London the day before. The boy was called Charles, and the Prince showed his regard for Endymion by becoming the child's godfather.[29]

The next day Charles and Buckingham went to New Hall, the house in Essex that Buckingham had recently bought. On the morning of the 18th they started off for Dover. Donning false beards and assuming the names of John and Tom Smith, they rode to Tilbury, attended only by Graham, Buckingham's master of the horse.

Their first mishap occurred when they crossed the river to Gravesend. One of their false beards fell off. This naturally roused the suspicions of the ferryman as to the bona fides of the travellers in such fine riding coats. These suspicions were enhanced when one of the travellers handed him a gold piece and rode off without waiting for the change. The ferryman at once informed the local magistrates who sent off to Rochester to have the party stopped, but their messenger failed to catch up with the well-mounted travellers. As they left Rochester, however, they were unlucky enough to meet the Spanish Ambassador to the Netherlands on his way from Dover to London. The Ambassador's escorts, Sir Lewis Lewknor and Sir Henry Mainwaring, were surprised to see three strange hooded figures carrying pistols leave the road as they approached and gallop off across the fields. Mainwaring at once sent a messenger to Canterbury with orders to have them stopped. On arrival in Canterbury the travellers were therefore met by the Mayor, and 'Jack' and 'Tom' were only allowed to proceed after 'Tom' had removed his beard and told the astonished official that he was the Marquis of Buckingham, the Lord Admiral, on his way to a surprise inspection of the royal ships.

At six in the evening the three horsemen at length reached Dover, where they found Cottington and Endymion waiting for them with the news that their ship was ready. The night was stormy, but the little party was up early and embarked at five o'clock, with a fair wind to carry them over.[30]

Two days later, by hard riding, the travellers had reached Paris and found lodgings above a hostelry. On the road, they had a narrow escape from being recognized when they had the ill-luck to meet two German gentlemen who had recently seen the Prince and Buckingham in England. The Germans gave signs of recognition, but so improbable was it that such great personages should be found as ordinary travellers on a French road that Graham had little difficulty in convincing the Germans that they were mistaken.[31] The next day (February 22nd) the travellers rested in Paris and, in the afternoon, wrote their first letters home. Charles and Buckingham wrote a joint letter to James, their 'dear Dad and Gossip', signing themselves 'Your humble and obedient son and servant, Charles', and 'Your humble slave and dog, Steenie'. They told him how Charles had been the first one to be sick on the crossing, but how Buckingham had gone on being sick the longest; how they got to Boulogne in six hours, after as fair a passage as anyone ever had; and how the sight of land made them feel so much better that they made up their minds to set off riding as soon as they landed, so that they reached Montreuil that night and Paris two days later, with Buckingham falling off his horse four times, but with Charles holding up his horse when it stumbled with such mastery that he never had to stop. The letter went on to tell how, in Paris, they bought periwigs which overshadowed their faces and disguised them so effectively that they thought they might venture to have a look at the King of France, which they effected through the good offices of M. de Preaux 'the King's Governor'. M. de Preaux's son then took them to look at the Queen Mother at dinner, and, as they related in a second letter written later that evening, brought them to the Louvre again where they saw the young Queen and Princess Henrietta Maria (Charles's first glimpse of his future wife) with most of the beauties of the Court dancing in the rehearsal of a masque. The writers assured James that they had not been recognized. They were full of glee at the audacity of their adventure at the French Court.[32]

Endymion also had time to write to Olive to relieve the anxiety which she must have felt at his sudden and unexplained departure.

'My dear Olive,—Since my departing from you I have enjoyed very little content, although I have had health and everything I could desire, wanting nothing but your sweet company, by which you may perceive in how great a measure I esteem yours, that can prefer it before a Prince's and a Lord's, both of whom I honour and love as my life, and the worst of whom would seek for company to the best man living. I give God thanks we are all safely arrived in Paris, where it hath pleased His Highness and my Lord to stay this day to see the town. Tomorrow we set forwards from hence towards Spain and, good Olive, let us have your prayers every day along with us to help to conduct us thither. I make no doubt but we shall have them the heartier for our return; because I fear there may be a grudge remaining still in you for not acquainting you first with my journey, but I was conjured to the contrary by my master, which I hope will fully satisfy you that I ought not to have done it.

I would have you send Charles and the Spaniard* along with the Prince's servants that come by sea. They are to be allowed as my men to come in the ship, and let them bring me one dozen of shirts, and little George his picture, and yours in the gold case which is at Gerbier's, and half a dozen pairs of silk stockings, three black and three colours, and your chain of diamonds, and let me entreat you to make much of yourself that I may hear of your health, which news will somewhat mitigate the pain of this absence.

Little George and Charles will serve to put you in mind how much you are to love me, and my own conscience shall make me remember that I am not to do anything that may offend the faith I owe to so good a wife. Farewell, sweet Olive, and God Almighty bless thee and thine. I will ever be thy true loving husband

Endymion Porter

Paris, this 22nd day of February, 1623.'

'You must not let it be known from me whither we are gone, but say you know nothing, nor speak to Charles till you hear further from me of coming, for the Prince will not have it spoken of, and I charge you not to tell anybody whither I am gone. Remember my humble duty to my Mother and burn this letter.'[33]

Next morning, the travellers were up at three o'clock, riding hard for the Spanish frontier, over the muddy, wintry roads that Endymion had so recently traversed. Buckingham had a heavy fall at Orleans. At Bordeaux, they bought riding coats all of one fashion and colour, and avoided the courteous attentions of the Governor by pre-

* His servants.

79

tending not to be of sufficient rank to meet him. It was Lent, and the hungry travellers could not get any meat at the inns. Shortly after leaving Bordeaux, they came on a herd of goats. Hearing Graham say that he would steal one of the kids and carry it with him to their inn, Charles called out, 'Why, Richard, do you think you may practise here your old tricks upon the Border?' While Buckingham and Graham dismounted and chased the kid, Charles killed it with a shot from his pistol.

In six days from Paris the party had reached Bayonne. There the Governor, de Grammont, had his suspicions that the travellers were of higher rank than their outward appearance indicated, but let them pass. Just before they reached the Spanish frontier, they met Bristol's messenger, Gresley, riding with letters from Madrid to England. They ordered him to turn round and accompany them as far as Irun and across the border into Spain, so that he could take back to James a letter actually written on Spanish soil.[34]

'We are now got into Spain,' wrote Charles and Steenie, 'free from harm of falls, in as perfect health as when we parted, and undiscovered by any Monsieur.' They went on to say that Gresley's news, and what they read in such of his despatches that were not in cipher, only confirmed the need for their journey in order to cut through the endless delays in Madrid where nothing seemed yet to be settled.[35]

1   Charles, Prince of Wales, later Charles I, by Mytens

CHAPTER IV

(i)

FOUR days later, in the evening of March 7th, Buckingham, his portmanteau under his arm, was knocking at
the door of Bristol's house in Madrid, while Charles waited
in the shadow of the other side of the street. Cottington and
Endymion were a few hours behind. The party had covered
the seven hundred and fifty miles from Paris in thirteen
days, an average of nearly sixty miles a day.[1] By such hard
riding, they had outstripped any possibility of news of their
departure reaching Madrid. In England, however, the secret
soon leaked out. Hardly had the travellers embarked at
Dover before the rumour flew to Newmarket, where the
King had gone from Theobalds. The Council knelt to im-
plore the King to tell them if it was true. He said that it
was and put the onus on the Prince, because of his passionate desire to force a conclusion to the business that had
so long distracted the King's affairs. The Council had not
been told because 'secrecy was the life of the business'.
After long discussion, the Council persuaded James to send
some person of distinction after the Prince in case he had
been stopped in France. Anxiety over this risk was all the
greater because neither Endymion nor Cottington spoke
good French. Nor were the Prince and Buckingham very
fluent, Buckingham being the best, since Charles stam-
mered. Lord Carlisle was accordingly sent off. Arriving in
Paris, he found, of course, that the Prince and his party had
gone. He was, however, able to offer excuses for the Prince's
behaviour to King Louis, who was particularly offended at
the incognito visit to the Louvre.[2]

At home, the news was heard with universal consternation and apprehension except among the Catholics, since the

commonest rumour was that the Prince was to change his religion and be married at a mass. People argued that if the marriage plans were far enough forward to warrant the presence of the Prince in Madrid, why had he not gone with a fleet and with a following suitable to his rank; but if everything was still uncertain, why did he risk his person and give such an advantage to the King of Spain by putting himself into his hands? There was no answer to this obvious question, and, as a letter-writer remarked, 'Wise men are troubled and betake themselves to prayer rather than to inquiry'. On Sunday, prayers for the Prince's preservation were offered up in all the churches.[3]

The venture seemed equally fantastic to a neutral observer. The Venetian Ambassador wrote to the Doge that 'No action more remote from all imagination or belief ever took place, or less founded on likelihood, to say nothing of reason, utterly unknown to everyone and approved by nobody'. It was, he thought, 'a monster among decisions' and England was now in the hand of Spain.[4] Archibald Armstrong, the Court Jester, commonly known as Archie the Fool, summed up general opinion by clapping his fool's cap on the King's head. When James asked him why he did this, Archie replied because he'd sent the Prince into Spain. 'But,' said James, 'what if he should come back safe?' 'Why then,' said Archie, 'I'll take my cap off your head and put it on the King of Spain's.'[5]

James alone was quietly confident and busied himself with despatching suitable noblemen by land and sea to attend the Prince in Madrid, and with arranging for ships to be got ready to carry over further attendants, clothes and jewellery. Charles and Buckingham's 'Georges and Garters' were to be sent at once by special messenger, and James took a personal interest in selecting jewels from the Jewel Room in the Tower both for Charles's own wear and for presenting to the Infanta. Estimates of the value of the selected jewels varied from £80,000 to £200,000.

The choice of attendants was a matter of more difficulty.

Charles had left a list of people he wanted to follow him and James began to add others of his own choice, including a physician and two chaplains, Doctors Man and Wren, to whom he gave special instructions as to their behaviour. They were to preach the doctrines of the English Church, but not to indulge in polemical preaching or controversy. Another name added by the King was that of Archie the Fool.

Charles's original list of eighty-six had soon grown to one hundred and sixty-seven, each of whom wanted to take at least one servant with him. This far exceeded the available accommodation in the ships that were being prepared. Matters came to a head when even Archie the Fool demanded to take a servant along. The lists were pruned and the number of servants strictly limited. Among those to go was, however, Endymion's servant Sebastian Rowland.[6]

James also entertained himself by correcting and amending, if he did not solely compose, a set of eight verses commemorating Jack and Tom's journey. The last three ran as follows and well illustrated the King's mood.

'Love is a world of many Spains
Where coldest hills and hottest plains
With barren rocks and fertile fields
By turns despair and comfort yields;
　But who can doubt of prosperous luck,
　Where love and fortune doth conduct?

Thy grandsire, godsire, father too,
Were thine examples so to do;
Their brave attempts in heat of love,
France, Scotland, Denmark, did approve,
　So Jack and Tom do nothing new,
　When love and fortune they pursue.

Kind shepherds that have loved them long,
Be not too rash in censuring wrong;

Correct your fears, leave off to mourn,
The heavens shall favour their return!
Commit the care to royal Pan
Of Jack his son, and Tom his man.'[7]

(ii)

Meantime, in Madrid, 'Jack' and 'Tom' had been enthusi-astically received. Bristol's astonishment when his servant brought the two travellers up to his study must have been extreme, but long training had taught him self-command and he received his guests with all due deference.

Next morning Cottington and Endymion arrived and Gondomar was sent for. At the sight of the Prince he fell flat on his face, crying 'Nunc Dimittis!' Gondomar then hastened to Olivares who, in turn, hurried to the King. On one point they all felt certain. Charles must have come to Spain to change his religion and all their difficulties would be solved. Small wonder they were delighted at the unex-pected turn of events and eager to give the Prince a royal welcome. Olivares at once arranged for Buckingham to have a private audience of the King and accompanied Bucking-ham back to Bristol's house in order to pay his respects to Charles.[8]

The next day's events were fully recounted by Endymion in his first letter to Olive from Madrid. As the Prince's sole attendant and as the only member of the party thoroughly familiar both with the Spanish language and with Spanish ways, Endymion had little time for letters home.

'My sweetest love,' he began, 'Although I have so much employment here at Madrid, that I have scarce time to dress myself, yet if I should not watch and lose my sleep to write to thee, I were unworthy of such a wife and could not deserve the smallest part of thy inestimable love to me. Oh that you did but know how great a grief it is for me to live without you, for then you would believe that nothing but you could give me content, nor any but the want of you cause sorrow in me. Had I but expressions for my love, they should satisfy you and ease me, but if you can give faith to an honest heart, then be assured that my life only depends on that love which I hope for from you, and all the happiness this world can give me leans upon the same.

The Prince and my lord are well and have been the braveliest received that ever men were. Yesterday the King and Queen came publicly abroad, and the Infanta with them in the coach, where my master and my lord with the ambassador and myself in another coach (with the curtains drawn in the street) stayed to see them go by, and the Prince hath taken such a liking to his mistress that now he loves her as much for her beauty as he can for being sister to so great a King. She deserves it, for there was never seen a fairer creature.

Although the Prince was private and the curtains of his coach drawn, yet the searching vulgar took notice of it, and did so press about the coach to see him, that we could not pass through the streets, insomuch that the King's guard was forced to beat them from it and make way through the multitude. They all cried "God bless him", and showed as much affection generally as ever was seen among people, only they took it ill he showed not himself to them in a more public manner.

Last night, the King of Spain had a great desire to see the Prince, and, in a coach only with the Conde Olivares, my lord Marquis and myself, he came privately at eleven of the clock at night, and met the Prince in the fields without the town, who came there with the two ambassadors* only, and the King used him with so much love and respect, giving him the better hand still, that he is as well affected to his Majesty's nobleness and courtesy as to his sister's beauty.

Dear Olive, all these things I thought fit to acquaint you withal, that you may not say I never tell you anything, but all these things, compared with the desire I have to see thee,

* The Earl of Bristol and Sir W. Aston.

are nothing but vanity, that is the real felicity only which makes me breathe, and God Almighty grant me leave that it may be quickly, and His blessing light on you and George and Charles, and I pray you send me word how you do and which is the prettiest boy. Good Olive, entreat my mother to pardon me, for the Prince having but one alone here, I have so much to do that I cannot awhile to write to anybody. Entreat her to send me her blessing, and commend me to my sisters. I will never fail to be

Thy true loving husband
Endymion Porter.

Madrid, this 10th day of March, 1623.'[9]

The rest of Charles's first week in Spain was spent in resting and, in the afternoons, riding and hawking with Bristol. On the Friday, however, Philip and Charles met again in the fields and rode together watching Philip's servants shooting running rabbits and partridges on the wing.[10]

Then came the Prince's solemn official entry into Madrid, when Charles and Philip rode into the city under a canopy supported by twelve noblemen of high rank and followed by a resplendent train, among whom rode Endymion. Charles and Buckingham described the event in their letter to James, written the next day, March 17th.

'Yesterday, being Sunday, your baby went to a monastery called St. Jeronimo's, to dinner, which stands a little out of the town. After dinner came all the Councillors, in order, to welcome your baby; then came the King himself, with all his nobility, and made their entry with as great a triumph as could be, where he forced your baby to ride on his right hand, which he observes always. This entry was made just as when the Kings of Castile came first to the Crown; all prisoners set at liberty, and no office or matter of grace falls, but is put in your baby's hands to dispose.'[11]

Madrid was *en fête* for the event. For four nights, fireworks lit up the city and the bells pealed till midnight.

Among the lucky prisoners freed were all the English galley slaves. Only the Infanta, reported the Venetian Ambassador, wept and lamented to realize that the marriage was so imminent. She again declared that she would rather take the veil with the barefooted nuns than marry a heretic.[12]

Charles, Buckingham, Cottington and Endymion (Graham had been sent home with their letters) were now lodged in apartments provided by Philip in the Royal Palace. Rich presents were showered on them, including perfumes and a dressing gown for Charles in a large gold coffer. Not so useful a gift, which was to be sent on to James, was one of four camels—two he's and a she and a young one—and an elephant. These eventually reached England in July and roused much curiosity, although they were driven through London in the middle of the night.[13]

Behind these scenes of festivity, there now began the long game of duplicity which both sides were to play for the next six months.

Almost at their first meeting, Olivares had suggested to Buckingham that all further delays to the marriage could be avoided by Charles's immediate conversion. Faced by Buckingham's protests against such an idea, Olivares had said that the only other course was to send a letter to the Pope to try to hasten the dispensation. By stressing the Pope's reluctance to grant this, Olivares hoped to force Charles to agree to conversion. But, if Charles proved obstinate, the Papal Nuncio in Madrid and the Pope could be made scapegoats for delaying the marriage, thus lessening the risk of Spanish rejection of the Prince's suit leading to war with England.

Charles and Buckingham, on the other hand, thought it good policy to temporise and to allow hopes to be entertained of the possibility of a conversion which they never intended should be realised. Morover, Charles had now seen the Infanta even if he had not yet spoken to her, and his infatuation had been still further increased. As Buckingham wrote to James, 'Baby Charles is so touched at the heart, that he confesses all he yet saw is nothing to her.' Charles was thus most anxious not to give the Spaniards any offence.

When Buckingham and Olivares got down to discussions, Olivares started with an attempt to undermine the Infanta's reluctance to marry a heretic by getting Charles to agree to liberty of worship for Catholics in England as a concession to hasten the dispensation. To this proposal Buckingham had to return a firm negative, knowing, as he did, how it would outrage English opinion. The Papal Nuncio, Massimi, however, told Olivares that it must be a condition of the Pope's granting the dispensation and went so far as to display his utter ignorance of England by proposing that King James should hand over some fortified English town to the Catholics, as a security for their freedom of worship. On Buckingham's scouting such a fantastic idea, Olivares quickly put the blame on the Nuncio and assured Buckingham that the Pope would be pressed to hurry the dispensation. Ostensibly for this purpose, the Duke of Pastrana was despatched to Rome after kissing Charles's hand and telling him that his chief object was to do Charles's service.

Buckingham and Charles felt that they had won a diplomatic victory. Writing to James they told him that their arguments had succeeded in preventing any further demands in exchange for the dispensation and had safely banished Spanish hopes for Charles's conversion. 'To conclude,' they wrote on March 27th, 'we never saw the business in a better way than now it is.'

What they did not know was that the Duke of Pastrana had been given secret instructions from Philip to urge the Pope to refuse to grant the dispensation, which Philip no longer desired since there seemed no likelihood of Charles's conversion.[14]

(iii)

It was, however, no longer possible to go on keeping Charles from speaking to the Infanta, at least in public.

At last it was decided that his visit to her should take place on April 7th, Easter Day. Such was Charles's state of mind that he even submitted to be dressed as the Spaniards told him. He had arrayed himself in gala costume with blue hose and a collar in the latest English fashion. The Royal Chamberlain objected to this attire and Charles had to put on a collar in the Spanish style and other clothes that Olivares lent him.

Thus suitably clad, Charles was accompanied by the King to the Queen's apartment. The Venetian Ambassador in Madrid, in a despatch to the Doge, described what happened. After offering his salutations to the Queen, Charles approached the Infanta to whom he began a somewhat lengthy compliment in an affectionate manner. This caused whispering in the room. The Queen also looked annoyed and the Infanta showed signs of boredom. Charles had, therefore, to cut his speech short. The Infanta coldly answered him in a few formal phrases. The bystanders were astonished at her self-control 'because it is notorious that she regards the marriage with extreme aversion and dread, her only consolation being that she says she will die a martyr'.[15]

Even such a chilly reception did nothing to cool Charles's ardour or to dispel his romantic illusions. The next day Endymion wrote to Secretary Conway in London, 'The Prince my master and our lord are very well and here receive all manner of love and respect. I make no doubt we shall have a good success. His Highness visited the Infanta yesterday whose beauty gives him a just occasion to love her and whose goodness may make us all pray for the match.'[16]

But if, in the midst of all his duties, Endymion felt that official affairs were prospering, he had his own personal troubles to contend with. In a fit of jealousy, Olive had written to him accusing him of misbehaving with an inn-keeper's daughter in Boulogne. Even if any such idea had entered Endymion's head, there would certainly have been no opportunity, since the Prince and his party had left Boulogne for Montreuil as soon as they had landed. Writing to Olive, Endymion poured out his lonely and aggrieved heart to her.

'My dear Olive,

'Since my coming to Spain I have received four letters from you, and the two first with such kindness in them, as I thought my love rewarded; but the two last are so full of mistrusts and falsehoods, that I rather fear you have changed your affection than that you have any sure grounds for what you accuse me of in them; for, as I hope for mercy at God's hands, I neither kissed nor touched any woman since I left you; and, for the inn-keeper's daughter at Boulogne, I was so far from kissing her, that, as I hope to be saved, I cannot remember that I saw any such woman. No, Olive, I am not a dissembler, for I assure you that the grief which I suffered at the parting with you gave me no leave to entertain such base thoughts, but rather lasted in me like a consumption, increasing daily more and more. But seeing you have taken a resolution without hearing what I could say, never to be confident of me again, I will procure to be worthy of your best thoughts and study to have patience for any neglect from you.

I understand that you sent me two kisses by a gentleman. God reward you for them, and since your bounty increases, I think it unfit my thanks should diminish. I perceive you would be glad to hear of my kissing inn-keepers' daughters every day, that you might have some excuse to do that which nothing but my unworthiness and misfortune can deserve.

Alas, sweet Olive! Why should you go about to afflict me. Know that I live like a dying man, and as one that cannot live long without you. My eyes grow weary in looking upon anything, as wanting that rest they take in the company and sight of thine; nor can I take pleasure in sports, for there is none that seems not a monster to my understanding when my Olive is wanting. With thee, I only entertain myself and were it not for the force of remembering thee, I know not how any life should have maintained itself so long.

You have a great deal of advantage of me in this absence, your two little babes and less affection. They serve to entertain you and it teaches you to forget me. Yet for pity in this banishment and misery let me hear of your health and theirs, and I assure you it will be no small comfort to me.

Good Olive, let me receive no more quarrelling letters from you, for I desire but your love, it being the thing that only affords me pleasure in this vile world. Send me word how the children do, and whether Charles be black or fair, and who he is like; but I am sure that the nurse will swear that he hath my eyes or nose, and that you may perchance be angry and say you never saw anything so like some brother of yours as he. I would to God I could hear thee discourse, I would never come to Boulogne to kiss any host's daughter although you would entreat me.

The Prince visited the Infanta yesterday, whose beauty gave him a just occasion to like her. The marriage will be as yet I know not when, but if my desires to see you could hasten it, I assure you I would make bold to trouble you before the two months' end which you allow me in your last letter.

I have sent my Lady Villiers a tobacco box. I hope she will esteem it as a token of my love and that you will deliver it with the best grace your father has taught you, which is 'Hold up your head, Olive'. Now I am sure you laugh and forget the just cause I have to be angry with you, but till I receive more kisses from you I shall not be well pleased.

I would have you send me word whether my lady* be with child or how my little lady† doth. I pray you remember my humble service to my lady and tell her that my lord

* The Duchess of Buckingham.
† Lady Mary Villiers, her eldest child.

and I wish you were both here very often, for which I hope you will pardon us. We live very honest and think of nothing but our wives. I thought to have sent you a token of some value, but I found my purse and my goodwill could not agree, and I, considering that my letter would be welcome to you, I leave to do it, only this ring which I hope you will esteem if not for love, I think, for charity. The conceit is that it seems two as you turn it, and 'tis but one.

My dear Olive, be assured that I can love nothing but thee, nor can the times afford place for one thought that doth not let me know my happiness in having thee. Therefore let me entreat you that there may be a fair correspondence and that you will call to mind how often you have sworn you could love nothing but me. I hope you continue the same, for all your protesting never to be confident of me again.

I would have you send me my cutwork bands by the first and send me word what hopes you have to receive any money out of Ireland, which Dick Oliver will inform you, and if Sir Edward Villiers can receive the four hundred pounds of Sir Henry Fines. I would have you pay Bloxam out of that money. Howsoever let it be paid out of the money from Ireland, which you may advise with Dick Oliver and my Brother Canning.

I pray you pardon me this long letter, if you have patience to read hither. Howsoever, I will always do it till you forbid me, for this is the happiest time I pass in this country. I hope to have some employment that may bring me home before you look for me, and although I should not be welcome, I must needs be glad to come, having no other heaven nor joy, but the hope of seeing you. God Almighty bless you and George and Charles and give you His grace, and I pray you remember to pray for him that will ever be

Your true loving husband
Endymion Porter.'[17]

Endymion evidently hoped that he might be one of Charles's suite sent back to England with despatches or to make a personal report, as Graham had been and as Cottington was soon to be. But his knowledge of Spanish and the closeness of his personal service to Charles made his presence in Madrid indispensable.

News now came from Rome that the Pope had decided to grant the dispensation in spite of Philip's promptings to the contrary. On April 24th it was received in Madrid by Massimi, the Papal Nuncio. Important alterations had been made to the marriage articles. The age at which the children were to cease being educated by their mother was raised to twelve; the Infanta's Church was to be open to everyone; and all English Catholics were to substitute an oath prescribed by the Pope for the oath of allegiance settled by Act of Parliament. Like Olivares, however, the Pope wished, if possible, to avoid being blamed for a breakdown in the negotiations for fear of repercussions on the English Catholics. So he cleverly returned the ball into Olivares' court by making the handing over of the dispensation dependent on Philip's pledging himself, under a solemn oath, to be backed if necessary by the guns of the Spanish fleet, that James would carry out all his obligations.

As the easiest way out of this awkward dilemma, Olivares once more turned to the conversion of the Prince. In order to arouse feelings of edification and compunction, Philip showed Charles the spectacle of processions of flagellants scourging themselves, and of friars with their heads bleeding from their crowns of thorns. Charles's distaste for Catholic rites was only enhanced by such exhibitions, and he countered by arguing about the scriptural authority for the practice of confession. Soon after, Charles and Buckingham were confronted with four friars, whose attempts to enlighten the two heretics ended abruptly in Buckingham's jumping from his seat and stamping on his hat.

Meantime Charles and Buckingham continued to press Olivares for the immediate grant of the dispensation.

Olivares still wished to appear as the protagonist of the match, so he fell back on the obduracy of the Nuncio as the cause of the delay. As a further cover, he set up a Committee or Junta of theologians to report on how Philip's oath could best be kept. As to this, Olivares now had the idea that the best course would be to retain the Infanta in Spain until James had fulfilled his obligations under the articles.

If left to himself, Buckingham would have broken off the negotiations then and there. But the hint of the possibility of a return home without his bride was as hurtful to Charles's vanity as it was repugnant to him as a lover. He gave way over the articles on every point. Even so, Philip insisted on waiting for the Junta's report.

At last, on May 23rd, the Junta gave its decision. If Philip were to take the oath, the Infanta must remain in Spain for at least a year after the marriage ceremony, during which time all the reliefs for the English Catholics must be openly enforced.[18]

Buckingham was furious and Charles turned to Bristol to try to get concessions. When nothing came of such efforts, Cottington was despatched to England to report to the King, while Charles and Buckingham followed him up on June 6th with a letter to James, typical of Charles's shallow optimism and facile ideas of trickery. 'We make no doubt,' they wrote, 'but to have the opinions of these busy divines reversed, so your Majesty will be pleased to begin to put in execution the favour towards your Roman Catholic subjects, that ye will be bound to do by your oath as soon as the Infanta comes over, which we hope you will do for the hastening of us home, with this protestation to reverse all if there be any delay of the marriage. We send you here the articles as they are to go, the oaths private and public, that you and your baby are to take with the councils, wherein, if you scare at the least clause of your private oath (where you promise that the Parliament shall revoke all the penal laws against the Papists within three years) we sought good to tell your Majesty our opinions, which is that if you think you may do it in that time (which we think you may) if you do your best, although it take not effect, you have not broken your word, for this promise is only as a security that you will do your best.'[19]

They then sat down to wait for James's replies. Though Charles busied himself unavailingly in efforts to get the Spanish Government to alter its decision, he was still confident that he would carry the Infanta home.

(iv)

Time hung heavily on the hands of the little group of Englishmen as the summer heat began to scorch the wide streets of Madrid and the sun's rays were dazzlingly reflected from the white-washed walls of the mean two-storey houses. Very few of the gay train of courtiers who had sailed so eagerly to Spain to join the Prince's party had ever reached the capital. Philip objected to the presence of so many foreigners at his court, so most of them had to go straight home when their ships reached Santander. Of the few who got to Madrid, only one or two were allowed to stay, among them Archie the Fool.

Grand as were the state apartments in the Royal Palace, crowded with elaborate furniture and statues and hung with rich tapestries and with pictures by Flemish artists and family portraits by Titian, the rooms allotted to the Prince and his suite were few and small. Spanish food was tough or too sweet. Nothing was punctual. The chaplains sent by James had never got further than Burgos. In any case, Philip would not allow Protestant services inside his palace and the devotions of Charles and his party were confined to bedchamber prayers except when they once went to service in Bristol's house.[20]

Spanish Court life was ruled by the strictest etiquette. When Lord Carlisle with much difficulty got permission to kiss the Infanta's hand before leaving Madrid, he found her seated on a high throne with her ladies about her. For all his compliments, he failed to draw the least sign of recognition. She sat 'as immoveable as the image of the Virgin Mary'. After kneeling before her for over an hour, Carlisle took his leave.[21]

The deadly dullness of the Court was only relieved by a few plays stiffly performed for the Prince's entertainment, by an occasional wild boar hunt, and by bull fights.

By now Charles had really worked himself into the belief that he was deeply in love with the Infanta. Lacking sexual experience, his was a case of calf-love, and calf-love at the age of twenty-three. He would sit in a closed coach in the street for hours watching in the hopes of catching a glimpse of her. At Court functions, his eyes would be immoveably fixed on her (Olivares unkindly said that it reminded him of a cat watching a mouse).[22] But Spanish etiquette never gave him a chance of a word in private. Finally, he made a desperate effort to break through the barrier. Learning that the Infanta was in the habit of gathering may dew in the gardens of a royal summer house across the river, Charles rose early one morning and, taking Endymion with him, stole out of the palace. They were let into the summer house and garden, but were told that the Infanta was in the orchard, divided from the garden by a very high wall. Finding the door between bolted, Charles and Endymion scaled the wall and jumped down the other side. Terrified by such an unprecedented approach, the Infanta ran off shrieking, while her guardian, an old Marquis, fell on his knees before Charles and begged him to leave, since he would be beheaded if he admitted anyone. There was nothing left for Charles and Endymion to do but to retire through the door which the Marquis unbolted for them.[23]

Buckingham's mood, meantime, was growing more and more impatient. He had toothache and intermittent fever, and he and Bristol were hardly on speaking terms. Once when Buckingham and Charles were with Bristol in his coach, they met Olivares. Saying that the Prince wanted to speak to Olivares privately, Buckingham ordered Bristol out of the coach and called Endymion in as interpreter.[24] James finally had to order Bristol not to interfere in the Prince's business, which was to be left to Buckingham, Cottington and Endymion. Nor were Buckingham's relations with his Spanish hosts much better. His careless, easy manners and his amours were both equally offensive to the Spanish Court. He was, however, still trying to conceal his feelings. In this, Archie the Fool proved useful, the Venetian Ambassador reporting that Buckingham attributed some of his reputed remarks against the Spaniards 'to a buffoon who is here with his Highness'.[25] One consolation, however, for Buckingham's exile was James's gift of a Dukedom to him, the highest honour that he could bestow.

(v)

There was one absorbing interest which Endymion shared with his master—their love for the arts. Endymion was already familiar with the art treasures in Madrid. Now, when Philip showed his visitors the pictures in his palace, Charles, for the first time, was able to see assembled in one place a collection of some of the greatest masterpieces of Renaissance painting. The impact had a deep influence on the formation of his tastes, confirming his early affection for the Venetian school and inducing his life-long devotion to the work of Titian. Futile as it was in every other respect, Charles's Spanish visit had, at least, a lasting and most valuable result in widening and intensifying his love of pictures.

The Prince and Endymion went to meetings of art connoisseurs and attended sales. Charles bought at least two Titians and Cottington's account book records on July 14th a payment 'by Mr. Porter's order, being for a picture which was bought for the Prince's account'. Other entries in Cottington's accounts 'signified unto me by Mr. Porter' were payments for a picture by the contemporary Spanish painter Caxes and for a Dürer.[26]

Philip presented Charles with Titian's 'Venus of the Pardo', for which the Prince expressed particular admiration. Another gift from the King was Gianbologna's statue of 'Cain and Abel' which Charles later gave to Buckingham to stand in the garden of York House.

It was from Madrid that Charles wrote to Sir Francis Crane, the manager of the Mortlake tapestry works, founded five years earlier by King James, instructing him 'to send to Genoa for certayne drawings of Raphaell of Urbin, which were desseignes for tapestries made for Pope Leo X and for which there is 300 L to be payed, besides their charge for bringing home'.*[27]

Endymion himself bought some pictures. In a letter to Olive written in August he asks her 'to inquire after the picture, for I would not lose it. It is the picture of a Mary Magdalene with a pot of flowers by her. I pray you ask my Lady if it came not with the perfumes and the boxes of china with perfumes for you'.[28]

Gerbier had, by now, also joined Buckingham in Madrid, bringing his artistic enthusiasm and considerable knowledge to reinforce the party. It was Gerbier who probably painted the picture of the Infanta which was taken back to England.†

Another relaxation was music. In Madrid, Endymion made the acquaintance of a Spanish singer, Donna Francesca Juarez, and introduced her to Charles. Seven years later, Charles and Endymion still remembered her lovely

---

* These were the famous set of Raphael cartoons (now in the Victoria and Albert Museum on loan from H.M. the Queen) which are some of the finest examples of Renaissance art. They were part of a set of ten, commissioned from Raphael by Pope Leo X in 1515 for tapestries for the Sistine Chapel in the Vatican. On completion, they were sent to Brussels where the tapestries were woven. The Mortlake works made a number of sets of tapestries from them.

† According to the tradition in the Denbigh family, Buckingham gave this picture to his sister, the Countess of Denbigh, after the match was broken off. It is now at Parham Park.

voice. A cousin of Olive's wrote to Endymion from Madrid in 1630 that he had read a letter of Endymion's, in Spanish, to Donna Francesca and her father and that they were all exceeding glad to hear from him and that His Majesty was pleased to remember them. Donna Francesca's 'angelical voice', the letter went on, 'has far more power to give life to all creatures sensitive and vegetative than ever Orpheus's silver-stringed lyre had.'[29]

But Endymion's heart was with Olive in England. He was living, as he wrote to her, 'like a man without a soul.' And the ache grew sharper as the growing strain of their separation brought about misunderstandings. Olive blamed Endymion for not writing more often. She had fits of jealousy and believed all the stories that she heard about gay doings in Madrid. Nor was Endymion himself free from jealous fears.

'If you did but know how truly I love you,' he wrote, 'you would never be jealous of me, and had you such reports of me as you conclude for truths, yet if you loved me half so well as I deserve, you would not give credit so easily to them. I know you are not so sorry as you would make me believe for my absence, for I hear you are very merry and can take upon you to command other young men to travel from their wives. Long may you be merry, and if I thought my company would diminish it, I love you with that extremity that to give you as much content as I can, I would bar myself from the happiness of seeing you as long as my many desires would give me leave, and my master's business would keep me here.'

Olive had been short of money. Endymion hoped that Buckingham would write to the King on his behalf to arrange with Buckingham's wife to supply Olive with funds. Meantime, he arranged with Cottington for the payment of £400 to Olive when he got to London in return for monies advanced by Endymion in Madrid. Forty-five pounds was to be paid to his mother.

'Assure yourself,' he declared, 'it hath not little grieved

me to think you want, for there is nothing in this world that I would not do to make you see my care of you is greater than of myself. . . . However, be you contented, and although I dig for my living, you shall never want, but with our poverty we will love as richly as they that have the greatest plenty, and bread with thy company shall please me better than the greatest dainties of the world without it.'

He sent her presents from Madrid—a very pretty diamond jewel worth some hundred pounds to be worn 'every day to put you in mind of me'; a toy of gold and little rubies; purses and boxes of perfumes for Olive, her mother and sisters and for Buckingham's wife and his sister. 'I have no news to send you,' he said, 'nor secrets to write unto you, for which I am sorry, that you might discourse with the one and tell the other.'

Every line breathed Endymion's deep and passionate love for his wife. 'This last letter you sent me was the kindest I have yet received, with which I am so contented that I can vaingloriously brag of it. . . . Sweet Olive, remember what it is to be good, and forget not how often you have sworn you loved me, so shall you preserve my honour and your own and make your vows true with a pure conscience. I take no pleasure in any other thing but you, which makes me write you long letters. If they trouble you, pardon me, and believe that it proceeds from the love of him that will ever be

Your true loving husband
Endymion Porter.'[30]

Only Archie the Fool was thoroughly enjoying his Spanish visit. He was notorious for his quick tongue and his avarice and, in Madrid, he was able to satisfy both. At the end of April, he was writing to James that the King of Spain had received him in audience when neither 'men of your own nor your son's men can come near him'. The rules of etiquette that bound others were ignored by Archie. A letter from Madrid told how 'Archie hath more privilege than any, for he always goes with his fool's coat where the

Infanta is with her ladies of honour and keeps a blowing
and blustering among them and flurts out what he lists'.

Once when the Infanta and her ladies were discussing
how strange it was that the Duke of Bavaria's army, with
much inferior strength, should have routed the Protestant
forces and taken Prague, Archie interrupted to say that
something even stranger was that, in 1588, a fleet of one
hundred and forty sails should have come from Spain to
invade England and that only ten should have got back to
tell what became of the rest!

Archie was equally outspoken to his fellow countrymen.
He so discomfited Tobie Matthew in an argument at dinner
that the latter was forced to leave the table. He even dared
to speak his mind to Buckingham, blaming the inconsistent
and untruthful way in which the whole negotiations had
been carried on. When he ignored orders to be silent,
Buckingham threatened to have him hanged if he didn't
hold his tongue. To this Archie replied, 'No one has ever
heard of a fool being hanged for talking, but many Dukes
in England have been beheaded for their insolence.'

As for his avarice, he succeeded in getting gifts of rich
clothing from Olivares and Gondomar and a promise of a
pension from King Philip.[31]

(vi)

Back in England, preparations had been going on for the
Infanta's reception. Amongst these was the building in
St. James's of a new chapel for her use. Designed by Inigo
Jones, it was the first example in England of a truly classical
style in ecclesiastical architecture. The chapel was later
finished for Henrietta Maria.[32] James had, however, grown
anxious when no word came from Spain for a month. On
June 14th Cottington arrived and James heard with dismay
the news that it would be a year before the Infanta would
be allowed to leave, and, worse still, that Charles's own
return might be indefinitely delayed.

'My sweet boys,' he wrote, 'your letter by Cottington hath stricken me dead; I fear it shall very much shorten my days.' 'Alas,' he went on, 'I now repent me sore that I ever suffered you to go away. I care for match, nor nothing, so I may once have you in my arms again. God grant it, God grant it, God grant it; Amen, Amen, Amen!'[33]

Charles's safety was now James's only concern. 'Do you think,' he said, bursting into tears, 'that I shall ever see the Prince again?' He at once sent off Sir William Croft to Spain with his promise to agree to the articles as they stood and with orders for Charles's immediate return.

When Croft reached Madrid on June 26th, Charles and Buckingham sent for Olivares to ask his advice on how best to comply with James's wishes for their return without breaking off the marriage. Olivares continued to screen himself behind the Junta, but promised to do his best for them. On July 6th he came back with the final word of the Junta and Philip. The only concession that could be made was to shorten the delay by four months. The marriage could take place in September and the Infanta come to England in March.

Shocked by this end to his hopes, Charles declared his intention of breaking off negotiations and leaving at once. The next day he went to see Philip. To everyone's astonishment, instead of saying good-bye, he told the King that he had resolved to accept all the terms rather than abandon the match.

All was now rejoicing in Madrid. Once again the streets were illuminated and the Infanta was referred to as the Princess of England.

Endymion hastened to send the news to Olive. 'Our business here,' he wrote on July 7th, 'is not likely to hold. We are to come home suddenly, which I desire for nothing but to see you. And as I was writing this, the Prince concluded the business himself with the King, so that it is now finished, and I hope we shall all receive a great deal of comfort in it, for sure there never was a better creature than

the Infanta is. He (the Prince) is to be contracted presently
and then he means to go away hence within these three
weeks so that we shall all be at home suddenly. She is to
be delivered in March next. God be praised for so great a
blessing as we shall all receive by it.'

Endymion had need of such cheerful news. He had had
no letters from home and was feeling miserably neglected.

'How happy was I, dear Olive,' he wrote, 'when I lived
at home, secure of your love, and never did suspect that
anything could have made you forget me. But now I see
your memory fails and my misfortune increases, and I fear
that absence hath made you neglect writing to me, and
changed that constant love which, in my opinion, was
wholly mine. But it may be that I lived deceived then, and
God hath been pleased with this occasion to open my eyes
that I may see how little you esteem me. Here have come
two posts and I have received no letters from you. It may
be mine have been so long, that because I should not
trouble you with so much letter, you thought good to for-
bear writing, thinking I could not be so shameless as to do
it without correspondence.

I left my heart within your sweet breast at my departing
from you, and am united there with you in spite of this
tedious intermission of my joy, which makes me live here
like a man without a soul, therefore you ought to love that
love which is in me, though you have none yourself. Let me
entreat you to have a care to let me know how you and
your children do, though you write not to me, for that is
some comfort and makes me enjoy myself a little. I wonder
my mother would forget me, but sure she knew not of the
posts coming.

I sent you by Dick Graham a chain of gold which is the
prettiest making that ever I saw. I pray you wear it and
let nobody know how kind I am to you, lest they laugh at
me for my fondness. By Killigrew I sent you a feather, but
I fear I shall trouble you with tokens as I do with letters.
Yet I would willingly have nobody come without some

small remembrance to you, which makes me send you this poor token now. I want a better, but cannot tell when to have anything rich enough for my desire, which could not be satisfied, though I were powerful to send you the King of Spain's wealth.'[34]

James, in England, had had many hesitations before he summoned the Council to ask their advice over keeping his promise to sign the marriage articles. The Council, too, were more than hesitant, but Williams, the Lord Keeper, argued that relaxing the penal laws against the Catholics could not violate the King's conscience. On July 20th, the articles were solemnly sworn by James and the Council in the presence of the two special Spanish ambassadors who had been sent from Madrid in June. The Infanta's household was to be nominated by Philip; a bishop and twenty-four priests, all outside the jurisdiction of English law, were to minister to her; there was to be a public church wherever she might live in which only English Catholics could worship. The Council further swore to refrain from enforcing the penal laws against the Catholics. Later that evening James also undertook to try to get Parliament to confirm these concessions.

Nothing, of course, could have been more disastrous to the future cause of toleration in England than thus to make it a private bargain with a foreign government against the wishes of almost all Englishmen. No wonder that it was rumoured that, for the sake of the marriage, the Anglican faith had been betrayed to the Pope.

James was now also much concerned about money. The expense of keeping his ships ready to go to Spain had already proved a heavy burden, and nothing definite had been settled about the Infanta's dowry, on which James was relying to ease his finances.

'Since it can be no better,' he wrote to Charles and Steenie on July 21st, 'I must be contented; but this course is both a dishonour to me and double charges if I must send two fleets; but if they will not send her till March, let them, in God's name send her by their own fleet . . . forget not to make them to keep their former conditions anent the portion, otherwise both Baby and I are bankrupts for ever.' A few days later he was again writing, 'I protest I know not what to do if she come not this year; for this very refreshing of my fleet with victuals hath cost me £8,000; and therefore ye have need to hasten the payment of the dowry.'

But in the same letter James gave the reassuring news that the Spanish ambassadors were opposed to the delay in sending the Infanta and would try to get this revoked. His letters also urged Charles to press for a settlement of the question of the Palatinate and also that of Holland, as soon as the marriage arrangements had been fixed.[35]

The question of Holland was a new development. Dutch men of war, in hot pursuit of a Dunkirk privateer seeking to evade the Dutch blockade, had actually sailed into Leith harbour, where they had shot their prey to pieces, killing a Scottish bystander in the process. To make matters worse, the unfortunate crew of the Dunkirker, struggling ashore, were beaten up by the mob whose sympathies were all with the Protestant Dutch. James was furious and wrote to Buckingham and Bristol telling them to try to secure the aid of Spain in making war on Holland. Luckily his instructions were ignored. James's anger soon cooled and before long he was speaking of the Dutch in cordial terms.

But the Palatinate was another matter. Here, the position of James's unfortunate son-in-law, the Elector Frederick, had steadily grown worse. At the end of July, his latest hopes of regaining his inheritance were shattered by the rout at Stadtloo of his ally, Christian of Denmark, at the hands of the Catholic forces under Tilly. Both James's daughter and the whole Protestant cause in Germany stood in dire need of help.

Charles, meanwhile, was enjoying the atmosphere of goodwill prevailing in Madrid. He felt sure that now that he had given in on all points the Infanta would be allowed to go back with him in September, especially if James made no difficulty about his oaths. More cheerful letters went from Charles and Buckingham to their Dad. 'I, your Baby, have since this conclusion been with my mistress, and she sits publicly with me at the plays', and 'we can now tell you certainly that, by the 29th August, we shall begin our journey, and hope to bring her with us'.[36]

But Endymion grew increasingly miserable and was very worried because he had heard from Olive that she was ill.

'But why should I blame anybody,' he wrote to her, 'for that which was in mine own hands to have remedied, and had I known we should have stayed thus long I would not have left thee, though the Prince, my master, had given me one of his kingdoms. For what can I wish more than content which I did enjoy in thy company, beyond all that the world can give me. In thee I am rich, and without thee nothing but misery. I curse the slow time that helps to lengthen this bitter absence.'[37]

A fortnight later he was writing again, in distress that the Duchess of Buckingham had taken a gold chain that he had given Olive. He could not, he said, buy her another such for five hundred guineas, but he sent her a pair of earrings. Absence, he wrote, was punishment enough, without further wrangling. 'I beg you,' he concluded, 'not to beat George so much unless he be very like me. I will never beat Charles for being like you.'[38]

Charles and Buckingham now felt that they had Olivares on their side. 'He is working underhand with the divines,' they wrote to James, 'and, under colour of the King's and Prince's journey, makes preparations for hers also; her household is a settling, and all other things for her journey; and the Conde's own words are, he will throw us all out of Spain as soon as he can.'[39]

Olivares had, indeed, been compelled to change his tactics. Till now, he had believed that his extravagant demands would eventually be bound to lead to the breakdown of the marriage negotiations. But Charles and James had swallowed them all, and now, to Olivares' astonishment, Charles even held out hopes of his future conversion by agreeing to further articles, one of which bound him willingly to listen to the arguments of Catholic divines whenever the Infanta so wished. Having successfully driven such a hard bargain over the marriage, Olivares believed he could drive an equally hard one over the Palatinate. With the aid of his wife, he had therefore set to work to convince the Infanta of the desirability of the marriage.

On July 25th the marriage contract was signed by Charles and Philip although the Infanta was not to leave till the spring. The marriage was to take place as soon as news arrived that James had sworn to the articles and the Pope had agreed to the actual celebration. But some short delay was inevitable in respect of the latter, since Pope Gregory XV had just died.

It was now Buckingham's turn to try his persuasive skill to secure the Infanta's departure with the Prince. This he urged in interviews with Olivares, with Olivares's wife and finally with the Infanta herself. In spite of the Countess Olivares's assurances that all would be well, nothing came of Buckingham's efforts. It was Philip who would not budge. Not perhaps without reason, he had doubts about the fulfilment of English promises once the Infanta was out of his hands. But he suggested that if Charles stayed till Christmas he might marry the Infanta then and take her home with him in the spring.

Charles still could not make up his mind whether to go or to stay. Buckingham's patience had run out, but there were limits to his ability to influence a Charles still entangled in his love and vanity.

There was, however, something else on which Charles had equally set his heart. This was the restoration of his sister's fortunes. Twice since he came to Spain he had sent special messengers to her with the assurance that her interests would not be forgotten.

When Charles and Buckingham now raised the question

of the Palatinate, Olivares proposed that, as a condition of restoring his lands, though not his Electorate, Frederick's son should marry the Emperor's daughter and be brought up in Vienna, where he would almost certainly become converted to the Catholic faith. But Olivares firmly refused to back any such proposal with the force of arms. Once again—as he had told Endymion nearly a year before—he insisted that the King of Spain would not in any circumstances fight against the Emperor. 'If you hold yourself to that,' replied Charles indignantly, 'there is an end of all; for without this, you may not rely upon either marriage or friendship.'

Charles's disillusionment was complete when, at another interview, Olivares, in an unguarded moment, gave away the long deceit by producing letters that he and Philip had written in November of the year before, showing that it had not really been intended to allow the match to take place.[40]

At last Charles gave way to Buckingham and announced his intention of leaving. 'We have wrought what we can,' he wrote to James on August 20th, 'but since we cannot have her with us that we desired, our next comfort is that we hope shortly to kiss your Majesty's hands.'[41]

Endymion, at least, was overjoyed at the news. 'Now the happy time for me grows near,' he wrote to Olive the same day, 'for now I am sure it will not be long before I shall see that face of thine wherein all the joy and content the world can afford me lieth. . . . The 30th August we are to set forwards from hence, so that I hope within these six weeks I shall be with thee. . . . My dear Olive, you cannot believe with what extremity I am joyed that I shall now come home and stay there till you bid me go away. I am resolved never to leave thee now, but to live with thee free from the troubles of this wicked world. I protest to God I am happier in thee than in my life, and I am sure that nothing can afford me any content till I see thee again. God of his great goodness give me leave to come safe home.

I would have you cut George his hair somewhat short and not to beat him overmuch. I hope you let him go bareheaded, for otherwise he will be so tender that upon every occasion you will have him sick. . . . Farewell, my sweet Olive and I must entreat you to make much of yourself that I may find you merry and well when I come to you. God of Heaven bless you and send you all the happiness He can, and as much content as I wish for my own soul, and believe it that whilst I breathe I will ever be

Your true loving husband
Endymion Porter.

Mr. Secretary Cottington is very sick.'[42]

It was time that Endymion and Olive were reunited. The misunderstandings between them continued to grow. In the same letter, Endymion took Olive to task for her jealousy. 'And for your suspicion of my having any other creature here,' he wrote, 'I know you writ that but to make up your letter. I will have so charitable an opinion of you that I dare swear you have not such a thought, nor can be guilty of so much malice. No, dearest love, I cannot forget how much reason I have to be constant to you; what pawns you have of mine to oblige me to be so, and what a George and a Charles, the memory of whom were sufficient to keep me chaste, though mine own devilish disposition might lead me to any unworthy act. Believe me that nothing shall ever have power to make me offend you in a thought, for as I hope to be saved I cannot endure the sight of any woman. And good sweet love, do not find new ways to vex me; let it suffice that I live from you, which is so great a punishment that death cannot be greater, this absence being every hour accompanied with grief enough to make an end of my days.' He also felt hurt that she had not acknowledged his gifts. 'You might take the pains to tell me you had received them although you did not esteem them.'[43]

The strain of Endymion's relations with Olive was only a shadow of the strains which had been developing in

Madrid between the Spanish and Charles and his English companions. Charles himself, however disillusioned and sore at heart he had become, continued to maintain every outward show of respect and affection to Philip and the Infanta. But Buckingham no longer took any pains to disguise his disgust at Spanish double-dealing. There was trouble, too, with others of Charles's suite. Cottington, as we have seen from Endymion's letter, was taken seriously ill. Believing himself to be dying, he had himself received into the Church of Rome. A few days later, however, when he began to mend, he again declared himself a Protestant. Then a youth called Washington, one of the pages, fell ill and in his dying state sent for a Jesuit priest. His English companions stood outside the door of his room barring the entrance, and Sir Edmund Verney hit the priest in the face. Only Gondomar's intervention prevented a serious riot breaking out.

From the Spanish point of view the English had, indeed, long outstayed their welcome and Philip was only too eager to get them out of Spain. The Spanish Court found Buckingham's arrogance and insolence so intolerable that Bristol was constrained to write to James that 'distastes betwixt them all here and my lord of Buckingham cannot be at a greater height'.[44]

Besides, James was not the only one who was finding the marriage business extremely costly. The expenses of giving hospitality to Charles and his suite, with all the lavish festivities and entertainments, were proving a terrible drain not only on the Spanish exchequer, but equally on the private resources of the Spanish nobility who had come to Madrid to impress the visitors with the splendour of their persons and their households. As the Venetian ambassador wrote, 'The Prince has sacked Madrid without any army and produced scarcity.'[45]

Philip, accordingly, did his utmost to speed his parting guests. Charles could no longer wait for the instructions from the new Pope (who had been ill) to his Nuncio in

Madrid to hand over the dispensation. He took, on August 28th, a solemn oath binding himself to the marriage, and left, in Bristol's hands, a proxy to be used within ten days after the arrival of the Pope's consent from Rome.

Splendid gifts were now exchanged. Philip gave Charles a present of more than fifty horses with rich saddlery, as well as a pistol, sword and dagger set with large diamonds. Buckingham, too, was given horses by Philip and a girdle of diamonds, worth 30,000 crowns. Olivares presented Charles with pictures. Charles, in his turn, gave Philip a sword set with diamonds, worth £6,000, and the Infanta diamond pendants and a string of 250 rare pearls.* Endymion was given 'jewels of good value and six excellent swords' by Olivares.[46]

Gerbier saw to the packing up of the pictures and sculpture that the Prince and his party had bought and it was arranged that two of Gerbier's men should be detailed to take charge of them on the journey.[47]

On August 29th Charles took his leave of the Queen and the Infanta, and Endymion sent a hasty note to Olive to say that he had no time to write more than that he was well, and, tomorrow, was to set forward 'for the happy place where I shall see thee'.[48]

(vii)

The next day Charles and his attendants, accompanied by Philip, left Madrid.

Two days were spent at the Escurial, the great royal palace thirty miles from Madrid. Cottington's account book has the following entry under the date of September 8th— 'paid unto a painter for drawing the Prince's picture, signified by Mr. Porter from the Prince'.[49] Although it has never been found, it is known that Velasquez made a sketch of Charles.[50] So it seems likely that it was during

* A good deal of the jewellery was subsequently returned by the Spaniards in December 1624.

these parting days at the Escurial that Philip brought in the young Velasquez, then twenty-four, to paint his guest's portrait and that Charles and Endymion met the greatest artist of their age. Then, after a last boar hunt and a picnic in a wood, Charles and Philip parted with every outward appearance of friendship, while Endymion and Charles's other attendants kissed Philip's hand. In this exchange of courtesies Buckingham took no part. His farewell to Olivares was marked by loud and bitter recriminations, after which he rode away.

Charles was equally resentful. At its height, his infatuation for the Infanta had been largely vanity; and now he was being sent back to England without the prize for which he had risked and sacrificed so much. But Charles's pride would not allow him to betray his feelings until he was safely out of Spain. So he preserved his outward air of courtesy and friendship in his farewells to the Infanta and to Philip, and on his stately royal progress to the sea, accompanied by members of the Spanish Council of State and a splendid retinue. At each stopping place he was greeted with costly entertainment by the local notables. At Valladolid he displayed a special interest, which Endymion no doubt shared, in the pictures there by Raphael and Michael Angelo.

On September 12th the Prince and his party reached Santander, where they had the welcome sight of the English ships, under the command of Buckingham's father-in-law, the Earl of Rutland, lying some way out from shore. Although it was late in the afternoon, they at once put off in boats to visit Rutland's flagship, the *Prince*. Going ashore again, after dark, they found that a strong off-shore wind had blown up, and, with the swift tide running out, they could not make the land. As they tried to get back to the *Prince* they got lost in the stormy night, and their boats were in imminent danger of being swept out to sea or of being sunk through running foul of the ships' cables. Luckily, the Captain of the *Defiance* put out lighted buoys

2   The Infanta Maria Anna of Spain

The original portrait brought back from Spain
by the Duke of Buckingham

roped to his ship and the crew of the Prince's boat managed to get themselves and their passengers onto the *Defiance*. A moment later the boat was smashed against the ship's side. Eventually all the boats succeeded in reaching one or other of the ships, and the passengers, Endymion among them, spent the night on board, wet and fearful of the fate of their friends.

Contrary winds kept the fleet in Santander for nearly a week. Charles slept aboard the *Prince*, though entertainments were given both on the ships and in the town.[51]

While waiting at Santander, Charles was met by the Secretary of his sister, the Queen of Bohemia, bringing letters from her. There was good news of the birth of her son, but her letters were a bitter reminder of the utter failure to achieve anything for the relief of her situation.

Charles wrote back to Elizabeth by her messenger. His letter made it clear that he had every intention of breaking off the match, and, in it, he openly expressed his disgust at the treatment he had received in Madrid and his desire for revenge.[52]

The first step in his revenge had already been taken a few days before in Segovia, on the way to the coast. It was as deceitful a move as anything the Spanish had conceived. After writing a friendly note to Philip, Charles sent Clarke, a confidential servant of Buckingham's, back to Madrid. He was ordered to say he had merely returned on Buckingham's private business, but he carried with him, in secret, a letter to Bristol which he was not to hand over until the arrival of the Pope's consent to the dispensation. Under pretext of guarding against the possibility of the Infanta's taking refuge in a nunnery after the proxy marriage, the letter commanded Bristol not to deliver the proxy to Philip until Charles had full security that the Infanta would not take the veil. Charles had thus made it impossible for his solemn promises to be redeemed.[53]

On September 18th the wind at last changed and the fleet set sail for England. Unfavourable winds accompanied them and it was not until September 26th that they put into the Scillies, where Charles and his attendants had some difficulty in landing at night in a rough sea and where they stayed four days. It was near the Scillies that they had a further adventure, when the fleet intervened to stop a running fight between five Dutch ships and four ships from Dunkirk, all men of war. Charles sent for the rival commanders and made them shake hands and promise to be friends on land and not to cut each other's throats at sea. The Dunkirkers were sent off first, but as soon as the Hollanders were let go, they again set off in full chase of their enemies.[54]

On the afternoon of Sunday, October 5th, the fleet reached Portsmouth. It was raining, but the Prince and his attendants, Endymion amongst them, at once landed and set out by coach for Guildford, where they spent the night. By eight o'clock next morning they reached London, crossing the river to York House. As soon as they had breakfasted, they drove straight on to Royston to greet the King.

The news of the Prince's return spread like wildfire. He was safe home; he had left the dreaded Infanta unwed in Spain; he had freed himself from the toils of Spanish and Papist influence and had come back to help his people in their resistance to Popery. A wave of spontaneous and almost hysterical rejoicing, unparalleled in memory, swept over the whole country, shared by men and women in all walks of life. Along the route which Endymion followed in Charles's train, the crowds dragged the horses from any carts carrying wood, and flung carts and contents onto the blazing bonfires. It was only with the greatest difficulty that the royal party made their way along the Strand through the press of people cheering and shouting 'Long live the Prince of Wales'. When they neared Tyburn, they came across a group of condemned felons—six men and two women—on their way to be hanged. The lucky prisoners were at once released.

As the news reached each shire and town, the church bells were rung and bonfires lighted. In Cambridge, for instance, the bells were rung for two whole days. For three nights bonfires and fireworks lit the sky, while an extra dish was served at the College suppers.

In London, in spite of pouring rain, a hundred and eight bonfires blazed merrily between St. Paul's and London Bridge. Tables, laden with food, were set out in the streets by the wealthier citizens, together with hogsheads of wine and butts of sack. All day long the feasting and drinking went on, and, when night fell, the revellers poured wine onto the fires so that flames of every colour of the rainbow lit up the scenes of revelry. At St. Paul's Cathedral a solemn service of thanksgiving was held, at which the 114th Psalm was sung as a special anthem, 'When Israel came out of Egypt, and the House of Jacob from the barbarous people.'

When Charles and Buckingham reached Royston, the King fell on their necks and they all wept for joy.[55]

It seemed to most Englishmen that the Deity himself was giving a striking demonstration of his support of the Protestant cause when, a few days later, a crowd of some four hundred people assembled in a large room in the top storey of part of the French ambassador's house in Blackfriars to hear a sermon by Drury, a Jesuit priest. As Drury began to speak of God's mercy and how His longsuffering even endured the blasphemies of the heretic English, the floor support, a beam of sound oak (to show how clearly it was God's hand) suddenly broke in two. The floor collapsed, carrying with it in its fall the floor of the room below. Priest and congregation were hurled twenty feet down. Ninety-one people, including Drury, were killed and most of the others badly injured.[56]

(viii)

Although James was now persuaded to order Bristol to tell Philip that the restitution of the Palatinate must be a condition of the marriage so as 'not at the same time to give joy to his son and to give his only daughter her portion in tears',[57] the old King, left to himself, would have clung on to his hopes of the Spanish alliance and the Spanish marriage. He was still as willing to be deceived by the Spaniards as the Spaniards were anxious to deceive him; and Bristol, from Madrid, was still urging that the marriage should be completed.

But James's growing feebleness was no match for the combined pressure brought on him by Charles and Buckingham, who were determined to revenge themselves by a complete break with Spain. To obtain this, they were even ready to persuade James to summon Parliament, in the knowledge that Parliament would give the fullest support to any anti-Spanish policy. It was they and not James who now dictated the course of events.

On November 13th James wrote to Bristol ordering him, before he delivered the proxy, to obtain a written declaration from Philip of his intention to obtain a complete restitution of the Palatinate by force of arms if mediation should fail. While this ultimatum was on its way to Spain, the Pope's long-awaited approval of the dispensation arrived in Madrid and Philip fixed November 29th for the celebration of the proxy marriage. It was only three days before this date that James's letter of November 13th reached Bristol. At the very last moment, therefore, Bristol was forced, most unwillingly, to tell Olivares that the ceremony could not take place.

Not unnaturally, the Spanish regarded this as a public insult. When Bristol presented the ultimatum about the Palatinate he met with a firm refusal. The Infanta ceased to be styled Princess of England, she stopped learning English, and Bristol was recalled from Madrid.[58]

In February 1624 Parliament met and James asked for their advice about the Spanish alliance. But first, they were to hear the story of the Spanish visit from Buckingham's own lips. On February 24th he gave his narration before both Houses. In it he presented a full account of Endymion's abortive mission in the autumn of 1622. There were, of course, many omissions in his long narrative, but it gave conclusive proof that there had never been any serious intention on the part of Spain to help recover the Palatinate by force of arms. Attempts by the Spanish ambassadors to discredit Buckingham with James only added to his popularity. His triumph was complete and he received the unanimous endorsement of his conduct from Parliament, which proceeded to present a petition to the King begging that the treaties with Spain should be ended and offering assistance in case of war.

On March 23rd, James was finally persuaded by Charles and Buckingham to declare all negotiations with Spain at an end. Once more bonfires of joy blazed in the streets. A Spanish princess would not be Queen of England.

On the other hand, a happier fate awaited the Infanta than a life in a heretic country. Before long she was married to Ferdinand, son of the Emperor Ferdinand II. Her husband was a cultivated, scholarly man and a com poser of music. His personal life was blameless. Above all, his devotion to the Catholic religion matched the Infanta's. She bore him three sons, and, in 1636, her husband became Emperor on his father's death. She died in 1646.

Appropriately, perhaps, the last word may be left to Archie. In November, Sir Edward Zouche was saying that he 'dares not write what Archie the Fool said about the Spanish match'. Archie had, however, extracted the promise of a pension from Philip and, seven years later, he was boasting that he had received the arrears of the pension amounting to £1,500. So one person, at least, got something from Charles's visit to Madrid.[59]

CHAPTER V

(i)

THE Spanish journey had considerably enhanced Endymion's own position, his close attendance on Charles and their shared experiences bringing him more deeply into the Prince's confidence. Shortly after their return, a note from Conway to Middlesex, backing a petition from Endymion, significantly alluded to 'whose servant Porter was and whose he is'.[1]

But Buckingham's was the only version of the Spanish journey that had been given to the King and Parliament. Things might well look somewhat different if the other side were heard. Gondomar, in particular, knew much too much, as did Bristol. Lafuente, Gondomar's confessor, was now sent to England. On his journey a mysterious robbery at Amiens deprived him of his credentials, but his report of Buckingham's conduct and intentions alarmed James and caused scenes between the King and the Duke. The Privy Council, however, pronounced Buckingham innocent. Bristol was dealt with by being ordered to stay at home at Sherborne without being allowed to see the King. Finally Middlesex, the Lord Treasurer, who opposed war with Spain in the knowledge that the country's finances would not stand it, was impeached by the Commons at Buckingham's instigation and was dismissed.

It was to France that James, Charles and Buckingham now turned both for an ally against Spain and for a wife for Charles in the person of Princess Henrietta Maria, King Louis's sister. But, once again, it looked as if the proposed marriage would split on the rock of toleration for the English Catholics, on which Louis insisted, although James had given Parliament an undertaking that no concessions would be made. The new French ambassador found, however, an ally in Buckingham, who was so bent on French help for the recovery of the Palatinate that he was prepared to agree to almost any terms for the marriage. After long haggling, the marriage treaty was signed in November. While Louis only gave a verbal promise of support to Mansfeld, whom James and Buckingham proposed to send with English troops to attack the Palatinate, Charles had to sign a private engagement promising toleration to the English Catholics.

Meantime, the Progress in the hot, dry summer of 1624 had taken Endymion with most of the Court to the Midlands. Olive stayed in London, at their house in the Strand, or with her parents at Woodhall. Endymion's letters to her show his efforts to control her difficult and independent nature, and how his passionate love was still tortured by his long absences and by Olive's jealousy, which was once more harping on the attractions of the Crofts ladies at Saxham.

'My dear Olive,' he wrote, 'I hope that you have forgotten all the unkindness of last night, although I must confess I did suspect by your letter there was something remaining in your mind . . . Olive, believe me, that whatsoever I am, being angry, when it is past, I love nothing in the world near a comparison to you. All the joy and comfort I have is in you. Therefore, blame me not if I desire to have you according to my own heart, and assure yourself we shall never agree if we seek not to please one another. . . . God knows how unwilling I am to show any kind of distaste when you cross me, but to prevent a greater mischief, I think I had better make show of anger for small offences than conceal them and let greater be the ruin of our loves.

We have been four years married and God hath blessed us with children. . . . Before I gave you any hand of husband, you did engage your word to me that in whatsoever I should advise you, nothing should hinder you from following my directions and I swore to you that if you did so, no man breathing should love a woman more than I would you. I have kept mine oath, and whether you have kept your promise, that I leave to you; but, my dearest Olive, I wonder why you should suspect me for Saxum when, as I hope to be saved, I think of nothing but thy sweet love, which to me is above all the beauties that ever God created.'[2]

'I will ever endeavour to let you see that I esteem you above all earthly things,' he wrote again from Theobalds, 'but still I shall wish that you would know I must govern you and not you me.'[3]

Endymion's absence on the Progress was all the harder to bear, since Olive, in London, was shortly expecting her third child. The Court had moved north through Hertfordshire and Bedfordshire, reaching Buckingham's mansion of Burley-on-the-Hill at the beginning of August. At Burley a Masque was once again performed, this time 'Pan's Anniversary' by Inigo Jones and Ben Jonson, but the highlight of the Progress came next month on the way south at Woodstock, where, in a great hunt, 'Cropear a noted and notorious stag' was killed 'with so much joy and triumph as if it had been some great conquest'.[4]

During the Progress, Endymion wrote to Olive from Rufford.

'My dear Heart.

'This is the third letter I have sent you and the first I have received from you. I thank you for it, but I wonder you will urge me to come away sooner than the appointment we had agreed upon. I protest to God I have appointed to me business of so much importance which cannot be dispatched so soon as I could wish, but if you think my sudden presence might help you to any ease, I would leave anything that could import me to see you, for I look upon nothing beyond your health and comfort. You have with your letter amazed me and I wonder your love could give way to let you tell me that unless I presently depart from hence you cannot live . . . but so soon as conveniently I can, I will leave all and come to you.'[5]

At the end of September, Olive gave birth to another boy. He was christened Endymion at St. Martin-in-the-Fields. The register called the child 'filius sagacissimi viri' Endymion Porter. Endymion's reputation as a man of learning, which the register thus recorded, was already well established. This same year he was included by Edmund Bolton in his projected Royal Academy. Bolton had married Endymion's sister Margaret. He was a Catholic antiquarian and historian and had conceived the idea of a college of honour to hold its meetings in Windsor Castle. This Academy was to consist of three classes: the 'tutelaries', composed of Knights of the Garter together with the Lord Chancellor and the Chancellors of Oxford and Cambridge; the 'auxiliaries', made up of noblemen; and the 'essentials', drawn from the most notable gentlemen. The Academy was to superintend all secular learning in English. Bolton had already dedicated a historical tract to 'my good and noble friend, Endymion Porter Esq one of the gentlemen of the Prince's bedchamber', and Endymion was one of the 'essentials' for the Academy, along with such distinguished names as Edward Coke, Henry Wotton, Kenelm Digby, Michael Drayton, Ben Jonson, Inigo Jones and Tobie Matthew. Bolton's plan commended itself to King James, who was to be the Academy's patron, but Charles and Buckingham were apparently indifferent to it, and the scheme died with the King.[6]

Endymion had been in attendance on the Prince at Hampton Court when 'little Dim' was born, and shortly afterwards he had had to accompany Charles to Royston. From there he wrote to Olive on October 22nd, 'Your will be done, sweetheart, for otherwise we shall have but little quiet. You send me word that on Thursday you are to be churched. I entreat you heartily that it may be so, for on Friday I purpose to be with you, and, sweet Olive, remember that you love me still with that same affection you gave me first your heart, for I esteem it above all earthly pleasures. . . . Farewell, my dear love, on Friday night thou shalt have thy true loving husband.'[7]

The Court came to Whitehall for Christmas, as usual, and Endymion was able to be with Olive and the three boys. Although the customary Twelfth Night Masque was performed, the King 'kept to his chamber all this Christmas, not coming once to the Chapel, nor to any of the plays'.[8]

In the middle of January, Endymion moved with the Court to Newmarket. It was a warm unhealthy winter and Endymion had been 'very ill with an ague' when he wrote to Olive, 'Your kind letter came in good time to accompany me in this place which affords me no comfort but desires to see you. . . . You have the odds of me much, for the company of the little boys will help you to pass away this tedious time better than if I were with you. I beseech God to bless them and you and make me once able to enjoy you without this sense of absenting myself from you. . . . My dearest love, farewell, and believe that whilst I breathe I will ever be

Your true loving husband
Endymion Porter.'[9]

Towards the end of the year, the twelve thousand unwilling conscripts for Mansfeld's army to recover the Palatinate were being assembled at Dover. Money, food and equipment were all lacking and the wretched half-starved rabble roamed the country, mutinying, deserting and committing 'very foul outrages'.[10] Among those forcibly recruited were two men taken from Newgate gaol who had been arrested for 'breaking the house of Endymion Porter and stealing divers goods therefrom'.[11] The troops sailed at the end of January, but as the French would not allow them to land at Calais and march through France, they disembarked at Flushing. Frost and snow added to their miseries. Soon only a quarter of them were capable of carrying arms. Such was the fiasco of James's final attempt to restore his daughter's fortunes.

Endymion was with Prince Charles at Theobalds in March when the King was taken ill with a tertian ague. Although his constitution was not strong, he was not yet fifty-nine and there was thought to be no danger if he would listen to the advice of his doctors.[12] James was, however, a notoriously bad patient and the fever persisted. Buckingham and his mother then remembered the remedies that an Essex country doctor had given Buckingham in a recent illness. Sending for these, they applied them without consulting the King's doctors, who protested so vigorously that one of them had to be ordered to leave the Court.[13] The doctors, quite properly, refused to sign a statement that the remedies applied by Buckingham and his mother had been harmless. It was not, therefore, surprising that, however baseless the charge might be, some of Buckingham's enemies should have believed that the King had been poisoned.

James's strength gradually sank, and on March 27th, he died peacefully. His body was embalmed, his heart being found 'great but soft', and his head 'so full of brains, as they could not, upon the opening, keep them from spilling—a great mark of his infinite judgement'.[14] On April 4th, the body was brought to London to lie in state for a month at Denmark House.

The funeral took place on May 7th, 'the greatest that was ever known in England'.[15] A procession of nine thousand mourners accompanied the body from Denmark House to Westminster Abbey. Although the head of the procession started about ten in the morning, it was nearly five in the afternoon before all had entered the Abbey. Charles, as chief mourner, walked immediately behind the magnificent hearse, designed by Inigo Jones. Endymion's place in the procession was a little way in front. At the Abbey, where Bishop Williams preached a two-hour sermon, he was in close attendance on the new King, his master.[16]

Olive was not in London to watch, from their house, Endymion walking with the funeral procession to the

Abbey. She had gone to Aston, where, at the end of April, she gave premature birth to a boy. He was christened Villiers, but died in a few days.

(ii)

With the accession of his master to the throne Endymion was appointed one of the Grooms of the Bedchamber with £500 a year for life.[17] He was also given the lease of a number of manors belonging to the Duchy of Cornwall, together with the farm of a local tax on wines and certain customs duties on goods entering or leaving Duchy ports.[18]

The Bedchamber was a department of the Royal Household that King James had originated. It was an inner chamber, under the First Gentleman of the Bedchamber or Groom of the Stole, independent of the main Privy Chamber under the Lord Chamberlain. It furnished the King with his most confidential servants. The many other regular officials of the Household had their formal and specific court duties, but the Grooms of the Bedchamber were the King's most personal and informal attendants—'personal assistants' is perhaps the nearest modern equivalent.[19] Five other grooms were appointed at the same time as Endymion. They were Andrew Pitcairn, James Livingstone, William Murray, George Kirke and Thomas Cary.[20] Pitcairn was a Scot who had been in King James's and Prince Charles's service. He was also Master of the Hawks. He died in 1642.[21] Livingstone and Murray were also Scots. The former was made Earl of Newburgh in the Civil War. The latter, the son of the Provost of Eton, was just King Charles's age and had been brought up with him. He was made Earl of Dysart in 1646.[22] Kirke came from an old Derbyshire family.[23] Others then or later in the Bedchamber[24] were Patrick Maule, who was made Earl of Panmure in 1646, James Maxwell, Henry Murray and John Ashburnham who, like Endymion, became a member of the Long Parliament.

Endymion's position differed in some important respects from that of his fellow Grooms. For one thing, thanks to his travels and Spanish experience and connections, he was the only one to be employed overseas in diplomacy. Nor were the other Grooms wits and connoisseurs of the arts or used by Charles to assist in his picture buying. He also seems to have been more closely in the King's confidence than were his fellow Grooms, except perhaps William Murray. Certainly he was the only one whom Parliament specifically exempted from any pardon because of his supposed influence with the King. Nor was any other Groom of the Bedchamber so richly rewarded in the way of grants and patents. It may well have been because the King's appreciation of Endymion's services was so conspicuously shown in this material manner that he never received a Knighthood or other honour.

The Royal Household, outside the small group of the Bedchamber, was as large as it was diverse. There were the Gentlemen, Grooms, Ushers and Pages of the Privy Chamber and the Esquires of the Body, all in regular attendance by rota with the cupbearers, carvers and servers. There were the embroiderers, sempstresses and laundresses for the King's clothes, the shoemaker and the spurrier, the goldsmiths and jewellers, the large staffs in the kitchens who had to prepare not only the royal meals but board for all the courtiers; the bell-ringer, the wood-bearers, the porters at the gates and the vermin killer. There were the chaplains, the librarian and picture keepers, the musicians, the five physicians, four apothecaries, five surgeons, a herbalist and a French operator for the teeth, the Serjeants at Arms, Yeomen of the Guard and Band of Pensioners, with bow, gun and gunpowder makers. There were the equerries, the footmen, coachmen, littermen and farriers, and forty-four watermen and a barge-maker and a joiner under the Master of the Barges. There was a separate hunting stable and thirty falconers, twenty-four huntsmen for the buckhounds and sixteen for the harriers, as well as a keeper of the King's spaniels and two brothers who looked after the cormorants. In all, the regular household numbered a full thousand, not counting the unpaid 'extraordinary' members such as some three hundred Gentlemen of the Privy Chamber, eighty Esquires of the Body, chaplains and others.[25]

When the Court moved, as it was continually doing, harbingers under the Knight Harbinger went ahead to arrange the rooms for the inner Court circle and billets in the neighbourhood for the others. Small standing staffs were kept in all the residences and when the Court left, all had to give up the keys of their rooms so that everything should be 'cleaned and made sweet for the King's return'.[26]

The marriage of the new King with Princess Henrietta Maria was celebrated in Paris by proxy on May 1st, 1625. A fortnight later Buckingham arrived in Paris to fetch home the bride. He also went to try to secure definite French action in the way of open war with Spain for the recovery of the Palatinate. But Louis was not to be drawn into taking any steps other than giving subsidies to the King of Denmark and to Mansfeld. Buckingham's anger at this rebuff to his sanguine hopes may have prompted his astonishing behaviour at Amiens. Louis had gone back to Paris from Compiègne, but his mother and his wife had accompanied the bride and Buckingham as far as Amiens. There, Buckingham openly paid amorous attention to the French Queen. On one occasion he even broke into her bedroom, and addressed her in impassioned tones on his knees.

There was, however, one good result of Buckingham's visit to France. Through Gerbier, who had accompanied him, he met Rubens in Paris and the artist made the drawing of the Duke's head which served as the model for the magnificent equestrian portrait which Buckingham commissioned for £500.[27]

The new Queen landed at Dover on June 12th, late in

the evening. Charles, with Endymion accompanying him, had been waiting at Canterbury. Early the next morning, he rode to Dover. When he met his bride 'he wrapped her up in his arms and kissed her with many kisses'. 'Nimble and quick, black eyed and brown haired,' she was not yet sixteen and her head only reached her husband's shoulder. Although Charles had never been seen 'to look so merrily',[28] the difficulties that were to strain the young couple's early relations began within a few hours of their meeting. The Queen wanted to have her old lady-in-waiting in the coach with her on the drive to Canterbury, but this was not allowed and Buckingham's mother and sister rode with her instead.

Endymion, too, had been having his difficulties with Olive. From Canterbury he wrote to her—

'My dear Olive,
    'I did not think to have received such a swaggering letter from you, but I see you can do anything now, for time hath worn out the kindest part of your love, which I did hope would have lasted longer. I am glad you had not the keeping of mine towards you, for so we might have been without by this time, but be it spoken to your comfort or your grief, I will preserve mine whilst I have breath, nor shall age nor time make me forget my Olive.
    The Queen is expected this night at Dover and on Wednesday we shall be at London; the King will not come to Greenwich at all. I pray you have a care of my children and suffer not Guittens* to come in the house, for he runs into all the ale-houses in town. God bless George and Charles and Dim and you, and so, in haste, I rest
                    Your loving husband
                    Endymion Porter.'[29]

Two days later, he wrote again. 'This last night the King and the Queen did lie together here at Canterbury; long

---

* A servant.

may they do so and have as many children as we are like to have. I have sent you two of the King's points, one for yourself and another for a friend, and I have sent you this little ruby ring which I would have you wear for my sake. On Thursday I hope we shall meet at London, and although I desire infinitely to see my children, yet I would not have you let them come to London; you and I will go to them on Friday. God almighty bless them and you, and fail me when I fail to be

Your true loving husband.'[30]

Endymion's references to keeping his servant out of the house and to stopping the children coming to London were due to fear of the plague. London was always unhealthy in summer, but this year (1625) the plague was already assuming alarming proportions. It had begun as early as April and, in spite of an exceptionally cold May, thirty-two parishes had been infected before the end of June, and deaths had mounted to two hundred and fifty a week.[31]

The royal party came to London by river, going to Whitehall and then to Hampton Court. Endymion, it is hoped, was able to go with Olive to pay a quick visit to see their children in the clean country air of Aston, where Endymion's mother, Angela, still lived.

The Manor house of Aston-sub-Edge lies among orchards in the vale at the foot of the Cotswold escarpment. It stands today, as it stood when Endymion owned it, a lovely example of a small Elizabethan manor, part of it of an earlier date, but forming a harmonious whole with its two stories and gabled attics above, its mullioned windows and mouse-coloured stone-tiled roof, and its stone walls mellowed to that soft shade where undertones of pink and yellow suffuse the grey. Inside, there are two wide staircases and the rooms are spacious and cheerful. The farm buildings with their stone barns and sheds lie behind and give on to rich pastures.

Endymion's freehold property at Aston comprised nearly six hundred and fifty acres.[32] He had also re-acquired some

Mickleton leaseholds from Sir Edward Fisher to whom he paid a 'chief rent' of ten shillings a year.[33]

Edmund Porter, Endymion's father, had died in 1623 and grandfather Giles had not lived to see his grandson's rise to wealth and importance, but Endymion's mother had made her home in the manor house at Aston, while his sister Mary, who had married William Canning, lived a mile or two away at Foxcote. Canning rented the Aston manor house garden and orchards and the home farm from Endymion, whose total rentals at Aston and Mickleton brought him in nearly £300 a year.[34] Richard Bee, the steward, looked after Endymion's Aston affairs. He was a faithful and trusted servant who remained at Aston all through the wars and after Endymion's death.[35]

Apart from the Cannings, Endymion's chief neighbours were Sir Baptist Hicks, the rich city merchant who had acquired the manor of Campden and built Campden House; and Sir Nicholas Overbury of Bourton-on-the-Hill, who leased some of Endymion's Aston land.[36] There were, too, the Keytes of Ebrington, and the famous Robert Dover had a house in Aston itself.

This remarkable character was a native of Warwickshire. About the time of King James's accession, Dover, then some thirty years old, 'being full of activity and of a generous free and public spirit',[37] had conceived the idea of reviving the Olympic games, probably with the aim of countering the rising tide of Puritan opposition to sports and pastimes. He was able to get the sport-loving King's backing and his leave 'to select a place on Cotswold Hills in Gloucestershire'.[38] The superb site that he chose was in the parish of Weston-sub-Edge, next to Aston-sub-Edge and about a mile from Chipping Campden. Still known as Dover's Hill,* it comprises the upper slopes of a section of the escarpment where the Cotswold plateau falls steeply down to the plain, which stretches away far into the distance. On the left lies the vale of Evesham, flanked by

* Now National Trust property.

Bredon Hill. In the centre, fifty miles away on the horizon are the shadows of the hills of Clee. To the right, only ten miles distant, lies Stratford.

Dover's Cotswold Olympic Games flourished from about 1610 until the Commonwealth, when they were, of course, suppressed. Dover himself died in 1641, but his Games were revived at the Restoration and were carried on with full spirit for the rest of the century. Under the Georges, the Games still drew large crowds, but seem to have lost their character. In the nineteenth century they so degenerated that, in 1853, Dover's Hill was enclosed to put an end to them.

The Games were held every year on the Thursday and Friday of Whitsun week and 'were frequented by the nobility and gentry, some of whom came sixty miles to see them'.[39] They were opened by the unfurling of a flag from the battlements of a sham wooden castle that Dover had built on the crest, the firing of cannon from its sides and the blowing of trumpets. Dover directed the proceedings in person and Anthony Wood records that to encourage Dover and add to the splendour of the occasion, 'Endymion Porter, Esq., a native of that county and a servant of the King, a person also of most generous spirit,' gave Dover 'some of the King's old clothes, with a hat and feather and ruff purposely to grace him and consequently his solemnity'.[40]

The programme included all the country sports of the day—running, jumping, throwing the hammer and pitching the bar; dancing, football, skittles, quoits and single stick fighting; bull-baiting, cock fighting, bell ringing, horse racing and hare coursing.

In 1636, the Games were commemorated by the publication of a small quarto volume of sixty-eight pages—the *Annalia Dubrensia*. The volume was prefaced by a woodcut of the Games. At the top, 'the portable fabricke of Dover Castle' stands on the crest of the escarpment, elevated on what looks like the stem of a mushroom. An enormous banner flies from the centre cupola, and cannon are firing from each of the castle's sides. Below are depicted various of the Games. Three ladies dance sedately to a musician; two men are fighting with single-sticks, while another stands upside down on his hands, and another is jumping down the side of the hill. Two more are wrestling, and a hare is being pursued by greyhounds. In the left centre, the company is feasting at a large table on which enormous tankards are prominent. Below, another hare is being chased by hounds and horsemen, while competitors are engaged in throwing the hammer and tossing the pole. Occupying the whole of the lower centre of the page, Dover himself surveys his Games on horseback. He is richly dressed and an enormous black hat with feather surmounts his bearded face. He is wearing, no doubt, the royal attire that Endymion procured for him.

In the *Annalia Dubrensia* more than thirty poets each contributed a set of verses in honour of Dover and the Games. Although the poets included Drayton and Ben Jonson, the verses are hardly worthy of the occasion. They are, in fact, sadly pedestrian. Ben Jonson's lines

'But I can tell thee, Dover, how thy Games
Renew the glory of our blessed James
How they do keep alive his memory
With the glad country and posterity
How they restore true love and neighbourhood
And do both Church and Commonwealth the good,'

are matched by Drayton's

'And under written, lo this was the man
Dover that first these noble sports began.'

D'avenant's contribution, 'In Celebration of the Yearly Preserver of the Games Cotswold', was a thirty-three-line poem, 'sung by a poet that conceals his name.' It was added, unsigned, to the end of the collection. In his verses, D'avenant praises,

> 'Dover that his knowledge not employs
> T'increase his neighbours quarrels but their joys,'

and goes on to tell of the material rewards that Dover's enterprise should bring.

> 'Money at Cotswold Games shall early fly
> Whilst the precise and envious shall stand by
> And see his mineral fountains never dry.
> His girls shall dowerless wed with heirs of birth
> His boys plough London widows up like earth,
> While Cotswold Bards carol their nuptial mirth.'

Only Randall's lines,

> 'The Nemean and the Isthmian pastimes still
> Though dead in Greece, survive on Cotswold Hill,'

breathe a faint anticipation of Byron.[41]

But the Games may also have been referred to by Shakespeare himself. In the opening scene of the *Merry Wives of Windsor*, Slender says to Page, 'How does your fallow greyhound, Sir? I heard say he was outrun on Cotsall.' Although these lines first appeared in the 1623 folio, Shakespeare must have been familiar with Dover's Games. What, indeed, is more likely than that Shakespeare, in the years of his retirement, should have ridden over from Stratford through the fields and orchards in the early summer sunshine, perhaps with Ben Jonson or Drayton as his companion, to see contests inspired by classical Greece yet so very English in character; and, from Dover's Castle, to look down over the wide expanse of that green and wooded heart of England that he loved so well? And there, just returned home from his years in Spain and surrounded by Porter relations, Endymion might well have met him.

In fact, Endymion had a link with Shakespeare through the person of Thomas Russell, whose friendship with the poet was so close that Shakespeare chose him as one of the two overseers of his will. Russell, who was born in 1570, was the younger son of Sir Thomas Russell of Strensham, some twenty miles down the Avon from Stratford. Inheriting estates at Broad Campden and Alderminster, he became a neighbour and friend of the Porter family and, in 1595, stood godfather at Aston to Endymion's cousin Russell Porter, one of Uncle Nicholas's sons. This family friendship was maintained by Endymion. It was to Endymion that Thomas Russell turned in 1625 to try to persuade the King to make his great nephew, William Russell, a baronet. The honour was granted in 1627 and Sir William well repaid it by his gallant defence of Worcester in the Civil War. In 1630, Thomas Russell was corresponding with Endymion about a dog which the latter had promised to procure for him.

'Noble Sir,' Russell wrote from Rushock, his Worcester-shire home, north of Droitwich, 'Your letter sent by Phipps* was more welcome than any fortune I have lately encountered. I was never acquainted with compliment; but if I were subject to it, the carrier would not afford me opportunity of writing, only this. These are to tell you that by Phipps I understand you have now got the Tumbler† into your possession which you long ago promised me and I have zealously expected; wherefore if you please to send him by this carrier Payton, he has vowed to bring him safe to me. And thus with the remembrance of my true love and service to you and your lady Olive my Captain, with whom it shall please you else, I commit you and yours to God's protection and ever remain him whom you most command,
Tho. Russell.
Rushock this Xth of May, 1630.

* Russell's servant.
† A kind of small greyhound, renowned for skill in catching rabbits.

We understand here in the country the plague much to increase in London. I believe both you and your lady to be daily courtiers; for God's sake, if you come not down yourselves, send the children to me and I shall have a fatherlike care of them.'

This letter shows how familiar were the relations between Russell and Endymion. Even if Endymion never met Shakespeare, there can be little doubt that their mutual friend must have shared with Endymion, the patron and lover of poets, his memories of the greatest poet of all.[42]

(iii)

At Aston, the children were under the devoted care of Endymion's mother. 'I wish you could see me,' she wrote to Endymion, 'sitting at the table with my little chickens, one on either side; in all my life I have not had such an occupation to my content, to see them in bed at night and get them up in the morning. The little one is exactly like what you were when you were of his age, and if it was not for tiring you, I would give you such a sermon, but I take up too much time when speaking of them.

'You may rest assured that you need not be anxious; this situation is healthy, and no care that can be bestowed upon them is wanting to keep them in health. In reference to what you say regarding their food you must know that they have here butter and cheese in abundance. They have also very good cows and, before the children came, they killed a sheep once a week and sent it to market, for beef they do not kill on account of the heat, and veal and lamb sometimes they buy in the market; other times they kill when the cows breed. . . . I must now go and see my little ones to bed. The Lord bless you and allow me to see you as I would wish.

Your mother
Angela Porter.'[43]

After a few days with the children, Endymion's duty had called him back to plague-stricken London, where Charles's first Parliament assembled on June 18th, 1625. The King and Buckingham wanted funds to support their foreign policy. But Parliament was equally concerned with fears of concessions to the Catholics at home and drew up a petition asking for the execution of the full rigour of the penal laws. In respect of money, they would only vote a fraction of Charles's needs and even refused to grant for more than one year the export and import duties, known as tonnage and poundage, which had hitherto always been voted to a new sovereign for his lifetime. With the plague still spreading fast—one peer had to excuse his absence from Parliament because his shoemaker had fallen dead when putting on his boots[44]—Charles adjourned Parliament to meet at Oxford on August 1st.

Endymion was with Charles when he went to Woodstock for the meeting of Parliament at Oxford. There, the Commons turned again to the question of the English Catholics, facing Charles and Buckingham with the difficult choice of going back on the undertaking given to Parliament or of breaking their promises to France. They preferred to risk the French alliance and agreed to the Commons' petition for the enforcement of the anti-Catholic laws. But the Commons' mistrust of Buckingham and his foreign policy of continental alliances was too strong to allow them to vote subsidies before first ascertaining how they were to be spent. It was a naval war against Spain and not the recovery of the Palatinate that they favoured and, meantime, Moorish pirates were seizing English ships off the Devon and Cornish coasts, and Dunkirk privateers preying on English commerce in the Channel, while the English fleet lay inactive with part of its strength on a discreditable loan to the French King.

Charles's faith in Buckingham was, however, unshakeable, and he had no intention of allowing his minister's authority, and his own, to be subject to Parliament. Only twelve days after its Oxford meeting, he dissolved Parliament.

The plague in London had now reached its peak, with nearly three thousand five hundred deaths a week. A correspondent wrote that the city at one o'clock in the afternoon was as deserted as at a normal three o'clock in the morning —'no trading at all, the rich all gone, housekeepers and apprentices of manual trades begging in the streets'.[45] At the beginning of September, however, the plague started to decrease and by the end of the year it was almost over.

The Court, Endymion with it, had gone from Woodstock to the New Forest. The King was hunting at Beaulieu, while the Queen stayed at Titchfield, fourteen miles away, as the guest of Buckingham's sister, Lady Denbigh. Henrietta Maria's spirited independence, coming into conflict with Charles's autocratic ideas of a wife's duty of obedience to her husband, had already caused their estrangement. She resented Charles's attempt to force her to accept, as ladies of her bedchamber, Buckingham's female relations whom she regarded as spies, and she was deeply aggrieved at her husband's failure to protect the English Catholics. Her own French lay and priestly attendants did all they could to encourage her in the role of a martyr to her Catholic faith. One Sunday at Titchfield, when the local parson was holding a service for the Protestant members of the household, the Queen and her French attendants interrupted the service by noisily marching up and down the room. There was also an unedifying scene when the King and Queen were at dinner, with the rival Protestant and Catholic chaplains trying to shout each other down while saying grace.[46]

Early in September, Charles met the Dutch Commissioners at Southampton and signed a treaty of alliance for the blockade of Spain's Flemish and Spanish ports. A little later, Endymion accompanied the King from Salisbury to Plymouth for a review of the fleet and troops. In numbers, the eighty ships made a formidable array, but most of the ships were old, patched-up merchantmen, pressed reluctantly into service, and the whole fleet was ill-found and ill-provided by fraudulent contractors. The troops were pressed men, unwilling, untrained and unpaid. When the fleet finally put to sea early in October, Cadiz was chosen as its objective. But procrastination and muddle robbed the landing in Cadiz Bay of any chance of success. After failing to intercept the Spanish treasure fleet returning home from the Indies, the leaky and storm-battered English ships straggled home, one by one. The costly expedition, on which Charles and Buckingham had pinned such high hopes, had achieved precisely nothing.

Charles's and Buckingham's war plans also embraced a continental Protestant alliance, with the King of Denmark at its head, subsidised by England. Since Parliament had failed to vote the necessary funds for the subsidies, money was to be found by pledging the crown jewels with Amsterdam merchants as security for a loan. In November, Buckingham arrived at The Hague to negotiate the treaty. There he was shortly joined by Endymion, who had been given the task of taking the jewels to Holland.[47] They included 'a great jewel of gold, called the Mirror of Great Britain, having 2 fair table diamonds, 2 other large diamonds cut lozenge-wise, garnished with small diamonds and a pendant of a fair diamond cut in faucets without foil'.[48] Unfortunately the Amsterdam merchants refused to advance money on the crown jewels without security for their redemption.

The mission was not, however, entirely fruitless. Buckingham had already sat to Rubens in Paris. Now, accompanied by Endymion, he visited the painter's studio in Antwerp, where Endymion met Rubens for the first time. They saw Rubens's splendid collection of Italian masters and Buckingham persuaded the painter to sell him the complete collection together with thirteen of Rubens's own canvases.[49]

This was not Endymion's only connection with pictures

in 1625. In London, he had got to know Daniel Mytens, who had come to England from Holland about 1618 to paint for Arundel. In 1624, Charles had bestowed a pension of £50 a year on him 'for his better encouragement in the art and skill of picture drawing'[50] and, in 1625, Endymion procured him the office of one of the King's picture drawers in ordinary with the fee of an additional £20 a year.[51] For nearly ten years Mytens was to be engaged in painting a succession of official portraits for the King and in copying some of the masterpieces in the royal collection.

Another painter to be befriended by Endymion about this time was Orazio Gentileschi, whose work was much admired by Charles and Buckingham. Charles invited him to England in 1626, gave him a pension of £100 a year and treated him with great liberality. According to a thoroughly spiteful document compiled by the jealous Gerbier, his house was furnished for him 'from top to toe' at the staggering cost of over £4,000. Gerbier went on to state that Endymion had solicited Buckingham for money on Gentileschi's behalf, hinting that some of the proceeds had remained in Endymion's hands. Besides painting religious pictures, Gentileschi executed nine canvases, representing the Muses and the Arts, for the ceiling of the hall in the Queen's house at Greenwich.[52]

It was not only painters who found a valuable and sympathetic friend in Endymion. By 1625, the name of Robert Herrick was becoming well known as a poet. Four years younger than Endymion, he had taken his degree at Cambridge and, after being ordained in 1623, had come to London.[53] Herrick's poems attest his warm affection for Endymion and his admiration for the encouragement which Endymion was ever ready to give to the arts. One poem, addressed to 'The Patron of Poets, Mr. End: Porter', begins

'Let there be Patrons; Patrons like to Thee
Brave Porter! Poets neer will wanting be.'

The poet goes on to praise the way in which Endymion gave

> 'Not only subject matter for our wit
> But likewise oil of maintenance to it.'[54]

Another poem to 'The honoured Master Endymion Porter' runs

> 'When to thy Porch I come and (ravisht) see
> The State of Poets there attending Thee:
> Those Bards and I, all in a chorus sing,
> We are thy Prophets, Porter; Thou our King.'[55]

A few years later, when Herrick was in deep sorrow over the death of his brother, he wrote an ode to Endymion in which he called him his 'chief preserver' and blessed 'that hand which makes me stand'.[56]

But the most charming of the poems which Herrick addressed to Endymion are those describing the country life that Endymion, tied by his Court duties, could so rarely enjoy. There is 'An Eclogue or Pastorall between Endymion Porter and Lycidas Herrick', in which 'Lycidas' Herrick reproaches Endymion for forsaking the country for the Court.

> 'Thou leav'st our Hills, our Dales, our Bowers
> Our fine fleeced sheep:
> (Unkind to us) to spend thine Hours
> Where Shepherds should not keep.'[57]

In a long poem, 'The Country Life, to the honoured Mr. End: Porter', Herrick gives a picture of what well might be the life at Aston that Endymion sometimes must have thought of with longing in the midst of the endless Court round.

'Sweet country life, to such unknown
Whose lives are others, not their own:
But serving Courts and Cities be
Less happy, less enjoying thee.

*   *   *

No, Thy ambition's master piece
Flies no thought higher than a fleece:
Or how to pay the Hinds and clear
All scores, and so to end the year.
But walk'st about thine own dear bounds,
Not envying others' larger grounds,
For well thou know'st tis not th'extent
Of land makes life, but sweet content.
When new the cock, (the ploughman's horn,)
Calls forth the lily-wristed morn,
Then to thy cornfields thou dost go,
Which tho' well soiled, yet thou dost know
That the best compost for the lands
Is the wise master's feet and hands.
There at the plough, thou midst thy team
With a hind whistling there to them:
And cheer'st them up, by singing how
The Kingdom's portion is the plough.
This done, then to th'enamelled meads
Thou goest, and as thy foot them treads
Thou see'st a present godlike power,
Imprinted in each hub and flower,
And smell'st the breath of great-eyed kine
Sweet as the blossoms of the vine.
Here thou behold'st thy large sleek Neat
Unto the dew-laps up in meat:
And, as thou look'st, the wanton steer,
The heifer, cow and ox draw near
To make a pleasing pastime here.
These seen, thou goest to view thy flocks
Of sheep (safe from the wolf and fox),

And find'st their bellies there as full
Of short sweet grass, as backs with wool,
And leav'st them (as they feed and fill)
A shepherd piping on a hill. . . .'[58]

It is not only Endymion's 'general learning', and 'admirable wit' to which Herrick's poems pay tribute. They show, too, his 'sweet temper' and that side of his nature, so often apparent in his letters to Olive, that would gladly have exchanged worldly success for the contentment of the kind of family life that he had known at Aston as a boy.

(iv)

On February 2nd, 1626, Charles, dressed in white, was crowned in Westminster Abbey. The Queen, pleading religious scruples, refused to attend the ceremony, but watched the procession from a window, 'her ladies frisking and dancing in the room'.[59] Four days later, Charles opened his second Parliament, confident that the Commons would now vote him the money needed for prosecuting the war with Spain. But the opposition found a new leader in Sir John Eliot. He had been a friend of Buckingham's until, as Vice-Admiral of Devon, he had seen with his own eyes the chaos and misery of the Cadiz expedition. Now, his patriotism demanded that inquiry should be made into past mistakes before more funds were voted. When Charles insisted that Parliament should vote the money and ask no questions, the Commons attacked Buckingham by name as the author of all the failures. Regarding this not only as unfair but also as an attack on the Crown itself, Charles defended his favourite, only to be met by the Commons proceeding to amass evidence against Buckingham. In this, they were encouraged by the arrival in London of the Earl of Bristol. He had been confined in his house at Sherborne ever since his return from Spain, two years before, having obstinately refused to admit any errors in his conduct as

Ambassador. Now, he petitioned for a trial. Charles's reply was to accuse him of high treason.

On May 1st, Bristol was brought to the bar of the Lords to hear the Attorney General's charges against him. They were mostly vague and included the accusations that Bristol had tried to bring about Charles's conversion to Rome and that it had been Bristol's advice to continue the marriage negotiations that had obliged Charles to go to Madrid. Bristol asked leave of the Lords to speak. When this was granted, 'Then, my Lords,' he said, 'I accuse that man, the Duke of Buckingham of high treason and I will prove it.'[60] With these bold and contemptuous words, he presented his own charges. The first was that Buckingham had 'secretly combined and conspired' with Gondomar to take the Prince to Spain for his conversion to the 'Roman religion, so that the true religion established in England might be the more easily destroyed'.[61]

The second charge read 'that Mr. Endymion Porter, being duly instructed, was sent to Spain with messages so constructed that they might well serve as the foundation for putting this conspiracy into practice, which had been arranged months previously, thus abusing the confidence of the King and Prince by inducing them to give their consent to the expedition, which consent was obtained on the return of the said Porter'.[62]

Endymion was thus drawn into the full limelight of the contest between Parliament and the King and Buckingham. Absurd as was the charge that Buckingham had ever had any wish or intention to procure Charles's conversion to Catholicism, the awkward fact remained—and Bristol knew it—that Charles and Buckingham had indeed secretly made plans with Gondomar, which they had concealed from the King and the Council, for Charles to visit Madrid; while Gondomar, at least, had believed that the visit was to be the prelude to Charles's conversion.

In spite of Charles's efforts to silence Bristol, the Lords determined to continue the hearing, while the Commons proceeded with Buckingham's impeachment. Their grounds included his multiplicity of offices, the vast sums of money he had amassed and the honours and wealth he had showered on his relations, his failure to guard the Channel against privateers and pirates, and the loan of ships to France to be used against the Huguenots of La Rochelle. Finally, James's death was brought up, with the hint of poison in the medicine that Buckingham had administered.

Buckingham sat 'outfacing his accusers, outbraving his accusations', while Sir Dudley Digges compared him to 'a comet, exhaled out of base and putrid matter'.[63] Eliot summed up in a speech of bitter invective, comparing Buckingham to Sejanus, which led Charles to draw the conclusion that Eliot intended the comparison to include him as Tiberius.[64]

Grave as were Buckingham's faults of character, the picture drawn by his accusers was a false one. It was in his incompetence, rather than dishonesty or selfish aggrandisement, that responsibility lay, and Charles, believing implicity in the wisdom of his minister, knew that he shared Buckingham's responsibility to the full.

On June 8th, Buckingham laid his defence before the Lords. In its support and in support of the Attorney General's charges against Bristol, Endymion was summoned to appear the next day before the Committee of the Lords. In his examination on oath, Endymion told the full story of his mission to Madrid in 1622, bringing out Bristol's reluctance to assist him to force an answer out of the Spaniards, and the Ambassador's equivocal conduct in respect of Olivares and the disclosures that Endymion had wrung from him. Endymion also related that, on his departure from Spain, Bristol had told him that King James must do 'some main thing' to satisfy the Spaniards on the question of religion, while Gondomar had assured Endymion that Bristol had promised more in the way of religious concessions than Gondomar had dared to ask when he was in England. 'They held me here a greater heretic than Bristol,' Gondomar had said. Finally, Endymion repeated a conversation between Buckingham and Gondomar, when Endymion was acting as interpreter and when Gondomar had said that Bristol had told him that 'in his heart he was a Catholic'.[65]

Bristol at once replied by petitioning the Lords that Endymion, Tobie Matthew, Cottington, Gage and Kenelm Digby should be examined in his defence.[66] From a paper which he subsequently drafted,[67] we know that his interrogation of Endymion would have been a searching one. The questions that he drew up showed that he had in his possession and would quote from translations of Buckingham's and Endymion's letters to Gondomar and Olivares. There were, as well, to be questions about the hints that Endymion had conveyed regarding the Prince visiting Spain. Bristol was also going to put his earlier acquaintanceship with Endymion to good account by asking him about his service with Olivares and with Calley, together with such awkward questions as when and where Endymion had then frequented 'the public exercise of the protestant religion'. His final question was to be what present or gift had Olivares given to Endymion when he was last in Spain before the Prince's going and of what value.

Luckily, perhaps, Endymion was to be spared Bristol's interrogation. The Commons, by a large majority, resolved, before voting the King any money, to present their Remonstrance, demanding the dismissal of Buckingham, whom they called 'a common enemy of Church and State'.[68] Compliance with this demand, on the grounds that the Commons had no confidence in Buckingham personally and disapproved what he had done on the King's orders, would have been, in Charles's eyes, the abandonment of royal authority. The Commons had failed to prove any criminal charges against the Duke. Their function was to advise the Crown but not to control it. Anything else would lead to anarchy.

Sending Bristol to the Tower, Charles made up his mind to dissolve Parliament. When the Lords unanimously urged him to prolong the sitting if only for two days, 'Not a minute,' he replied.[69]

The general feeling of disaster at the breach between King and Parliament was echoed by the Heavens. In a thunderstorm of unprecedented severity, the waters of the Thames were whipped up into a huge waterspout. Travelling down river, it broke in a thick smoke on the garden wall of York House, Buckingham's residence.[70]

(v)

Endymion's master's quarrel with Parliament was not the only source of trouble. There was other strife that affected Endymion and the inner Court circle even more closely. Time had not improved Charles's relations with his little Queen, whose French attendants disliked England and the English and whose priests—'the most superstitious, turbulent and jesuitical that could be found in all France'[71]—made her submit to ostentatious penances and humiliations in the name of her faith, even interrogating her as to 'how often in the night the King had kissed her'.[72]

One day in June the priests persuaded her to walk on foot from St. James's to Tyburn 'to visit the holy place where so many martyrs, forsooth, had shed their blood in the defence of the Catholic cause'.[73] To Charles, this was the final straw. He now resolved to get rid of the whole pack of his wife's French attendants, who numbered over four hundred.[74] Entering the Queen's apartments in Whitehall and finding some of her Frenchmen 'unreverantly dancing and curvetting in her presence',[75] he took her to his own apartments, locking the door behind him, while Conway, aided by the Yeomen of the Guard, had the Bishop, priests and attendants removed to Somerset House, the women 'howling and lamenting as if they had been going to execution'.[76] Hearing the uproar, the Queen broke a window with her fist in anger.

Thirty coaches and fifty carts were sent to Somerset House to carry the French to Dover, but they refused to depart until the Yeomen of the Guard were marched down to eject them. The Queen was left with only her French nurse, lady's maid, cook, dressmaker and two other French servants. One French and two English priests were allowed her, and her French ladies-in-waiting were replaced by Buckingham's old mother, his sister Lady Denbigh, and other English noblewomen.

Charles's treatment of his wife did nothing to improve the steadily worsening relations with France in which maritime rivalry was a principal factor. This culminated in the seizure at Bordeaux of the whole English and Scottish wine fleet. But money remained Charles's and Buckingham's most pressing problem. An economy drive was carried out in the royal household and the courtiers were put on board wages instead of receiving free board. The City of London, however, refused to lend money on the security of the crown jewels. A forced loan, to which courtiers such as Endymion had to contribute with a good grace, afforded some relief, but it was the cargoes captured in a successful sweep off the French coasts and sold to Burlamachi, the London financier, for £150,000,[77] that enabled arrears of wages to be paid to sailors and dockyard workers, and preparations to be begun for a great expedition against France.

Endymion and Olive had suffered a sad loss at the end of 1626, when their two-year-old 'little Dim' had died in London. In February 1627, however, Olive gave birth to another boy, who was christened Mountjoy after Lord Mountjoy, soon to be created Earl of Newport, who married Olive's youngest sister Anne at Whitehall in the same month.

Throughout the spring and early summer of 1627, ships and men were being assembled at Portsmouth. The troops were levies, ill-clothed, ill-armed and often mutinous for lack of pay. Fifteen hundred raw Scotch recruits, billeted in the Isle of Wight, proved a particular terror to the local inhabitants.[78] Early in June, Endymion accompanied the King to Portsmouth, where Charles carried out a thorough inspection of ships and men, going on board every vessel and watching the troops drilling in the country round.[79] Buckingham followed soon afterwards, bringing £10,000 to encourage the troops with arrears of pay.[80]

The expedition of nearly one hundred ships and six thousand soldiers set sail at the end of June. Buckingham was in command, with Sir John Burgh, an experienced soldier, as his deputy. Endymion's brother Tom commanded one of the ships, and amongst the chaplains was Endymion's friend, Herrick the poet.[81] Buckingham's instructions were first to sweep the French and Spanish from the seas and then to proceed to La Rochelle to offer assistance to the Huguenots in their resistance to the French King.

The fleet met no French or Spanish ships on the sea and on July 10th Buckingham anchored off the Isle of Rhé, which commanded the entrance to La Rochelle. The island's main defence was the town and port of St. Martin, held by a strong garrison. Buckingham's landing was hotly disputed and only his personal bravery and energy succeeded in getting his unwilling and undisciplined force on shore, after the first wave had been hurled back into the sea by the French cavalry. The Rochellese showed no great enthusiasm over Buckingham's arrival, but the Duke at once set about the siege of St. Martin. The fort was too strong for assault and a French army had neared La Rochelle. All depended, therefore, on how quickly the English blockade could compel St. Martin to capitulate. By the end of September, St. Martin was on the point of surrender, but, at the last moment, a change of wind enabled the French to break the sea blockade and supply the citadel with another month's provisions.

Charles was straining every nerve to send further assistance. In spite of the emptiness of his treasury, he had succeeded in assembling ships and men at Plymouth, though their arms were defective and their supplies in confusion. Endymion was ordered by the King to accompany Lord Holland with the relief expedition, but when they reached Plymouth, a south-west wind prevented the fleet from sailing. On October 29th, the wind at last dropped. Against the advice of the seamen, Holland forced the fleet to put out into Plymouth Sound. Endymion was on board with him that night, when 'the cruellest storm almost ever seen'[82] drove the ships back. They were in great danger and many vessels were damaged. Holland at once sent Endymion to London to report to Charles that the fleet's departure was now indefinitely delayed.[83]

It was, in any case, too late to help Buckingham. By mid-October, the weather had turned cold and wet and the troops were in a wretched condition. The French army was now beginning to land on the island, and when a despairing attempt to take St. Martin by assault had failed, Buckingham had no option but to evacuate his forces. But retreat had been delayed too long. The fresh French troops attacked while the English were retiring, and surrounded and massacred part of the English forces. Thirty-four officers were killed and over twenty taken prisoner, including Endymion's brother-in-law, Lord Mountjoy.[84] Forty-two captured ensigns were hung in Notre Dame in Paris. 'The greatest dishonour that our nation ever underwent' was the typical opinion of a letter-writer.[85]

Buckingham had behaved with great courage and had seen all his surviving troops on board before he left the shore,[86] but his return to England was the signal for an outburst of public anger that threw the entire blame for the disaster onto his shoulders. Only Charles and his Court circle remained unshaken in their trust and admiration, putting the blame where, in fact, it largely lay, on the muddles at home, that had delayed the sending of supplies and reinforcements.

(vi)

The end of 1627 saw Endymion engaged in a very different enterprise from that of the Isle of Rhé. With his accession to the throne, Charles had pursued his picture collecting with increasing zeal. Purchases from abroad were the chief source for his collection, and the resources of the royal diplomatic service were deployed to help in his acquisitions. Sir Dudley Carleton and Sir Henry Wotton, the ambassadors at The Hague and Venice, and Sir Thomas Roe and Sir Peter Wyche at Constantinople, were the outstanding examples of this dual function of diplomat and collector. Courtiers going abroad also combined diplomatic missions with picture buying. Nicholas Lanier, the Master of the King's Music, was sent on the quest for pictures to Italy, where Daniel Nys, a merchant of Venice of indeterminate nationality, was Charles's principal agent. In Antwerp, the business side of picture buying was looked after by Lionel Wake, the English merchant with whom Endymion had corresponded when in Calley's service in Madrid. At home, the finance of the purchases went through the hands of Burlamachi, the Rothschild of the day. In all of this, Endymion acted as Charles's personal representative and its business formed one of his special functions at the Court.

The greatest purchase to enrich Charles's collection was now to be made. Daniel Nys, in Venice, had seen the opportunity in the ruined finances and corrupt government of the collapsing Gonzaga dynasty in Mantua. With great secrecy he had opened his approaches to Duke Ferdinand in 1624, and, when the Duke died in 1626, he had continued negotiations with the new Duke, Vincenzo. Finally, in the autumn of 1627, Nys persuaded the Duke to sell the greater part of his collection.

It was a great coup. In a letter to Endymion, 'his most esteemed patron,' Nys wrote triumphantly, 'since I came into the world, I have made various contracts, but never a

more difficult one than this, and which has proceeded so
happily. In the first place, the City of Mantua, and then
all the Princes of Christendom, both great and small, were
struck with astonishment that we could induce Duke Vincenzo to dispose of them. The people of Mantua made so
much noise about it, that if Duke Vincenzo could have had
them back again, he would readily have paid double and his
people would have been willing to supply the money. . . .
In treating for them, I used every artifice to obtain them
at a moderate price; as, had it been known that I was
acting for his Majesty, they would have demanded so much
more.'[87]

A few days later, the enthusiastic Nys wrote again to
Endymion describing the pictures that were being sent to
England. There were two Correggios and a Raphael, 'the
finest pictures in the world and well worth the money paid
for the whole'. There was a Raphael Madonna, 'for which
the Duke of Mantua gave a Marquisate'. There were 'the
twelve Emperors of Titian, a large picture of Andrea del
Sarto, a picture of Michelangelo di Caravaggio; other pictures of Titian, Correggio, Giulio Romano, Tintoretto and
Guido Reni, all of the greatest beauty. In short, so wonderful and glorious a collection that the like will never again
be met with; they are truly worthy of so great a King as his
Majesty of Great Britain. In this negotiation I have been
aided by divine assistance, without which success would
have been impossible; to Him then be the glory'.[88]

In his letters, Nys also told Endymion how Lanier, whom
Charles had sent to Italy, had helped 'to repair and trim
up' the pictures and had had them packed and put on board
ship, except for the two Correggios 'in tempera' and a
Raphael which Lanier was taking home with him over-
land.[89]

Ambassador Wake's services were called upon as well.
He reported to Secretary Conway how he personally saw
the cases safely stowed on the *Margaret*, 'a tall ship, very
strong and well manned with thirty-seven mariners';[90] how

he got Lanier and the *Margaret's* captain to agree to rate the cases of pictures at a bulk hundred tons; and how he gave the captain a note to say that his ship was on the King's business. Wake also arranged for the shipment to be free of customs duty, and helped Lanier on his overland journey with transport and with a passport.

The *Margaret* sailed from Venice on April 15th, 1628. After surviving a furious storm in the Adriatic, she reached London safely. But, on unpacking the pictures, a number were found to have been damaged on the voyage. 'Quick-silver' had got into them and made them black. Jerome Lanier was put to cleaning them. According to his own account, he first tried 'fasting spittle'. Then he mixed this with warm milk, but to no effect. Finally he cleaned the pictures with 'Aqua vita alone being warmed and that took off all the spots and blackness'. Unfortunately, a few of the pictures had suffered irreparable damage.[91]

Nys was not, however, content to rest on his laurels. As he wrote to Endymion, 'as companions it will be necessary to have the Marbles of the Duke of Mantua, the list of which you have, with certain pictures comprised therein'. Apart from his sculptures and these pictures, the Duke had also retained Mantegna's nine large canvases of the Triumph of Julius Cæsar. These Nys determined to acquire, since, in his own words 'not having the Triumph of Julius Cæsar, I had nothing at all'.[92]

Both Nys and Lanier thought that the Duke was asking too much for the sculptures and other pictures, but Nys said nothing to Lanier about the Mantegnas. After much haggling, aided by Duke Vincenzo's death and the even greater impoverishment of his successor, Nys acquired the whole lot, including the Mantegnas, for £10,500.[93] So eager was he, that he made the bargain without asking for authority from England, and when he drew on Burlamachi for the money, the London financier refused to honour his drafts. Nys's purchases could not, indeed, have been made at a worse moment so far as payment was concerned. As we have seen, Charles was in desperate straits for money and the Isle of Rhé expedition had exhausted every financial resource. In October 1627 Burlamachi had written to Endymion, 'I pray let me know his Majesty's pleasure, but above all where money shall be found to pay this great sum. If it were 2 or 3000 £ it could be borne, but for 15,000 £ besides the other engagements for his Majesty's service, it will utterly put me out of any possibility to do anything in those provisions which are so necessary for my Lord Duke's relief.'[94]

In the long and tangled story of poor Nys's financial troubles that ensued, it is clear that he was not fully trusted either by Burlamachi, by Charles's court, or by Rowlandson who had succeeded Wake in the Venetian Embassy. Their suspicions seem to have been not altogether unjustified. To start with, Nys only sent to England what he later admitted was 'the refuse of the collection'. And when, eventually, Nys's creditors broke into his house, he was, so he wrote, 'greatly astonished and also rejoiced' to come across, 'in a back place', a number of pictures and sculptures belonging to the King. These hidden treasures included a Raphael, three Titians and three sculptures of children by Michelangelo, Sansovino and Praxiteles 'above price'![95]

Charles was determined to obtain the whole collection, but his advisers were not prepared to recommend payment until all the pictures and sculptures had arrived in England and had been approved; and the Lord Treasurer, Weston, had genuine difficulty in finding money to meet bills which Nys drew on Burlamachi. Nys wrote despairing letters to Dorchester and even to Charles pleading his imminent financial ruin. He sent drawings of the sculptures and paintings to London; he even sent his servant over, but he still delayed shipping the bulk of the purchases, and he and Burlamachi were involved in such a wrangle over bills that litigation was threatened. Four years, in fact, elapsed before, in July 1632, the *Assurance* sailed from Venice, carrying to England the last batch of pictures and statues. A month later, Charles signed the warrant for the final instalment of the total of £18,000 12s. 8d. that was paid to Nys for the Mantua collection.[96]

The transport of large pictures back to England involved, of course, considerable hazards. Mostly, they were sent by sea, in cases covered with waxed waterproof cloth. When overland transport was used, as with the three Mantuan pictures brought home by Lanier, or with the ten pictures that Gerbier brought from Italy for Buckingham in 1621, the frames were sent by sea and the canvases rolled up in cases. From Turin, their passage over the Alps was accomplished on mule back, assisted by man-handling over the steeper stretches of the rough track. At Lyons, the pictures had to be unpacked and repacked for the Customs. From Lyons, the route was by Paris to Boulogne and thence to Dover and London. In the case of Gerbier's ten pictures, the cost of frame-making and packing was £37, while the transport cost £40, including customs.[97]

Poor Nys eventually settled in England. In 1635, in a petition to Charles, he drew a woeful, if no doubt exaggerated, picture of his fortunes. He related how he had served Ambassadors Wotton, Carleton, Wake and Carlisle in Venice; how he had bought the Mantua pictures and statues, keeping Lanier in his house free-of-charge; how he could have re-sold the Mantua collection to Richelieu at a large profit; and how, his bills not being met, he had had to abandon his business and, on the verge of complete ruin, to settle in England. He now put forward various ways of getting money, amongst others by improving the streets and health of London. He also offered to show the King how to prevent frauds in the Customs, on condition that he was granted a fifth of the increase in the Customs' yield.[98]

(vii)

In spite of the Isle of Rhé disaster, Charles and Buckingham were determined to continue the war and relieve Rochelle, now completely blockaded. But there was no money left even to repair the leaky ships and pay the soldiers and sailors and the unfortunate countrymen on whom the starving troops were billeted. Charles had finally to agree with Buckingham that Parliament must be summoned to vote supplies.

In February, Endymion accompanied Charles to Theobalds and Newmarket, leaving Olive ill in London. 'Unless I be assured that you are very well, I must be ill,' he wrote to her from Theobalds, 'for I protest to God nothing can please me but what hath a relation to your content. . . . Let me, so soon as you can, know how you do, but trouble not yourself to write, for I know the hanging down of your head will hurt you.'[99]

Not having heard from Olive, Endymion wrote to her from Newmarket a few days later, 'Send me word, I beseech you, sweetheart, whether your face mend or no, that I may the better endure this affliction of absence from you, which, if you be well, I purpose to suffer till the King return, but otherwise I will endure it no longer, but speedily remedy my own torment by coming to you.' 'Send me also word,' he ended the letter, 'how my little partridges do . . . kiss all my little boys for me and ask Mun* half a dozen to send me as a token.'[100]

The new Parliament met on March 17th. Charles in his opening speech merely requested subsidies for continuing the war, but the Commons turned at once to past misgovernment, and, once again, showed their determination that redress of grievances must precede the granting of supplies. Under Wentworth's practical and conciliatory leadership, supplies were to be voted, but to be accompanied by a bill in which, without reciting past grievances

* "Mun" was their year-old baby, Mountjoy.

3   Endymion's home, Aston-sub-Edge, Gloucestershire

or entering into constitutional theories, Charles was to undertake in specific terms to observe past statutes for the protection of the liberties of his subjects. But Charles would not agree to any bill. All that he would offer was his general promise. Wentworth's attempts at reconciliation had failed and the Commons proceeded to draw up a Petition of Right, its substance being their protests over forced loans, arbitrary imprisonment, compulsory billeting and martial law. On May 28th, both Houses passed the Petition.

Only by consenting to the Petition could Charles obtain the promised subsidies, but he first tried to return an evasive answer. Eliot would have none of it. Reminding the Commons of all the disasters into which mismanagement had led the country, he asked that a Remonstrance should be prepared. Even if he did not mention Buckingham's name, all his hearers knew to whom his bitter words referred. Charles replied with a sharp message demanding the passing of the subsidies bill. Only when the Lords also demanded a clear answer to the Petition, did Charles give way. On June 7th, he gave his formal assent to the Petition of Right. As soon as the news spread, 'the bells began to ring, bonfires were kindled, the number whereof at length equalled those at His Majesty's coming out of Spain.'[101]

Charles had got his subsidies, but the Commons would not drop their Remonstrance. In it they stated that the cause of all the evils was 'the excessive power and greatness of the Duke of Buckingham and the abuse of his greatness'.[102] They then went on to break new ground by discussing Charles's right to tonnage and poundage, on which nearly half of his normal revenue depended. Charles's answer was to prorogue Parliament. His confidence in Buckingham remained unshaken either by Parliament or by popular hatred of the favourite, and now that the subsidies had been voted, the war could be pursued, La Rochelle relieved and assistance given to the Protestants in North Germany. But Buckingham's plans also included the opening of peace negotiations with Spain in the belief that Spanish jealousy of France might be used to bring about the restitution of the Palatinate and the acknowledge-ment of the independence of the Dutch republic. Once again, the man chosen to prepare the ground with Olivares was Endymion, whose Spanish affiliations and sympathies made him, as the Venetian ambassador reported, 'the very man for such an important negotiation.'[103]

Endymion's own fortunes had continued to prosper during the summer of 1628. The more Buckingham was attacked, the more Charles showed his personal favour to those, like Endymion, who were loyal to the Duke. This summer, Endymion's pension of £500 a year was converted into an annuity of a similar amount for his and Olive's lives.[104] He also received an important new source of in-come in Charles's grant to him, for his life, of the office of Receiver of the Fines in the Star Chamber. This allowed Endymion to keep for himself half of the fines collected over £743 5s. 0d. a year. Since, three years later, an account for two and three-quarter years showed that Endymion's half share amounted to just over £2,000, the office was worth £750 a year.[105] In addition, the King assigned him the manor of Alfarthing, near Wandsworth Common in Surrey, with the reversion to brother Tom for a payment of £300 down and a rent to the King of £40 a year, which was later reduced to £26 13s. 4d. Endymion and Olive never seem to have lived there, but the rentals Endymion received came to over £300 a year, apart from sales of timber of nearly £20 a year.[106]

Endymion had also begun to enjoy a share of spoils from Ireland. In 1621, he had acquired through Buckingham a grant of 1½ tenths of the profits of the Irish Customs after the Duke, as lessee, had paid the King £6,000 a year. The amount due to Endymion for the half year ending Easter 1625 had been £180 2s. 10d., so this grant was worth fully £350 a year, but, as in the case of so many of the grants, payments were always in arrears. Through 1628, Charles was writing to Falkland, the Lord Deputy of Ireland, instructing him to order the farmers of the Customs to cease obstructing payments to Endymion. The King finally ordered that the Customs' officers and farmers were to be allowed no entertainment until they had met the arrears.[107]

About this time, Endymion was also granted mining rights in gold, silver, copper and lead over all Ireland except Munster, for a royalty of 1 tenth to the King.[108] Other Irish grants that he had lately acquired were of lands belonging to the dissolved Franciscan Abbey in Dundalk and of fishing rights in Lismore.[109] Apart from such sources of income, there were occasional special payments such as the £500 at the end of 1626 in respect of Endymion's visit to The Hague,[110] and a grant in the summer of 1628, which he shared with two other officers of the Court, of a part of the proceeds of certain Irish accounts due to the King.[111]

There were also, no doubt, 'presents' to Endymion for favours that one so near to the King and Buckingham could perform. A hint of what these could mean is given in a jocular private letter to Endymion from Ireland at the end of 1627. In it, Sir William St. Leger, the President of Munster, a personal friend, wrote that he had told the Earl of Cork that he would not be excused coming to England to defend a suit over land unless he gave Endymion £1,000 in addition to a present of £3,000-£4,000 to Buckingham![112]

Altogether, Endymion's gross income must already have grown to nearly £3,000 a year—a quite exceptional amount for a commoner apart from the very wealthy city merchants, and a remarkable one for a man who had started his career only ten years earlier without any landed or other resources.

The summer of 1628 also brought domestic happiness to Olive and Endymion in the birth of another child—once again a boy, born in London in July and christened Philip.

All through July, rumours had been circulating about Endymion's mission to Spain. Its object—to start peace negotiations—was correctly surmised, but it was reported first that he was going to Italy to buy pictures for the King and then that he had actually left for Genoa in the company of a Jesuit priest![113]

Endymion, in fact, left London early in August. With him went Gerbier and the Abbé Scaglia, the Savoyard ambassador in London. The party sailed to The Hague in Endymion's brother Tom's ship *Warspite*, to command of which he had been promoted from command of *Convertive* in 1627.[114] At The Hague, Endymion paid his respects to the Elector and Electress Palatine but without discussing his mission. He and Tom then hurried on to Brussels where he met the Spanish Regent, the Infanta Isabella.[115]

From Brussels the brothers paid a visit to Van Dyck's studio in Antwerp. Endymion had last seen the painter in London at the beginning of 1620. In the interval, Van Dyck had spent nearly seven years travelling in Italy, studying the works of the great Italian masters and, in Genoa, painting the portraits that had so enhanced his reputation that, on his return to Antwerp in 1627, the Archduchess Isabella had made him her Court painter. From Van Dyck, Endymion commissioned the first of the artist's pictures that Charles was to acquire. It was the story of Rinaldo and Armida.* A year later Van Dyck wrote Endymion an affectionate letter to say that the picture was finished and had been delivered to Mr. Perry, Endymion's Antwerp agent, who had paid the artist's fee of £72. Endymion was recouped by a payment from Charles of £78 which covered the packing and transport. From a letter to Captain Tom Porter from Perry, it would also seem that both Endymion and Tom had bought pictures from Van Dyck for themselves.[116]

At the beginning of September, Tom went home from Brussels and Endymion started for Madrid, accompanied by one of the Infanta's gentlemen, and travelling post so as to avoid recognition. According to one report he also shaved off his beard for greater secrecy. At Basle, Endymion met

* Now in Baltimore.

158

Scaglia and Rubens. There, a courier from England brought them the shocking news of Buckingham's murder. They heard the story 'with exclamations and tears'.[117] To Endymion, the sudden and tragic death, in the prime of life, of the man to whom he owed so much of his fortunes, was a shattering blow.

Charles had gone down to Portsmouth about the time of Endymion's departure from England and stayed at Sir Daniel Norton's house at Southwick, while he tried to speed up the preparations for the sailing of the great new fleet which Buckingham was to command for the relief of starving La Rochelle. On August 17th, Buckingham followed him down to Portsmouth. At the end of July, Olive had written to her uncle wishing him good fortune with the new expedition. 'Your noble imagination give you to understand,' her letter had ended, 'that the rest can be nothing but prayers and good wishes for your happiness and safe return, a sacrifice of a grateful heart which owes your goodness all that I and mine have and shall be daily offered by your servant—Olive Porter.'[118]

Buckingham was lodging at a house in Portsmouth High Street. On the morning of August 23rd, he was about to start for Southwick to meet Charles and had come down into the crowded hall of his house, when a man stopped him and stabbed him in the left breast. Buckingham had only strength to pull the knife out, crying 'Zounds villain', before he fainted. A friend lifted him up and leant him against the hall table, over which his blood spurted from his mouth. In a few minutes, he was dead. His wife, distraught with grief and shock, tried to throw herself over the gallery into the hall.

The assassin at once gave himself up. He was Felton, a lieutenant who had served with Buckingham in the Isle of Rhé, and had a grievance over his failure to gain promotion. Arrears of pay had brought him deep into debt and his private bitterness had been inflamed by Parliament's Remonstrance naming the Duke as the public enemy responsible for all grievances. It was in the spirit of an executioner that he had murdered Buckingham.

Charles was at prayers at Southwick when the terrible news was brought to him. Saying nothing, he went on with his prayers and then retired to his chamber 'and came not out in two days'.[119]

In spite of the news of Buckingham's death, Endymion continued his journey to Spain, probably in the company of Rubens who arrived in Madrid at about the same time as Endymion in the last week of September. Rubens's mission was also a pacific one—to explore the ground for a truce with Holland. Although news of the capture of the Spanish treasure fleet in the West Indies by the Dutch had not yet reached Spain, Olivares was very conscious of Spain's weakness and was anxious to secure England's neutrality, if not her alliance, against France. Endymion was therefore well received and Olivares held out rosy prospects of the result of a Spanish alliance. Endymion's letters home told of his good reception. He was well, he wrote to Olive, asking her to intercede with the King for his speedy return. Charles at once ordered Captain Tom to fetch his brother from Santander, but contrary gales kept him from sailing.[120]

On December 1st, Endymion wrote to Olive from Madrid, 'Now, my dear soul, I could wish myself wings to fly unto thee, for this day I set forward towards the sea side to seek a ship to carry me to England and if I find one ready I shall quickly be there, but if in the port I go to there be none, you must not expect me so soon. Therefore if this letter come to you before you see me, be not affrighted with anything, for by the Grace of God I shall come safe unto you. You cannot believe of what comfort your letter was to me, for till I saw it, I had none since the ill news of the loss of my Lord Duke, nothing no man can suffer so much as I and my very soul has been sensible of it. Good, sweet Olive, make much of yourself that by seeing of you I may receive a remedy for the hurt that grief has caused in me. And my

Lord . . . sends me word of Mun's being ill, which hath not a little troubled me, for you know how dearly I love him. I wonder you would not let me know of his sickness. God of his great mercy and goodness bless him and keep him with the rest, for none I shall never joy in anything but you and them. My cousin Butler* takes unkindly that you forgot him in your letter but it seems you were in haste and so am I to come to you and I therefore with a thousand kisses rest

Your true friend and loving husband.'[121]

Reaching Santander, Endymion found a Biscayan ship about to sail and took passage on her. It was an unfortunate choice. Coming up Channel at the end of December, the ship went ashore below Burton Cliffs on the Dorset coast and broke up.

Endymion and the crew and passengers, one hundred and thirty people in all, managed to struggle safely to land. But they were at once set upon by the inhabitants of Burton Bradstock, who had run down to the shore in the hope of plunder. Finding the wreck to be Spanish, they not only robbed the castaways of all their possessions, but even stripped them of their clothes, leaving them shivering in the cold. Endymion's loud protests that he was no Spaniard, but an Englishman on the King's service were disregarded, and it was some hours before a Catholic gentleman from the nearby village of Puncknowle came to his rescue, giving him and his companions shelter and arranging for a messenger to be sent in haste to London.

Charles was much annoyed when the news reached him. He at once issued a warrant for the punishment of the offenders and the Council ordered Sir Thomas Freke, the Member of Parliament for Dorset who lived near Blandford and who owned property at Burton Bradstock, to go to the spot and render assistance to Endymion and his companions. Freke reported to the Council on January 3rd that

* George Butler, a poor cousin of Olive's, employed in the English embassy in Madrid.

he had attended on Endymion and the shipwrecked Spaniards and had done all he could to recover what they had
lost, but had only been able to get back fifty damaged
muskets, nine cannon, two sails and an anchor.

Endymion arrived in London on January 5th, bringing
the ship's captain with him, while Freke distributed clothes
to the ship's company and arranged for their food and
lodging for two months. In the end, Freke paid out £626,
of which the Exchequer provided £600. Charles gave the
Spanish captain a new ship and Freke and Endymion were
granted leave to sell any rescued cannon, rope and sails to
defray their own expenses. On Freke's suggestion, three or
four of the cannon were mounted to guard the Dorset
coast.[122]

During Endymion's absence abroad, La Rochelle had at
last fallen to the French royal forces. The English fleet
under the Earl of Lindsey had reached La Rochelle in
September but found that the approaches to the blockaded
city had been made virtually impassable. Two ineffective
attacks were attempted before Rochelle surrendered on
October 18th. Sixteen thousand of its twenty-two thousand
inhabitants had died of starvation.[123]

No one ever took Buckingham's place in Charles's confidence. After Buckingham's death the influence of the
Lord Treasurer, Weston, increased and, through him,
Arundel and Endymion's old companion Cottington joined
the Council. The King, too, obtained an adherent from the
ranks of the opposition leaders. Shortly after the end of the
last session of Parliament, Wentworth had been raised to
the peerage, and, at the end of December, he went to York
as President of the North.

On January 20th, 1629, Parliament opened its new
session. Charles was anxious to avoid further quarrels and
tried to conciliate Parliament by renouncing his claim to
tonnage and poundage as his hereditary right, but the
Commons postponed the bill for passing the grant and
turned to matters of religion. Eliot's speeches made it clear

that he intended the Commons and not Charles and his Bishops to be the arbiters of doctrine. After an unseemly struggle over the question of whether the King had the right to order the Commons' adjournment, and after Eliot had proposed Weston's impeachment, the Commons on March 2nd defiantly voted their own adjournment. Two days later the King issued a proclamation for Parliament's dissolution and committed nine members, including Eliot, to prison. It was to be eleven years before a Parliament re-assembled.

In foreign affairs, Charles's one object was now to try to obtain the restitution of the Palatinate for his sister and her family, whether with the aid of France, of Spain or of Sweden and Denmark. In April peace was signed with France. In May, Rubens arrived in London to discuss peace with Spain and, in the autumn, Cottington was sent to Madrid to try, as the price of peace, to obtain Olivares' engagement to help restore the Palatinate. Endymion, after his return from Madrid, had written frequently to Olivares but without receiving any reply. Now he wrote again, commending Cottington and the good and reasonable intentions of his mission.[124] Although Olivares would not commit himself over the Palatinate, peace with Spain was finally signed at the end of 1630. In fact, none of the warring powers on the Continent were under the illusion that they had much either to fear or to hope from the impoverished King of England's vacillating policies.

But, while the horrors of one of the cruellest wars in history were still ravaging large parts of the Continent, the next decade was one of peace and prosperity for the great majority of the subjects whom Charles ruled under his personal authority, without the aid of Parliament. If Charles's problems were only shelved, and if the opposition to his ideas of his prerogative had only been temporarily driven underground, the surface was one of contentment and security. These were the years in which, as Hollar, the drawing master to the royal children, once said to Aubrey, 'the people both poor and rich did look cheerfully';[125] the years of Marvell's 'dear and happy isle, the garden of the world erewhile'. They were certainly years of good fortune and happiness for Endymion.

CHAPTER VI

(i)

IN the summer of 1632, the artists Stalbempt and Bel-camp painted a conversation piece showing Charles and his court in the park of his palace of Greenwich. The small and elegant King and his little Queen have just ascended a rise; two-year-old Prince Charles holds his mother's hand, while the chattering ladies-in-waiting climb the slope behind her, and the Marquis of Hamilton is coming up to join the King. On top of the rise, on the right, stands Lord Treasurer Weston, gravely attired in black, talking to a courtier; and on the left, Arundel converses with the smiling Endymion, hand on hip and resplendent in white satin.

The Court, where Endymion had now become the closest and most trusted of Charles's personal attendants, mirrored the King's own character in its dignity, its strict formality and its elegance. Articles drawn up by the King 'to establish order and government in the Court' forbade 'tippling houses or selling or taking tobacco' in the vicinity of the palaces. Only 'sober people of honest birth' were to be employed, and the profane, drunkards or quarrellers were to be banished from the Court. No play at chess, cards or other games was to be allowed within the Privy Chamber. The duties of the various officers were carefully prescribed. Precise regulations were even made for seating in the chapel, with its daily morning and evening services with 'solemn music'.[1]

Charles's unhappy relations with Henrietta Maria had vanished on Buckingham's death, when the King, in his grief, had turned to his wife and had begun to centre on her all the single-minded devotion which he had felt for Buckingham. Warmed by her husband's love, the neglected and forlorn girl, who was only eighteen when Buckingham died, had blossomed afresh, and her wit and gaiety and love of plays and masques, dancing and music brightened the ceremonious Court. A miscarriage in 1629 had endangered her life, but in May 1630 she had given birth to an heir to the throne. In 1631, Princess Mary had been born and, in spite of delicate health, the Queen was to bear Charles four more children. An ivory complexion and large dark eyes were her only claim to beauty, but Charles had no thoughts for any other woman, and in her quick if superficial mind he found the foil for his own slow and hesitating thinking, so that he came more and more to rely on her advice. His love was fully returned and even when he caught smallpox she refused to leave him by day or night.[2] Deep as was the bond between them in all else, in religion they went their own ways. Charles's devotion to the Church of England was no more to be shaken than was that of the Queen to Rome.

The King's reticent character, coupled with the slight impediment in his speech, never allowed him to assume the easy, genial manners that would have made for general popularity in the Court circle or outside. In Charles, however, Endymion found a just, if reserved and strict master, with whom increasing familiarity of personal attendance only bred increasing respect and affection, while, in Endymion, Charles found a completely loyal servant whose manners, early trained in Spanish etiquette, conformed to his own ideas of courtly elegance, and whose intellectual and artistic interests were well suited to support his own tastes. No doubt, too, the King and Queen viewed with approval Endymion's devotion to Olive and the good example set by a love match whose bonds had not been weakened by time.

In his lodgings in Whitehall, Endymion must have followed the pattern of decorum that Charles set and demanded in his personal company. But another and more human Endymion showed himself in his and Olive's

4   Charles I with the Queen and Court at Greenwich
by Stalbempt and Belcamp

hospitable house in the Strand, in the taverns frequented by the wits and poets, and in the gay, extravagant life of the courtiers when away from the restraint of the royal presence. There, Endymion was the jovial man of the world of the double portrait with Van Dyck; the man of 'sweet temper', whose charm and good fellowship made a host of friends of all sorts and conditions, and whose many correspondents wrote to him in terms which, allowing for all the hyperbole of contemporary methods of address, show a warmth of affection that make it clear that they did not value him only because he was a useful person to know; the man who shared the tastes and pleasures of the poets and painters of whom he was the patron and companion and who was credited by gossip with enjoying the favours of Van Dyck's mistress, Margaret Lemon;[3] the friend to whom Sir William St. Leger wrote from Ireland, 'Noble Don, I hope you are in as good a fooling vein as when you wrote your last to me. My wife sends her love to you and swears that, however much I ask her, she will never give you such a kiss as she did when you were drunk with backrag* at the Augustine Friars.'[4]

Although Endymion was so close to the King, he wielded little political influence. Only once again, indeed, was he employed on a diplomatic mission overseas. It was in the talented intellectual and artistic life that so distinguished the English Court that he played his main role. Of this life, Charles himself was the active and discerning inspiration.

Even as a young man, Charles had been 'very interested in inventions', and like so many of his contemporaries had eagerly studied mathematics.[5] While physicians such as Harvey and Mayerne enjoyed the royal patronage, mathematics was the science in which the King took the most interest. Amongst his mathematicians was Richard Delamain, whom Endymion assisted in 1630 by writing to Secretary Dorchester to procure for him the sole right of making an instrument which he had invented and given

* A German wine.

167

the King, and of printing a book about it. The instrument was a ring which, through the movement of concentric circles, solved 'mathematical questions only by the eye with such facility and expedition as that the like had never theretofore been produced'. Charles so valued it that one of the personal relics which, on the morning of his execution, he entrusted to the weeping Herbert for presentation to his children was Delamain's ring, to be given to the Duke of York.[6]

Among the arts, music, in which the King was 'not unskilful',[7] enjoyed a prominent place at the Court. Employed in the royal household under Nicholas Lanier, the Master of the Music, were nineteen wind instrumentalists, thirteen violinists, twenty-three performers for lutes, viols and voices, a harpist, a virginals player and a musical instrument maker, as well as twenty trumpeters and nine men for the drums and fifes under a Drum Major.[8]

The drama was encouraged both by Charles and by the Queen. They themselves took part in a number of masques, and plays were performed before them at Court on royal birthdays and on other occasions in the little royal theatre in Whitehall called the Cockpit (not to be confused with the Cockpit playhouse in Drury Lane) or in other of the palaces. The Queen was even known to attend the public performance of plays at Blackfriars,[9] and it was her influence that caused the introduction from France of a new fashion for the portrayal of love in masques and plays. Howell described it in a letter to a correspondent in Paris. 'The Court,' he wrote, 'affords little news at present but that there is a Love called Platonic love, which much sways there of late. It is a love abstracted from all corporeal gross impressions and sensual appetite, but consists in contemplation and ideas of the mind, not in any carnal fruition. This love sets the wits of the Town on work and they say there will be a masque shortly of it whereof her Majesty and her maids of honour will be part.'[10]

Henry and William Lawes furnished the music for

masques and wrote settings to poems, while Lanier excelled musically both as composer and performer. Lanier held Endymion in high regard, addressing him as 'still the same best friend, to be by me for ever religiously beloved and honoured above all others'.[11]

Poets and dramatists, too, found in Endymion their most loyal and generous patron and friend at the Court. In 1631, Thomas May dedicated his 'Antigone' to Endymion in the following words, 'To speak of you as you deserve, I dare not, since your known modesty would check my pen; but this I dare say, there are no wits or any other true abilities that ever had the honour to know you but will spread your worth and think you most worthy to stand as you do in the presence of a King, wishing you long blest in his Majesty's favour and the King blest with more such servants as you are.'[12]

Endymion's reputation as a lover and patron of literature was well established. In 1637, Sir John Suckling wrote his 'Session of the Poets', in which he commemorated the chief literary figures among his contemporaries. In the poem, the wits of the town met at a tavern to contest for Apollo's laurel crown. Ben Jonson, 'good old Ben', was there, and D'avenant, Falkland and Carew. Endymion was named as one of this distinguished company.[13]

His most outstanding literary association had begun some years earlier. William D'avenant, Shakespeare's godson, had left home in 1622 on the death of his father, the Oxford vintner and Mayor of the city, in whose house in the Cornmarket Shakespeare used to stay every year on his way from London to Stratford. Young D'avenant was aged sixteen and was fired with literary ambition. In later life he liked to hint to his cronies that it was, in fact, through the closest of blood ties that he had inherited the spirit of Shakespeare.[14] Coming to London, D'avenant had entered the service of the aged Elizabethan courtier, soldier and poet, Fulke Greville, Lord Brooke, the friend of Philip Sidney. As well as taking part in the wars—probably in the Isle of Rhé expedition—D'avenant had written some poems and two flamboyant and blood-filled tragedies, the second of which had been licensed and performed. The murder of Lord Brooke by his valet in 1628 left D'avenant without a patron. The Greville family were, however, old friends and neighbours of the Porters in Gloucestershire and Fulke had been godfather to one of Nicholas Porter's children. No doubt Endymion had met D'avenant while he was in Brooke's service, and it was to Endymion that D'avenant now transferred his allegiance.

In his poems and in dedications, D'avenant never tired of acknowledging the great debt he owed to Endymion, whom he called 'Lord of my muse and heart'.[15] Attaching himself to the Porter household in the Strand, he became the Porters' 'poet in ordinary', and no less than thirteen poems addressed to Endymion and his family are to be found in D'avenant's works. In one poem, he declares that Endymion's inspiration 'didst give to my weak members strength and joy to live';[16] in another he bequeaths Endymion as a legacy to other English poets.

> 'And they received thee not from bounteous chance
> Or me, but as their own inheritance';[17]

another poem celebrates Endymion's recovery from a long sickness.[18] In 'A journey into Worcestershire',[19] D'avenant describes an expedition with Endymion and two other companions. Endymion would have been on his way to his home at Aston, but the journey may have also had the object of attending Dover's Whitsun Cotswold Olympic Games, since the 'Captain' in the poem may well have referred to Robert Dover himself, and the inn at 'Wickham' where the convivial party made merry may have been at Winchcombe, where Dover had a house. No sooner had the party left London than the English weather overtook them—

'But from the South arose a busier wind
Which sent us so much rain, each man did wish
His hands and legs were fins, his horse a fish.'

When the tired horses stopped, the cheerful Endymion

'Cries away! What make we here,
To draw a map or gather juniper?'

Arrived at Wickham,

'He that tonight ruled each delighted breast,
Gave to the palate of each ear a feast,
With joy of pledges made our sour wine sweet
And nimble as the leaping juice of Crete
Was brave Endymion——'

Two of D'avenant's Porter poems stand out above the rest.
One is a duet between Olive and Endymion.[20]

Olivia
'Before we shall again behold
In his diurnal race the world's great eye,
We may as silent lie and cold,
As are the shades where buried lovers lie.'

Endymion
'Olivia, 'tis no fault of love
To lose ourselves in death, but, O, I fear
When life and knowledge is above
Restored to us, I shall not know thee there.'

Olivia
'Call it not heaven (my love) where we
Ourselves shall see, and yet each other miss,
So much of heaven I find in thee
As thou unknown, all else privation is.'

Endymion
   'Why should we doubt before we go
   To find the knowledge which shall ever last
   That we may there each other know?
   Can future knowledge quite destroy the past?'

Olivia
   'When at the bowers in the Elysian shade
   I first arrive, I shall examine where
   They dwell who love the highest virtue made,
   For I am sure to find Endymion there.'

Endymion
   'From this vext world when we shall both retire
   Where all are lovers and where all rejoice,
   I need not seek thee in the heavenly choir
   For I shall know Olivia by her voice.'

The other—addressed 'To the Lady Olivia Porter, a present upon a New Year's Day'—is as charming a set of verses as the age produced.[21]

   'Go! Hunt the whiter Ermine and present
   His wealthy skin as this day's tribute sent
   To my Endymion's love, though she be fair,
   More gently smooth, more soft, than Ermines are.
   Go! Climb that rock and when thou there hast found
   A star contracted in a diamond,
   Give it Endymion's love, whose glorious eyes
   Darken the starry jewels of the skies.
   Go! Dive into the Southern sea, and when
   Thou'st found (to trouble the nice sight of men)
   A swelling pearl, and such whose single worth
   Boast all the wonders which the seas bring forth,
   Give it Endymion's love, whose every tear
   Would more enrich the skilful jeweller.
   How I command! How slowly they obey!

The churlish Tartar will not hunt today!
Nor will that lazy sallow Indian strive
To climb that rock, nor that dull Negro dive.
Thus poets, like to Kings, (by trust deceived),
Give oftener what is heard of, than received.'

D'avenant had, indeed, good cause for his gratitude to
Endymion for his steadfast friendship and support. About
1630, the wild young man had the misfortune to contract
syphilis. According to Aubrey, it was from 'a black handsome wench that lay in Axe Yard, Westminster'.[22] The in-
fection was a bad one and the treatment, with mercury,
was almost as grave a menace to his health as the disease.
In the end, he escaped with the loss of his nose. Endymion
showed him kindness and care in his illness and perhaps
gave him lodging, which D'avenant gratefully acknowledged in the poem he wrote to his doctor, Cademan, the
Queen's physician.[23]

Having helped to save D'avenant's life, Endymion was
now to be largely instrumental in making his reputation as
a playwright. In December 1633, D'avenant finished his
new play. It was called *The Wits*, and was his first straight
comedy—bold, lively, without morals and full of ingenious
farcical situations. He sent it for licensing to Sir Henry
Herbert, the Master of the Revels, and as such, dictator of
the dramatic world. Herbert took offence at some of the
language used and refused a licence for the play's performance. D'avenant at once went to Endymion, who recognized
the play's merits and took the matter over Herbert's head
to the King. Charles consented to read the play himself.
On January 9th, he sent for Herbert and went over all
Herbert's excisions. Some he approved, but he refused to
agree that words such as 'faith', 'death' and 'slight' were
oaths and as such to be prohibited. Instead, the King
insisted that they were merely 'asseverations' and must be
allowed to stand. Herbert had to submit to his Master's
judgement, but, as he recorded in his office book, he stuck

to his view that the offending words were oaths. In order to assuage Herbert's ruffled feelings, Charles ordered Endymion to take the manuscript back to Herbert and commanded D'avenant to re-apply for his licence with proper civility. On January 19th, *The Wits* was duly licensed for performance and on January 28th it was acted at Court before the King and Queen. Herbert's grudging comment was that it was 'well-liked', adding that the King commended the language, but disliked the plot and characters.[24]

D'avenant awaited the play's first public performance at Blackfriars with some trepidation. Rumours of the controversy with Herbert had got around and D'avenant's wild conduct had made him enemies. In a poem to Endymion[25] he told how conspiracies had been laid

'To have my muse, her arts and life betrayed.'

but how Endymion had been there to 'appease and make their judgements less severe'. In his subsequent dedication of the play to Endymion, he addressed him as 'the chiefly beloved of all that are ingenious and noble', and went on to declare that 'his goodness hath preserved life in the author' and that his patron had 'rescued his work from a cruel faction; which nothing but the forces of your reason and your reputation could subdue'.[26]

The Wits, which owed so much to Endymion's support, marked the turning point in D'avenant's career. It was printed two years later and was frequently played. Seeing it for the first time in 1661, Pepys was 'most highly pleased' with it, calling it 'a most excellent play'. He was so taken with it that he saw it again the next day, and a week later took Mrs. Pepys to see it.[27]

It was not, however, to bawdy comedy, but to masques and plays illustrating the Queen's favourite subject of platonic love that D'avenant now devoted his talents. Ben Jonson, the poet laureate and doyen of masque librettists,

was old and had quarrelled with Inigo Jones, whose outstanding stage designs and costumes were still such an important element in the popularity of masques. On Shrove
Tuesday, 1634, the King presented a masque *Coelum Britannicum*, written by Thomas Carew with Inigo Jones's
scenery. Charles himself took part, accompanied by eleven
lords and ten pages. 'It was the noblest masque of my time
to this day, the best poetry, best scenes and the best
habits,' wrote Herbert.[28] It is possible that D'avenant may
have had a hand in the *Coelum Britannicum* libretto. At
any rate, when the Queen determined to present a masque
in which she and her ladies should themselves appear, it was
D'avenant she chose as the librettist, no doubt on Endymion's recommendation, and the subject was to be the
triumph of chaste love. D'avenant's *The Temple of Love*,
with Henrietta Maria as 'Indamora, Queen of Narsinga',
was presented in the Banqueting House early in 1635 with
great success. Meantime D'avenant had written a new play
Love and Honour, whose elevated story of male chivalry
and female virtue was entirely to the Queen's taste and
set a pattern for romantic drama for many years to
come.

Other plays from D'avenant's pen followed in quick
succession, and, in February 1636, his new masque—*The
Triumphs of the Prince d'Amour*, with music by Henry and
William Lawes, was given in the Middle Temple, the Queen
and her ladies attending the performance disguised as
citizens' wives.[29] The masque was in honour of the Elector
Palatine and his young brother Rupert who had recently
come to England.

Frederick, the exiled Elector Palatine and King of
Bohemia, had died in 1632 in his thirty-sixth year, dis-
appointed, poverty-stricken and heartbroken at the tragic
death by drowning of his eldest son. Charles Louis, the
next son, assumed the Electoral title when he reached the
age of eighteen in 1635. His Uncle Charles then invited him
to visit England and the serious-minded and somewhat

priggish young man arrived in October. Two months later he was followed to England by his sixteen-year-old brother, Rupert, who had already served with distinction in two campaigns. Writing to Rupert's mother, the Queen of Bohemia, the experienced Sir Thomas Roe who had done good service at the Mogul and Ottoman Courts, described Rupert as 'of a rare condition, full of spirit and action . . . whatsoever he wills, he wills vehemently'.[30]

Rupert's vivacity charmed his uncle and aunt, while the artistic and sensitive youth was captivated by the intellectual life of Charles and his Court. In particular, Rupert was attracted to Endymion, and the young Prince soon became a familiar visitor to the Porter home in the Strand, where he met all the brightest wits of the town. Charles Louis, however, did not approve of his brother's new friends. 'My brother Rupert,' he wrote in June 1637 to his mother in Holland, 'is still in great friendship with Porter.' There was a special reason for Charles Louis's and his mother's anxiety. The arrival in London, in the summer of 1636, of Father George Con, a Scotsman, as the Vatican's agent with Henrietta Maria's Court, had roused the Queen's desire to win over her friends to the Catholic faith. Olive Porter had been one of the first of the new Court converts, and the impressionable Rupert would have been a great prize for the Queen to capture. In his letter to his mother, Charles Louis went on to say that he had warned Rupert not to get involved in religious discussions in the Porter household, 'for fear some priest or other that is too hard for him, may form an ill opinion in him. Besides, Mr. Con doth frequent their house very often, for Mrs. Porter is a professed Roman Catholic.'[31]

Rupert's interest was, however, fully taken up with something very different from religion. In the spring of 1637, Charles and the Court were devoting most of their attention to the astonishing project of sending out a large force, under Rupert's command, to conquer the island of Madagascar.[32] Discovered by the Portuguese in 1500, nothing had come of Portuguese and Dutch ideas of colonising the island, which was still a place of mystery, known to be inhabited by warlike tribes and believed to be rich in gold, precious stones and spices. Rupert was now to become King of Madagascar. Arundel was the chief protagonist of the scheme in the Council and many courtiers saw themselves reaping fat profits from the enterprise.[33]

As soon as the idea was mooted, D'avenant rushed into verse to celebrate the coming conquest. His five hundred-line poem, 'written to Prince Rupert', drew a highly fanciful picture of future events. After the natives have submitted to Rupert without bloodshed, the English invaders have to face a rival body of European adventurers, presumably Spanish. The issue is decided by a combat between two champions from each side. The English champions are Endymion and D'avenant's other patron, Jermyn (in the poem he is called 'Arigo'), who, naturally, prevail and settle down, as Rupert's chief officers, to enjoy the fabulous riches of the land, while D'avenant is rewarded by being made a judge.[34]

More objective observers, however, realized the crazy nature of the project. Writing to the Queen of Bohemia, Roe called it 'absurd', and the Queen replied 'as for Rupert's romance of Madagascar, it sounds like one of Don Quixote's conquests, where he promised his trusty squire to make him King of an island'.[35] The Venetian Ambassador was also convinced of the idea's complete impracticability.[36]

Charles asked the East India Company for their advice and assistance. Their reply was tactfully evasive. Because they were so heavily in debt, they said, they could not take any part in the affair, though they had no intention of opposing it and were inclined to regard it as an honourable enterprise.[37] But a 'blunt merchant called to deliver his opinion', as Roe wrote to the Queen of Bohemia, 'said it was a gallant design, but such as wherein he would be loath to venture his younger son'. Such wiser council, at any rate, prevailed, and early in May Roe was writing to the Queen of Bohemia that the dream of Madagascar had vanished.[38]

Early in 1638, D'avenant published his first volume of poetry, *Madagascar and other poems*. 'If these poems live,' the dedication ran, 'may their memories, by whom they were cherished, End. Porter, H. Jermyn, live with them.'[39] D'avenant's own poems were prefaced by commendatory verses contributed by four of his friends. Endymion's contribution came first,[40] followed by that of Suckling and then by verses from Carew and Habington. Endymion's sixty-two lines of rhymed couplets are mainly devoted to a lively apology for his shortcomings as a poet.

> 'With the whole kennel of the alphabet
> I hunt sometimes an hour, one rhyme to get.
> What I approved of once, I straight deny
> Like an unconstant prince, then give the lie
> To my own invention, which is so poor
> As here I'd kiss your hands and say no more,
> Had I not seen a child with scissors cut
> A folded paper, unto which was put
> More chance than skill; yet when you open it,
> You'd think it had been done by art and wit.
> So I perchance may light upon some strain
> Which may in this, your good opinion gain.'

Endymion's verses show no sign of any poetic gift, but they have a pleasant wit and competence and are certainly no worse than many contemporary efforts. His only other published poem is a dull and stilted epitaph to Dr. Donne, printed in the 1639 edition of Donne's poems.

Ben Jonson's death in 1637 had left the laureateship vacant. Thomas May and D'avenant were the two most fancied successors. Charles chose D'avenant. Thanks in no small measure to Endymion's steadfast support, he had reached the top of the tree at the age of thirty-two. His rival, May, was so incensed that he turned against the Court and his former friends, and joined the opposition.[41]

(ii)

Important as was the place of drama and music in the life of the Court, painting and sculpture were the arts that provided its chief glory and furnished Charles with his greatest interest. The King's splendid patronage of art was not only inspired by a genuine love and enthusiasm for pictures. It was also firmly based on a very considerable knowledge of painting, combined with excellent taste and discernment. Charles 'delighted to talk with all kinds of artists. In painting he had so excellent a fancy that he would supply the defects of art in the workman and suddenly draw those lines, give those airs and lights which experience and practice had not taught the painter'. So wrote the royalist divine, Richard Perrinchief, some forty years later. The King 'had singular skill in limning', recorded the contemporary Lilly.[42]

Round the King was grouped a small band of connoisseurs, collectors and patrons. This intimate circle consisted mainly of great noblemen such as Arundel, the Pembrokes and the Hamiltons, Lennox and Dorset. Associated with them were men of specialist knowledge and experience such as Inigo Jones, Gerbier and Lanier, while, abroad, ambassadors such as Carleton, Wotton and Wyche formed the link with the sources of pictures and sculpture in Italy, the Low Countries and Greece.

It was with the King, at the centre of this court circle, that Endymion had his niche. Though no artist himself, he shared to the full his master's enthusiasm for pictures. He was the friend of artists and though, as a patron, his resources could not match the immense wealth of the great landed noblemen, he was, in a more modest way, a keen and discerning collector. In 1627, for instance, he had taken advantage of Lanier's mission to Italy on Charles's behalf to get his friend to make a little collection for him as well.[43] His knowledge and experience were recognized in the Court circle, as when Carleton in 1631 wrote to the young Duke of Lennox, recommending him to make Endymion his adviser on pictures.[44]

Charles's collection of pictures was one of the greatest in Europe. The Mantua purchase formed its core, but, in 1638, the King also bought a collection of twenty-three Italian pictures from William Frizell, a protegé of Arundel's.[45] The royal galleries were also enriched by exchanges and purchases from the other court collectors. Raphael's 'St. George and the Dragon',* for instance, was acquired by Charles from the Earl of Pembroke, in exchange for a book of Holbein portrait drawings.[46] The Duc de Liancourt, visiting England, gave the King Leonardo's 'St. John the Baptist' and a Titian Holy Family in exchange for Holbein's portrait of Erasmus.†[47]

Endymion took part in these transactions, exchanging a Palma Giovanne of 'a great naked Venus sitting by a table with a looking glass' for one of Charles's Mantua pictures. He also sold the King a number of pictures and *objets d'art* from his collection, including a 'Resurrection of Lazarus' with a landscape by Jan Breughel, and a flower piece by Seghers 'in a black ebony frame', as well as pieces of carved ivory, bronze statuettes, an enamelled box and a silver medal of Pope Urban.[48]

Gifts to Charles formed another considerable source for his collection. It was a sure way to the royal favour, and one that was not neglected by his courtiers and ambassadors. In Charles's collection were pictures presented by Carleton, Hopton, Cottington, Killigrew and others. The Earl of Ancrum brought back from Holland and gave Charles two Rembrandts—a self portrait and a portrait of the artist's mother—which were probably the first two pictures by Rembrandt to reach England.[49] Endymion

* Now in Washington, D.C.
† Now in the Louvre.

gave his master a picture in grisaille of soldiers by Peter Breughel the elder, and a piece by Isaac Oliver 'on a well seasoned board of pear tree' depicting the Burial of Christ. Isaac Oliver had almost finished painting it when he died and it was completed by his son Peter. Vertue described it as 'a piece of the greatest beauty and perfection as I think all Europe and the world can produce'.[50]

Nor was this method of approach to Charles's goodwill neglected by foreign governments. The King of Spain, as we have seen, presented Charles with pictures and statuary on his visit to Madrid. In 1636, the States General of Holland gave the King 'five pictures of rare workmanship, done by great masters', in order to help sweeten their negotiations with him over fisheries.[51] The city of Nüremberg, through Arundel, gave Charles two Dürers.[52] The Pope felt that a present of pictures might help to increase Charles's sympathy towards Catholics, and in January 1636 an important gift of pictures from Rome arrived in London. They were first shown to the Queen and her ladies. Then Charles was told and came hurrying to see them, accompanied by Inigo Jones and Lords Holland and Pembroke. Inigo Jones took his coat off, put on eye glasses and, with the aid of a candle, he and the King closely examined the pictures, both particularly liking those by Leonardo, Andrea del Sarto and Giulio Romano.[53]

The Pope also sought to please Charles when, as an exceptional favour, he arranged for Bernini to model a bust of the King from the painting of Charles's head in three positions which was specially commissioned from Van Dyck and sent to Rome for the purpose. Both Charles and the Queen were delighted with the bust, showing the masterpiece to all who came to the Court.[54]

The main source for old statuary was Constantinople, where the King's ambassadors, first Sir Thomas Roe and then, from 1628, Sir Peter Wyche, were employed in the arduous work of obtaining classical sculptures from all over Greece and Asia Minor for Charles and Buckingham's collections. Arundel's chaplain, William Petty, was also busy in those parts, assembling a rival collection for his master. Petty was an indefatigable collector. Though ship-wrecked on the Asian coast and imprisoned as a spy, he 'encounters all accidents with so unwearied patience; eats with Greeks on their worst days; lies with fishermen on planks, at the best; is all things to all men, that he may obtain his ends', wrote Roe, who suggested that Petty should share his spoils between Buckingham and Arundel since he was dependent on Roe both for getting and taking away his finds.[55]

A few years later, in 1629, Sir Peter Wyche wrote to Endymion to report that he had found two excellent statues, one supposed to be of Diana of Ephesus and the other of a grave matron, both of which Petty coveted and which two other collectors were trying to buy. He had also bought statues at Scio which were being forwarded on the next ship and he asked Endymion to get the King to send him £1,000 on account.

The year after, Wyche wrote again to Endymion to tell him that two statues from Scio had been put in chests on the *Rainbow*, and that nineteen statues, small and great, had been laden at Smyrna. He asked Endymion so to inform the King and to send further instructions.[56]

As well as forming his splendid collection of old masters, Charles made England a centre for contemporary art. In Buckingham's lifetime, Mytens, Gentileschi and Honthorst had been the most important painters attracted to England by Charles. Now, the names of Rubens and Van Dyck were to shed their special lustre on the years of Charles's personal rule. The King welcomed Rubens as the greatest painter of the age when he arrived in London in May 1629 on his diplomatic mission. Pictures as much as peace with Spain were the subject of their discussions. During his nine months stay, Rubens was lodged at Gerbier's house, the King paying Gerbier for his lodging and enter-tainment. Rubens is said to have corrected some of Charles's

own drawings,[57] and the King commissioned him, for a fee
of £3,000, to decorate the ceiling of the new Banqueting
House in Whitehall, which Inigo Jones had now finished
building. The apotheosis of King James was chosen as the
subject, and Rubens may have made some of his pre-
liminary sketches during his visit. Charles knighted Rubens
the day before he left England and gave him 'a sword
enriched with diamonds', as well as a diamond ring and
diamond hatband, which the King bought from Gerbier
for £500.[58]

Endymion saw much of Rubens that summer. On the
eve of Rubens's departure Gage wrote to Endymion, who
had just lost his little son, Mountjoy, 'I have been twice at
your house to wait on you and to tell you that Signor
Rubens parteth very well satisfied of your favour and
affection to him, and is very sorry for the affliction which
God hath sent you; but we both hope that by this time
your comfort is well advanced.'[59]

Rubens finished his magnificent canvases for the ceiling
of the Banqueting House in 1634. They showed symbolically
the glories of James's reign, with peace, plenty, wisdom
and virtue triumphant over rebellion, avarice, envy and
lust. In the centrepiece, James ascended to Heaven,
attended by justice and religion and crowned by victory
and honour. The canvases remained, however, rolled up in
the painter's studio in Antwerp for over a year—possibly
because Charles was short of ready money to pay for them
—and they were not sent to England until the end of 1635,
after Rubens had had to re-touch them. Eventually, the
two cases of pictures were delivered by Rubens to Lionel
Wake, the merchant, who sent them by wagon from Antwerp to Dunkirk, whence they were shipped to London,
Rubens sending an attendant with them 'to sett up the
pictures' on arrival. Nearly two years, however, elapsed
before Rubens began to get his money. In November 1637,
Endymion, on behalf of the King, paid Wake (to whom
Rubens had given his power of attorney) a first instalment

of £800. A month later Endymion produced a further £700.
In May of 1638 he made Wake another payment of £1,170,
and finally, at the end of the month, he wrote from Greenwich Palace to his steward, Richard Harvey, to say that
the money for the final instalment of £330 was now available and was to be handed to Wake, who early in June gave
Endymion his full discharge for the £3,000 owing to Rubens
'for pictures bought of him long since'.[60] Charles's final gift
to Rubens, through Endymion, was a gold chain with a
portrait of Charles on a gold medal, the whole weighing
eighty-two and a half ounces. But it was not until March
1641 that the chain was shipped from London to Dunkirk
on the *Mayflower*. By then, Rubens had been dead for
nine months, so the gift was presumably made to his
widow.[61]

In the spring of 1632, after an interval of twelve years,
Van Dyck returned to England. No doubt Endymion was
one of those who persuaded him to come to the English
Court. Charles welcomed him royally. He was knighted and
given a pension of £200 a year. The King also installed him
in a house in Blackfriars, with summer quarters in the
royal palace of Eltham, and with an allowance for household expenses. Van Dyck also proudly wore Charles's gift
of a gold chain with the King's miniature set in diamonds.

The Court circle took immense pleasure in this accession
to their ranks. So frequently did the royal barge go down
the Thames from Whitehall that a special new stair was
built at Blackfriars for the King and Queen's use. Except
for a year in 1634 and 1635, when he was back in Antwerp,
Van Dyck lived at Blackfriars until 1640. Here he painted
those portraits, almost wholly confined to the Court circle,
which mirrored for posterity the reserved dignity of the
King, the charm of the Queen and the royal children, and
the splendid elegance of the courtiers and their wives in the
happy years before the Civil War. The artist's output was
huge and was only made possible by the employment, as
was customary, of a number of pupils. It is believed that

he painted the King thirty-six times and the Queen twenty-five times.

Money poured into his studio, though like other creditors Van Dyck found that the King and Queen were very dilatory payers. At the end of 1638, for instance, Van Dyck presented an account (in French, in his own handwriting) of money owing for twenty-four pictures, mostly of the King and Queen and their children. Van Dyck's prices ranged from £200 for large portrait groups to £20 for small pictures. The total for the twenty-four came to £1,295. Charles thought the prices excessive. Going through the account, he crossed out Van Dyck's prices in the case of fifteen of the pictures, writing his own valuations in their place. Against the other nine pictures he put a cross. On the King's instructions, Endymion wrote the following note at the foot of the account.

'The total of all such pictures as His Majesty is to pay for in this account rated by the King, and what His Majesty doth allow of amounts unto £528. The other pictures which the King hath marked with a cross before them, the Queen is to pay for them and Her Majesty is to rate them.'

Charles's 'rating' had reduced the price of the fifteen paintings from £915 to £528. The £200 pictures were reduced to £100, the £50 pictures to £40 and the £20 pictures to £15, leaving the Queen to 'rate' the nine pictures she was to pay for. Van Dyck's price for them had been £380. Van Dyck's pension was, however, also sadly in arrears, so Endymion added £1,000 to the £528 the King had agreed to pay, representing 'the arrear of the pension being five years, amounting unto £1,000 at £200 per annum'.[62]

But money was pouring out of Van Dyck's studio as fast as it came in. The artist's international reputation and the favour in which the King held him, as well as his own charm and distinction, gave him a social standing such as no other painter living in England had enjoyed. The Earl of Newcastle, for instance, wrote to him in 1637 of the blessing of his company and the sweetness of his conversation and ended his letter 'passionately your humble servant'.[63] Women also found Van Dyck extremely attractive, and the painter entered fully into the expensive social life of London. He enjoyed extravagant entertaining, even though such a luxurious way of living, coupled with the constant work needed to maintain it, undermined his health.

Margaret Lemon, Van Dyck's mistress, at first presided over the Blackfriars household, but, in 1639, the King arranged for the painter's marriage to Mary Ruthven, a granddaughter of the Earl of Gowrie. Through the alliance, Van Dyck could claim kinship with some of Scotland's noblest families.

Endymion was, of course, brought into close and constant contact with Van Dyck. The friendship between them is attractively shown in the superb oval double portrait*—the only occasion on which Van Dyck chose an Englishman as his fellow sitter—where the artist's own features are contrasted with the robust worldliness of Endymion's expression. Van Dyck also painted, probably in 1633, a big family group of Endymion, Olive and their three elder boys.† There are also other portraits, both of Endymion and of Olive, attributed to Van Dyck or his school.‡

When Rubens died in 1640, Van Dyck became the head of the Flemish school. In September of that year, he left England for Antwerp to claim his position and the commissions which Rubens had left unfinished. Early in 1641

* In the Prado, Madrid.

† In the possession of the author's wife. See Epilogue. A drawing for the head of Endymion with the youngest boy is in the British Museum.

‡ One is the portrait belonging to the Earl of Mexborough and exhibited in the City of York Art Gallery, which is probably the portrait that formerly belonged to the Earls of Hardwicke. Another is a portrait sold at Christie's in July 1950, which came from Mr Alan Fenwick's collection and which was stated to have been bought from Porter descendants in 1844. A portrait, said to be of Olive Porter and from the same source, was also in this sale.

he went to Paris to secure the work of decorating the Louvre, but the commission was given to the native French artist, Poussin. In November 1641 Van Dyck returned to London, his delicate constitution broken with overwork and financial worries. On December 1st his wife gave birth to a daughter in the house at Blackfriars, where, eight days later, he died.

(iii)

Endymion's knowledge of Spain was only to be put to official use on two occasions during these years. The first was his mission to Brussels at the end of 1634.

Charles's foreign policy—although still based on his desire to restore the Palatinate to his sister and her son—continued to shift with every wind, and his efforts to balance one side against the other only brought the contempt of all the continental powers, who knew well that he had neither the will nor the money to wage war.

The death of Gustavus Adolphus on the field of Lützen in 1632, and the assassination of Wallenstein early in 1634, had profoundly altered the aspect of affairs in Germany. The Emperor's forces and those of the King of Spain were able to unite and, in August 1634, they routed the Swedes and their Protestant allies at Nördlingen. The old rivalry between France and Spain now dominated the continental scene.

Charles's current policy was to support Spain against France and Holland, especially since French troops had occupied the Palatinate, and since France and Holland were entering into an alliance for the invasion and partition of the Spanish Netherlands, which threatened to place Dunkirk, Bruges and Ostend in French hands. Charles was therefore urging a secret treaty on a distrustful Olivares, whereby Spanish money was to help equip the English fleet to join in the overthrow of the Dutch republic.

The Spanish Regent in the Netherlands, the Infanta

Isabella, had died in November 1633. The victory of Nördlingen enabled her successor, King Philip's brother the Cardinal Infante Ferdinand, to arrive with his troops in Brussels a year later. Endymion was now chosen by Charles to convey his congratulations to the new Regent. On November 23rd, Endymion set out for Brussels at the head of a splendid mission, his suite consisting of twenty gentlemen with a large retinue of servants. He was also accompanied by his two older boys, George and Charles, and by his brother, Captain Tom, in whose ship they made the sea passage. A French observer in Brussels wrote that he 'never saw so many complete gentlemen in his life and a neater equipage'.[64]

It had been expected that Charles would send an Ambassador of high rank—Arundel's and Lennox's names had been mentioned[65]—and in Endymion's selection his career reached its high water mark. Besides bearing Charles's complimentary letter to the Cardinal Infante, Endymion was instructed to take up the question of Spanish interference with English trade. He was also ordered to present Charles's compliments to the Queen Mother of France, Mary de Medici, who had sought refuge in Brussels in 1631, after the failure of her plot to overthrow Richelieu.[66]

At Brussels, Endymion was met by his old acquaintance Gerbier, now Charles's resident envoy there. Neither Gerbier's character nor his experience was likely to fit him for such a post, but he had been Buckingham's servant and, because of this, Charles had given him his complete confidence. It was singularly misplaced. Only the year before, the needy and greedy Gerbier, for a bribe of 20,000 crowns in hard cash, had betrayed to the Infanta all the details of Charles's secret negotiations with the Flemings and Brabanters who were planning to throw off the Spanish yoke.

Writing from Brussels to Secretary Windebank on December 5th, Endymion reported how cordially Gerbier had welcomed him. He went on to say that, after present-

5   The artist and Endymion Porter, by Van Dyck

In the Prado Madrid

ing Charles's letter to the Infante, he had secured another audience at which 'I represented unto him the complaints of our merchants for the laying of new impositions upon our cloths and other commodities here contrary to the articles of peace; and also of the excesses and robberies committed by those of Dunkirk upon our merchants in general and in particular upon the fishing busses, for all of which I hoped his Highness would give order to see his ministers here, that full satisfaction and remedy might be had, and to that purpose (with Mr. Gerbier's advice) I drew a remonstrance, and it is referred to the President of the Council of those countries, who seems to be a wise and honest man; and gives me hopes that all shall be done as is desired, which is the only cause of my stay now.'[67]

Endymion's hopes were not fulfilled and his mission ended acrimoniously. The Cardinal Infante was renowned for his hauteur[68] and he now took offence. Sir Thomas Roe, writing to Wentworth in Ireland, described what happened.

'Mr. Porter, sent to congratulate the Cardinal Infante, has returned, having received no great satisfaction, for the Prince never moved his hat or foot. What displeased him we may not guess and his friends excuse him that it is the style of Spain, and that he never veiled to any since his arrival, but to the Queen Mother of France. This, at the best, is a proud defence, but we think there is more in it, for he offered to write back, but not giving upon his letters the due title of Majesty to our King, Porter refused to bring it. Upon this it was formalised and a week was spent, but in conclusion persisting in the difficulty, Porter has returned without any answer. Some say that his Majesty subscribing "à mon tres cher cousin" and not "altesse", from thence grew the exception, but it is not the style of Kings to inferiors, but that of Majesty is due from all inferiors to them.'[69]

Roe went on to suggest that if the Infante failed to send an envoy to reciprocate Charles's greetings, it would be a scornful neglect, but if he did and still failed to address Charles properly it would be a great affront. In fact, however, the Infante did send an envoy six months later to return Endymion's compliments in a suitable manner,[70] and no doubt Charles's displeasure was mitigated by the knowledge that the Infante had behaved in a similar manner to the King of France.[71]

Endymion's spirited refusal to take back the Infante's letter did not prevent the haughty Spaniard from making him a very handsome gift on his departure, a brush set with diamonds and a diamond ring each for young George and Charles. The Venetian Ambassador in London wrote to the Doge that he thought that the value of the presents would privately compensate Porter for the official rudeness of his reception.[72] Nor did Charles attach any blame to Endymion who, a year later, received the sum of £2,000 from the King, half of which was on account of his mission to the Infante, and the other half for 'divers services due to his Majesty'.[73]

Although Endymion returned without a letter from the Infante, he may well have brought back with him two things of much more lasting value. Being in the Spanish Netherlands, Endymion would certainly not have missed the opportunity of paying a visit to the studios of Rubens and Van Dyck. It is therefore probable that it was on this occasion that Endymion acquired for the King Rubens's great 'Landscape with St. George'.* Rubens had painted it as a reminder of the happy months of his visit to England, and in the picture, with its imaginary English background, Charles and Henrietta play the parts of the Saint and the Princess.[74] From Van Dyck, Endymion obtained for Charles the splendid portrait of Henrietta of Lorraine with a blackamoor, now at Kenwood. It seems likely, too, that it was at this time that Endymion, in full finery, sat with Van Dyck for their double portrait.

It was not until 1639 that Charles again made use of

* Now in Buckingham Palace.

Endymion's services in foreign affairs. In the meantime, the French attack on the Spanish Netherlands had failed and Charles's futile diplomacy, shuffling between alliance with Spain against France and alliance with France against Spain, and seeking to use the fleet raised with ship-money as his bargaining counter, had brought him no nearer to his goal of restoring his nephew, Charles Louis, to the Palatinate.

During the summer of 1639 a great Spanish fleet had been assembling at Corunna to convoy 10,000 men and a large sum of money to Flanders. Coming up the English Channel, early in September, the Spaniards encountered part of the Dutch fleet and a running fight ensued. The next day the Dutch Admiral Tromp arrived on the scene with the rest of his fleet. There was a fierce battle off Dungeness in which, after losing four ships, the Spanish fleet, their powder spent, took refuge in the Downs, where the English fleet was lying. Pennington, the English Vice-Admiral, after making the Spaniards lower their flag to him, ordered Tromp to abstain from attacking the Spaniards and to keep to the south part of the anchorage.

Both sides now appealed to Charles, the Spaniards for protection, the Dutch for leave to attack their prey. To have two rivals bidding against each other for his favour was a diplomatic situation after Charles's heart. At first, Charles's inclination was to help the Spaniards and to allow them to sail two tides before Tromp was permitted to follow them. But he then decided that he would only agree to this if the King of Spain would pay him £150,000 for such protection. At the same time, the French Ambassador was told that Charles would abandon the Spaniards to Tromp if Richelieu would place Charles's nephew at the head of an army to recover the Palatinate. In order to gain time for these offers to be considered, Charles ordered Pennington to tell the Dutch that he would shortly be requesting both fleets to leave and that, meantime, he was confident that no acts of hostility would take place.

It was at this point that Endymion came on the scene, Charles making him his go-between in Secretary Windebank's negotiations with Cardenas, the Spanish envoy. The message from Charles which Endymion was instructed to give, through Windebank, to the unfortunate Cardenas was hardly encouraging.

'His Majesty,' wrote Endymion to Windebank from Windsor, 'commanded me to let your Honour know that he would have you make answer to the Resident (if he require it) that the King hath showed his care of the Spanish fleet, and that if the wind sit where it doth, it will be impossible for his ships to come to protect them against the Hollander, but his Majesty will do the best he can. Howsoever, he would have the Spaniards prepare themselves for the worst, for they cannot imagine but that he will be pressed to limit a time for their abode in his port, and, in the meantime, he shall keep them from hostility if it be possible; and his Majesty hath given the best order he can for that purpose.' But this cold comfort was nothing to the further instructions Endymion sent. 'And your Honour can inform them,' he went on, 'how great a prejudice it would be to the King if they should fight in the harbour, for if any ships should miscarry and be sunk there, it would be the ruin of the best harbour in the Kingdom; but it seems the Spaniard regards nothing but his own accommodation, nor will they look about them, until the King assign them a day to set sail, the which will be required from him; and when they are out of the port, they must trust to their own force, for his Majesty will protect them no further.' Endymion's own opinion of the Spaniards and their fleet was a low one. 'As for their making any proposition,' he ended his letter to Windebank, 'I think they are such dull, stupefied souls that they think of nothing, and when I acquainted his Majesty with their negligence in that particular, he told me that the Resident was a silly, ignorant old fellow.'[75]

Charles's belief in the likelihood of a Spanish victory

was waning, for, next day, Endymion again wrote to Windebank on Charles's orders.

'His Majesty having taken into his gracious consideration what should happen if the Hollanders should, in a hostile manner, fall upon the Spaniards in the Downs, and, by any such act drive them to run on shore for safeguard of their lives, and thereby those that scape may be much necessitated, both for victual and lodging and the King's subjects damnified by the unruly carriage of soldiers in want; his Majesty (out of his pious care to prevent disorder on all sides) hath commanded me to let your Honour know that it is his royal pleasure you signify unto the Lord Warden of the Cinque Ports and to the Deputy Lieutenants of Kent that they (in such case of necessity) see provision be made for the billeting of strangers in such places, as for their moneys they may have all necessaries of meat, drink and lodging, that thereby the world may see his Majesty's christianlike intentions to the subjects of his friends and allies. These are his Majesty's commands.'[76] In other words, Charles's christian goodwill to the wretched Spaniards was to consist of not allowing them to starve, so long as they could pay for their food and lodging!

While Cardenas was engaged in discussing with Windebank the terms of the Spanish payment to Charles, Richelieu had returned an evasive reply to Charles's proposal to France. He was under no illusions that he had anything to fear from the English King; and it was probably on his advice that Tromp now struck, attacking the Spanish ships under cover of a morning fog. In an hour, twenty Spanish ships had run ashore to escape the Dutch, and the rest had made off with Tromp in pursuit.

Pennington's hands were tied by Charles's instructions, even if he had wished to risk a mutiny in his ships by asking them to intervene on behalf of the Spaniards. As it was, the fog provided a sufficient excuse for his inaction and he contented himself with protecting the stranded Spanish vessels, while Tromp was sinking or capturing the rest of the

Spanish fleet, except for a few that managed to reach the safety of Dunkirk.

Charles's vision of choosing between £150,000 from Spain or an army for his nephew from the French had vanished. Indignant as he was at the Dutch flouting of his authority in his own harbour, he was powerless to retaliate. But there were great rejoicings on the part of his Protestant subjects, who had feared that the Spanish army was to be landed in England to assist the King in putting down rebellion, and who now thanked their Protestant God for such a happy deliverance.

CHAPTER VII

(i)

Although Endymion was not often employed in diplomacy, his life was an extremely busy one. His Court duties were far from light. In addition, his position —and clearly, too, his friendly character—made him the channel through which all sorts and conditions of people sought to gain the King's ear. Even members of the powerful Villiers family were not above seeking the help of their relation by marriage. Buckingham's brother, the Earl of Anglesey, writing to Endymion as his 'good door-keeper' and signing himself 'your loving uncle', asked for his good offices in explaining his absence from Court and in securing posts for other relations.[1] Buckingham's sister, Lady Denbigh, wanted help in securing the next presentation of a living.[2] The Duchess of Buckingham asked her 'good cousin' to intercede on behalf of her steward and of an old servant of the Duke's.[3]

There were, too, many requests for assistance from other than Villiers, Boteler or Porter relations. The Bishop of St. David's, for instance, begged Endymion to tell the King that illness had kept him in his diocese, 'that desolate place where there is not so much as a leech to cure a sick horse', and where the roads are 'steep, craggy and Welshly tedious'.[4] Sir William Russell wrote on behalf of his nephew, said by the best of the country doctors to be suffering from the King's evil, and only to be cured by the King's touch. He asked Endymion to find out when he might bring his nephew up to London to be admitted to the royal presence.[5] Humble folk wrote about preferments to livings, or a place as a purser's mate for a poor widow's son.[6] A cry from the heart came from the Mermaid Tavern from Thomas Grove, who was lying there 'under some charge and in fear of the plague'.[7] A number of friends wrote asking for a warrant for a buck from the royal forests. One hopeful suitor, William Jones, sought to ingratiate himself by sending an anagram on the name Endymion Porter, 'Ripen to more end', together with eight lines of doggerel verse.[8] Sometimes Endymion's good nature made him too importunate on behalf of his friends. In 1639 for instance, he had to explain that he could not deal as expeditiously as he wished with some business for Windebank, because Secretary Coke had complained about him to the King 'for intruding on business'.[9]

But next to attendance on the King, it was his own business affairs that occupied most of Endymion's attention. Under Charles, as under his father, the office-holding class still looked mainly to fees and perquisites, rather than to salaries and allowances, for the normal and legitimate emoluments of office. The permanently impoverished condition of Charles's exchequer aggravated the position, as payments to creditors fell more and more in arrears. In 1635, for instance, the purveyor of poultry to the royal children was owed £1,900, and the royal fishmonger £1,000, while a jeweller's bill of £2,000 had been outstanding for ten years.[10] Pensions and allowances were equally behind in their payment. As we have seen, even the pension of such a royal favourite as Van Dyck was five years in arrears. It was, in consequence, not only custom but necessity that drove courtiers more and more to compete as amateur financiers and business men in spheres belonging more properly to the merchant class.

The King's desire to add to his revenues also increased the courtiers' opportunities for profitable business. Charles was genuinely convinced that his care for his loving subjects needed to be constantly exercised for their good in every kind of matter which touched their lives. Brick-making, coal shipments to London, soap-making, salt, starch-making, malting and brewing, overcrowding in

6   Endymion Porter, Olive, George, Charles and Philip, by Van Dyck

In the possession of Mrs Gervas Huxley

London, smoke abatement, the traffic problem caused by coaches in narrow streets, the danger of the sea being denuded of fish through trawling, were some of the varied subjects which provided the King with well-intentioned reasons for irritating and generally disastrous interference, while at the same time opening up new sources of income for his exchequer, as well as opportunities for his courtiers' business talents.

The Parliament of 1624 had made monopolies illegal, but William Noy, the King's principal financial adviser, found a way out in the royal grant of 'patents' to those, known as 'projectors', who invented or sought to develop some new idea or process and who demanded protection from competition. It was in this shape that monopolies now returned. Grants of patents, from whose fruits the Crown would gain some revenue, provided Charles with needed money, while courtiers, having the King's ear, were not slow to take full advantage of their position to become 'projectors'.

Courtiers became, too, singularly solicitous in their search for abuses that others might be inflicting on the public, in order that they might get the King's permission to supply the remedy in consideration of a suitable financial recompense for their trouble. In 1635, for instance, Katharine Elliott, the baby Duke of York's wet nurse, made the distressing discovery that shopkeepers were selling low quality silk stockings and waistcoats at the price of the best quality. She asked, accordingly, for a grant for thirty-one years of the privilege of marking all silk stockings and waistcoats at a charge of one shilling for a waistcoat and sixpence for a pair of stockings.[11] At about the same time, Sir Francis Cornwallis was grieved to find that inferior parchment and vellum was being sold to lawyers. To remedy this, he was prepared to examine and mark all parchment and vellum for sixpence a roll of parchment and threepence a roll of vellum.[12] Nor, in these matters, did dog refrain from eating dog. Courtiers were equally on the alert to denounce and profit from abuses inflicted by other patentees.

Endymion was by no means backward in making such profitable discoveries. Amongst the abuses which he and his friends conveniently unearthed was that of the sheriffs whose deputies paid them for the privilege of acting as bailiffs and prison keepers. The deputies, in order to recoup themselves, then took bribes and perverted justice. Endymion and a friend asked to be given all the fines imposed on these lawbreakers.[13] On another occasion, Endymion hit on the happy idea that baronetcies might not be legally hereditary. If this were found to be the case, it would open up a fine field for Charles to confirm his friends in their titles and to mulct his enemies. In return for his suggestion, Endymion asked that he should function as prosecutor with an appropriate allowance for his labours.[14] A little later Endymion joined with the Marquis of Hamilton in getting Charles's leave to examine all accounts rendered to the King and, where they were found to be fraudulent, to take advantage of it either by prosecuting the accountants or by getting them to compound for their offences. Half the money thus obtained was to go to the King, Hamilton and Endymion keeping the other half. The alarm of the accountants was so great that it was reported that within a fortnight of the grant being given, many of them had already offered very large sums by way of composition.[15] Yet another abuse which Endymion discovered and exploited, this time in partnership with Lord Conway, was the lack of uniformity in length, breadth and quality of silk goods with gold and silver thread.[16] Earlier, Endymion had discovered that the patentees for making and registering policies of assurance, who were allowed to charge one shilling for making a policy and two shillings for registering every £100, had, in fact, been charging treble. He asked for a grant of all the excess money that had been taken.[17] When, however, Endymion and two friends had requested a commission from the King to inquire into offences committed by scriveners, brokers and usurers, they found that others had already begun to usurp their functions. They begged, therefore, that the King would lose no time in granting their petition.[18]

Nor was Endymion's search for wrongdoers confined to England. In 1632, the King wrote to the Lord Deputy of Ireland that Endymion and Will Murray, another groom of the bedchamber, had told him that laymen had appropriated many Irish church livings. Endymion and Murray having undertaken to restore these to the Crown, the Lord Deputy was to issue a commission empowering them to make inquiries and issue the necessary writs and to help them secure their rights. Endymion and Murray were to be granted all the rents and tithes which ought to have accrued to the Crown since the last year of Queen Elizabeth's reign, reserving a quarter of such profits for the King.[19]

(ii)

Endymion's business activities were not, however, confined to such profitable reforms of minor abuses. He was also a partner in some of the important projects of the time. The King himself, with the most laudable intentions, took a leading part in promoting most of these major ventures. Besides being supposedly in the national interest, they promised, on paper, good financial returns to the Exchequer and to the courtiers who invested in them. In practice, however, the courtiers lacked the experience and skill to make a success of large-scale commercial projects, and more money was lost than was gained by the projectors. One of the earliest of Charles's major projects with which Endymion was concerned was that of fisheries. It was an industry of which the Dutch had acquired a virtual monopoly. Bringing in a yearly profit of up to ten million pounds, employing, in all, over two thousand boats and twenty thousand sailors, the fisheries round the coasts of

Britain formed one of the main sources of Dutch wealth and maritime power. Charles resolved to break this Dutch monopoly by establishing a British fishing industry. Towards the end of 1632, he formed by charter 'The Association for the Fishery', with a monopoly of all sea fishing and trade in fish. The Association was to be managed by a Council of twelve, half English and half Scottish. The City of London prudently held off from investing in the new enterprise, and the Court found the initial capital, a number of courtiers becoming 'Adventurers' in the project. Lord Treasurer Weston put up £1,000, the Lord Chamberlain and the Earl of Rutland £500 each, the Duchess of Buckingham £300, and Endymion, with Tobie Matthew and a number of other courtiers, £100 each. In all, nearly £12,000 was thus subscribed or promised.[20]

The centres of operation for the Association were to be the Island of Lewis for cod and ling, and the East Coast for the much more important herring fishery, in which the highly-organized Dutch industry employed 600 to 1,000 'busses'—boats of 100 to 120 tons—accompanied by fast-sailing ships to bring the salt and take away the catches to market. This Dutch fishing fleet operated in convoys guarded by warships against attacks from Dunkirk privateers. In the Western Isles, the Association soon came to grief, owing to the active hostility of the local inhabitants who preferred to deal with the Dutch fishermen. Trouble likewise arose on the East Coast, four of the Association's first six busses being seized by the Dutch or by Dunkirk privateers. The King was extremely angry at the behaviour of the Dutch. He had Seldon's *Mare Clausum* published in support of his hereditary claim to the Sovereignty of the Seas, and he informed the Dutch that their boats could only fish if they obtained licences. In 1636, the Earl of Northumberland was sent to the North Sea fishery grounds with part of the Ship Money fleet to protect the Association's boats and to enforce the licensing of their rivals. But the Dutch declined to fight and Charles was also unwilling

to press his claims too far. Meantime the Association's
finances had got into low water. Their capital was quite
inadequate and losses had been incurred every year. In
1637 the Lewis fishery was abandoned and, in 1639, after
a loss of £5,000 from the capture by Dunkirkers of four
more busses, the Association collapsed.[21] It was probably
in connection with his interest in the Fishery Association
that Endymion, at the end of 1637, petitioned the King
for a patent to collect money all over Great Britain for
building a harbour and lighthouse at Filey. Endymion
was to have the profits for thirty-one years after paying
£20 a year to the Exchequer. His petition was referred to
the Lords of the Admiralty, who, in 1638, asked Trinity
House for their advice, but the failure of the Fishery
project seems also to have ended Endymion's scheme for
Filey.[22]

Endymion was also a partner in a salt project. This
essential commodity had been in short supply. With the
object of remedying this and of encouraging domestic
industry, the King, in 1635, granted a patent to a company in Shields for the production of salt, which all port
towns from Berwick to Southampton were to use in place
of salt imported from the Bay of Biscay. In return, the
company was to pay a royalty to the exchequer. But the
fishermen, for whose trade salt was vital, complained that
the company could not supply them with enough and that
what they got was inferior in quality. One Nicholas Murford had, however, invented a new salt-making process.
With Charles's support an influential company, with Lord
Maltravers at its head and with Endymion and Secretary
of the Admiralty Nicholas among its thirty-six 'assistants',
was formed in 1636 to exploit Murford's process. The new
company, called the Corporation of Salt Makers of Great
Yarmouth, was to establish works in that town and was
to be allowed to sell salt in spite of the monopoly previously given to the Shields company. This naturally led
to quarrels between the two companies, while the Scots

complained that the English monopolies had ruined their trade, and the farmers of a tax on salt imposed by the King asserted that they were losing money because every-one was using Scottish salt! In 1638, the Yarmouth company proposed to expand their operations to the neigh-bourhood of the Thames for the sale of salt in London. Endymion and the other assistants were called to a meet-ing at Arundel House to say what share they would take in the venture,[23] but the days for this and other royal projects were, by then, numbered.

Endymion had, too, an interest in a major project which brought the King into much trouble and unpopularity. It was that of soap. Soap making had been in the hands of the London and Bristol soap boilers, fish oil being the chief ingredients used. At the end of 1631, a patent was granted for the manufacture of soap by a new process, using home-produced vegetable oils and potash. Under the aegis of Lord Treasurer Portland, and with the ostensible object of checking imports and encouraging home employ-ment, a group of courtiers, Endymion amongst them, bought up the patent. Many of the group concerned were Catholics and Gage was at their head. In return for their undertaking to make five thousand tons of the new soap a year, for sale at the low price of 3d. per lb., and for guaranteeing a payment of £4 a ton to the exchequer, the King, in 1632, issued a proclamation incorporating the group as 'The Governor, assistants and fellows of the Society of Sopers in the city of Westminster'. This com-pany was given the sole right of manufacturing the new soap. It was also empowered to test the soap made by its competitors, the sale of which was to be prohibited unless it had been marked by the new company with a fleur de lys as being 'sweet and good'. The use of fish-oil for soap making was also forbidden, only olive or rape oil being allowed.

Thus placed at the mercy of the new Westminster com-pany and debarred from using their chief former ingredient, the old London and Bristol soap makers rebelled. They continued to make large quantities of fish-oil soap ('very noisome and unfit' declared the new company) and stoutly resisted the new company's searchers. Prosecutions, fines and even imprisonment failed to stop them. They had, however, the strong support of the public, and numerous petitions were presented complaining that the new soap was 'useless and unserviceable', and that it hurt the hands of its users and spoiled their linen.

The new company was compelled to resort to publicity to defend its product. In December 1633, a sample of the new soap together with a sample of the old was taken to the Guildhall. In the presence of the public and of a panel consisting of the Lord Mayor, the Lieutenant of the Tower and a number of aldermen, two laundresses, 'indifferently chosen', were put to work to scrub clothes with the rival soaps. After two days' scrubbing, the panel decided that the new soap lathered better and washed clothes 'as white and sweet' as the old soap. This verdict was not, however, popular with the public, and the Lord Mayor had to turn tail before 'a troop of women that clamorously petitioned against the new soap'. In a further effort favourably to publicise the soap, the company obtained testimonials from more than eighty ladies of note, including four Countesses and four Viscountesses, that their maids found that the new soap had no ill-effects on their hands or on the linen. The company also asserted that most of the petitions against the soap were fraudulent, being composed of names used without their owners' knowledge. Of the few genuine names, one was found to be bedridden and another in childbirth. Only one woman, Mrs. Sweeting, was prepared to say that the new soap, though all right for fine linen, was not so good as the old for her coarser wash.

Thus reinforced, the King issued a second proclamation in January 1634, reaffirming his earlier one and ordering the dismantling of works still making the old soap. If the public still found the new soap bad, it must be because it was being adulterated by the retailers. But the only result of the proclamation was the creation of a flourishing black market in the old soap, for which the public were prepared to pay as much as a shilling a pound. Under this stimulus, illicit soap makers sprang up all over the country, while many housewives began to make their own soap at home. There were, too, serious representations from silk-dyers, wool-combers and weavers that fish-oil soap was essential for their trade.

Next July, the King had to issue a third proclamation. The new company was to be allowed to make fish-oil soap to meet these trade needs, and its powers were strengthened. Home soap making was prohibited and the company's searchers were to be compensated for their trouble from the fines collected from infringers of the monopoly. The Bristol soap makers were to be limited to six hundred tons a year, all to be sold west of the Severn, and they were to pay the Exchequer £4 a ton.

By the beginning of 1635, in spite of the three proclamations, there was more illicit soap making than ever. The new company, moreover, had run into trouble. It had incurred very heavy expenses and was unable to meet its obligations to the Exchequer. It had also run foul of the Admiralty, who alleged that the company's agents were buying up all the wood ash, so that the saltpetre manufacturers were unable to get their supplies, and, as the Admiralty observed, saltpetre ought to be given preference over soap 'as the more necessary for King and public'. There were petitions, too, from the Greenland whale oil traders who found their business gone, and from the Newfoundland Fisheries, employing nearly twenty-seven thousand tons of shipping and ten thousand men, who used to sell their oil for cheap soap, but who now found themselves with six hundred tons on their hands.

Encouraged by these persistent complaints and by the death of Lord Treasurer Portland in March 1635, the old soap makers of London made an offer to the King to pay him £8 a ton instead of the £4 a ton being paid by the new company, if they could be formed into a corporation in place of their rivals. Archbishop Laud took their part, but Cottington's friends had formed the new company and he got his way with the King, although the new company had to agree to pay the Exchequer £6 a ton for two years and thereafter £8 a ton. In return, it was given the monopoly of all soap manufacture and no other soap was to be retailed. But in spite of fines and imprisonment, the manufacture and sale of old soap still went on. Finally, in May 1637, the old soap makers of London succeeded in persuading the King to incorporate them in a new Society, with the Lord Mayor of London at its head, which bought out the Westminster company for £40,000, of which the new Society contributed half, as well as agreeing to pay the King £8 a ton on all soap manufactured. They were to sell fish-oil soap at $3\frac{1}{2}$d. a lb. and the best crown soap of olive oil at $4\frac{1}{2}$d.[24]

(iii)

Endymion's most important commercial venture was, however, an overseas one.[25] The East India Company had been incorporated by Royal Charter in 1600 and had been given a monopoly of commerce with the East Indies in order to compete with the Dutch in the valuable spice trade. From the outset, disputes with the Dutch and Portuguese had hampered the Company's efforts. In 1623, Dutch rivalry had culminated in the massacre of Amboyna, when the English traders at that Dutch settlement were tortured and killed on the plea that they were planning to seize the fort. Since the massacre, the Company's business had been largely confined to the less profitable trade with the Indian mainland, based on their trading station at Surat.

In December 1634 Captain Weddel, the Company's representative, came back to London with the news that the

President and Council at Surat had concluded a truce with the Portuguese at Goa, by which the Company's ships could make use of Portuguese ports in the East Indies, thus opening up greatly enhanced possibilities of trade, particularly in pepper. Weddel, however, had his own ideas as to how the new situation might best be exploited to his advantage. Approaching a group of merchants in London, headed by Sir William Courten, he proposed that they should seek the King's permission to break the East India Company's monopoly by sending out their own trading expedition. The time seemed propitious, since dissatisfaction with the revenue accruing from the Company's operations had just been enhanced by the discovery that the Company's principals in Surat had been trading for their own private profit.

Courten, whose father had been a Protestant refugee from Menin, had started on his road to fortune by marrying the deaf and dumb heiress of a rich Dutch merchant. Later, his ships had discovered and settled Barbados and his family firm had lent large sums of money to King James and to Charles.[26] Even though litigation and bad debts had recently reduced his fortune, he was still a very rich man, with £200,000 in lands and money.[27] In order to help secure the King's support for an enterprise which was sure to provoke the East India Company's strongest hostility, Courten took Endymion into partnership. In February 1635, Endymion obtained Charles's authority for two ships, the *Roebuck* and *Samaritan*, 'to range the seas all the world over,' this wide scope being intended to disguise their real objective, the East Indies. Endymion engaged himself to assist Courten, Kynnaston and Bonnel, the other merchants in the partnership, in all things which might concern the voyage and was to allow them, out of his share of the profits, a quarter of any charges occasioned by the ships being detained or in trouble.[28] Endymion's value as a partner was also shown by his obtaining from his friend Nicholas at the Admiralty a special exemption from pressing for the Navy for the crews of the two ships.[29]

In April 1635, the *Roebuck* and *Samaritan* set sail for India, but Courten and Endymion had still more ambitious plans. Again approaching the King, who, in spite of the indignant protests of the Company, was by no means averse to creating some competition in the East Indian trade, they were granted a licence in December 1635 to trade with the East Indies, on the grounds that the East India Company had failed to establish fortified settlements, had only considered their own interests and not those of the royal revenues, and had broken the terms of their Charter.

In March 1636 the Courten Association, as the new venture was called, though the East India Company christened it the Interlopers' Association, sent out the *Dragon* and five other ships under the command of Weddel and Mountney, another former employee of the East India Company. They reached Surat in August, informing the astonished President and Council there that they represented a new East India Company and presenting a letter from the King saying that he had a particular interest in Weddel's voyage and that he wished the Company to give the new Association every assistance. Weddel and Mountney then proceeded to Goa and went on to trade with the Portuguese ports in the East Indies.

So far, everything seemed to have gone well with Endymion's new venture; but the week before Christmas of 1636 an East India Company's ship, the *Discovery*, put into Plymouth with a startling story. This was that the *Roebuck*, when in the Red Sea on the way to India, had seized and plundered two Indian dhows, one belonging to the Mogul and one to a Portuguese-owned port. The crew of the *Roebuck* were said to have tortured the Indian sailors by putting burning matches to their fingers in order to make them disclose the whereabouts of £60,000 in specie that they were supposed to be carrying. It was further reported that the East India Company's officers in Surat had been thrown into prison by the Mogul and their property confiscated in retaliation for the outrage.[30]

Naturally, the East India Company made the most of this story for the discomfiture of their rivals, and immediately petitioned the King for leave to sue those responsible for the *Roebuck's* voyage. Sir William Courten had however recently died and it was doubtful whether a charge could be laid against his son, William, who had succeeded him as head of the family firm. Nor did the Company like to involve Endymion personally, but a suit for £10,000 damages was brought against Kynnaston.[31] Endymion used all his influence to soften the charges, and when the question was referred to the Council they were evidently suspicious that the story might have been exaggerated and decided that any judgement must await the *Roebuck's* return home.

The *Roebuck*, in fact, put into Falmouth in May 1637. The *Samaritan*, it appeared, had been wrecked on an island in the Indian Ocean on the way home and her Captain, Oldfield, the commander of the whole expedition, had died with most of the crew.[32] Oldfield's death temporarily shelved the East India Company's attempts to get damages from their rival traders. In spite of the loss of the *Samaritan*, the *Roebuck's* voyage had been a profitable one,[33] and a little later that summer, Weddel and Mountney also returned home after a highly successful voyage, their ships laden with profitable cargoes.

The East India Company were more alarmed than ever by Weddel's success and again repeatedly petitioned the King that they were facing ruin through Courten's competition. It was, indeed, widely believed that they would be forced out of business. Writing to Wentworth, Garrard told him that, 'The East India Company here are giving over their trade. The disturbance they have received abroad by ships sent out in the name of Sir William Courten and Endymion Porter have so disordered their affairs, that except they receive present comforts from the King and

State here and be by them protected, they cannot longer subsist . . . and they are now resolving to call home men, goods and shipping.'³⁴

Their lamentations had, however, no effect on Charles and the Council who, in June 1637, made a fresh grant to the Courten Association, in which their privileges were extended for another five years. They were authorised to export £40,000 in gold and silver for the purchase of goods and the scope of their trade was now to include Goa, Malabar, China and Japan. They were also to search for a North East passage 'to the North point of the Californias on the backside of America', so as to meet the North West passage and enter the Atlantic via Hudson's Bay. Six ships, the *Dragon, Sun, Katharine, Planter, Anne* and *Discovery* were fitted out by young Courten, Endymion, Kynnaston and Bonnel. The King himself took a share in the enterprise ³⁵ and when the fleet sailed in the spring of 1638 he issued an express command to the East India Company, forbidding them to trade in any Indian ports where Mr. Porter, Mr. Courten and their agents had established connections.

Weddel was again in command. He pushed on from Goa to Sumatra and thence to China. At Canton, faced with Portuguese and Chinese opposition, he successfully attacked a fort before returning to India, where he settled new factories, entered into trading arrangements with local rulers and invested profitably in pepper and saltpetre. No attempt on the North East passage was, however, made.

In desperation, the East India Company made a final appeal to the King. Their threat to abandon their trade was genuine. It was also a serious one for Charles. Two years before, Garrard had written to Wentworth of the loss of customs that would ensue if the East India Company were forced out of business. Now in 1639 the King could less than ever afford to risk the loss of any source of revenue. The East India Company's petition was accordingly referred to a Committee of the Privy Council. After

Endymion and Courten, as well as the Governor and Deputy Governor of the Company, had given evidence, the King decided, at the end of 1639, to revoke the Courten Association's licence, though they were to be allowed time to withdraw their settlements, ships and goods. The East India Company were also now authorised to take proceedings against Cobb and Ayers, the surviving commanders of the *Roebuck*, and the King undertook to renew the Company's charter when they had succeeded in floating a new joint stock issue. The advantage to the royal purse in keeping the East India Company in business was shown next year, when Charles relieved some of his need for ready cash by selling for 1/8 a lb. the Company's whole stock of pepper—600,000 lb.—which he had bought for 2/1 a lb. on credit.

Endymion's connection with the Courten Association seems to have ceased with the revoking of its licence. Courten's ships, however, continued to trade to the East, but with their credit declining. In 1646, Courten had the unfortunate idea of establishing a colony in Madagascar, a task beyond his resources, in spite of locally coining counterfeit money. In 1649, as the Assada merchants, a settlement was made on the island of Assada, but not long after Courten's enterprise was merged in the East India Company.

(iv)

One project in which the Court took special interest was that of draining the fens in order to provide good corn-growing land in place of swamps. A start had been made in 1626 with Hatfield Chase, near the Humber. Vermuyden, a Dutch engineer, was brought over from Holland with Dutch labour and capital, and in spite of bitter opposition from the fenmen the drainage was successfully completed a few years later. An even more ambitious project was then advanced. It was for the drainage of the

Great Level, a large expanse of swamp round the Isle of Ely, inhabited only by fishermen, fowlers and reed cutters who moved about in boats or on stilts. Vermuyden was again the engineer, and the Earl of Bedford was induced in 1631 to head the project. He was to be given forty-three thousand acres of the reclaimed land, twelve thousand were to be set aside for the King, and forty thousand were to be for the maintenance of the works after they had been completed. A little later, Bedford divided the undertaking into twenty shares and the shareholders were incorporated by Royal Charter.

By 1637, Bedford and his partners had spent £100,000 and although they claimed that the work was finished, this was not the case. It was left for the King to intervene in 1638 and himself take over the project, Bedford and his partners being given forty thousand acres without the obligation to complete the scheme. But, by 1639, Charles had neither time nor money to give to the Fens and the project remained unfinished.

Shortly after the Earl of Bedford undertook the Great Level project, Endymion embarked on his own Lincolnshire drainage venture. In September 1632 he obtained a grant from the King of one thousand acres of marshlands, with some waste ground beyond the banks, in North and South Somercotes.[36] He took a friend, Sir Nicholas Fortescue, into partnership, but on Fortescue's death a few years later he bought his share out for £430.[37]

Troubles began almost at once. A labour force was collected and sent to Lincolnshire for the banking and draining, this work and the subsequent farming operations being put in charge of Richard Cutterice and Thomas Butler, a poor relation of Olive's. But the local inhabitants refused to supply the imported labour with food or lodging, and Endymion had to ask for a warrant to the Lincolnshire Justices of the Peace to bind over anyone who tried to stop the work.[38]

By the spring of 1638 the first five hundred acres were

ready for cultivation, but Butler and Cutterice had over-spent and they had to borrow £100 from the Vicar of South Somercotes to pay for the ploughing and sowing the oats and barley.[39] A good crop 'as dry and well as corn can be' was being harvested in September.[40] Meantime a dispute over tithes had arisen with Mr. Gray, the Vicar of North Somercotes; and Endymion's steward Harvey had to be sent down to try to settle matters. Eventually, after Gray had written that 'his creditors were so pressing that he daren't go to church', Endymion agreed to pay £50 down and sixpence an acre.[41]

The remaining five hundred acres were now leased to Cutterice for £200 a year, Cutterice agreeing to put up a house and farm buildings worth £300.[42]

In June 1639 the crops again looked like being good, but no money had been received from Butler on account of the 1638 harvest. Olive had taken charge of the Somercotes business while Endymion was away in the North with the King, and Butler's explanations to Olive were more elaborate than convincing. He had gone to Hull, he said, to get a ship to carry the oats to London, but had then found that a royal ordnance forbade shipments of corn to London. He had then proceeded to York, but had found Endymion gone north and the York prices bad, while at Newcastle the weather was so rough that no ship could come near the shore. The barn was so stuffed with corn that he did not know what to do with the forty acres of rape seed that was nearly ready for cutting. He assured Olive that the banks and sluices were all in good order and he promised a full statement of accounts.[43]

Olive was not impressed with her relation's excuses, and Endymion wrote from the North that Cutterice and Butler were 'both cozening knaves'.[44] Harvey was sent down to look into the accounts, and when he reported that he could not believe that the corn had yielded so little, Olive dismissed the unfortunate Butler, who wrote despairingly both to Olive and to Endymion that he was 'undone for ever', and had not even a horse to ride to London on. He claimed £88 10s. 8d. arrears of wages, without which he would starve.[45] He managed to get to London, however, to make his apologies 'hoping that the heat of anger will be over'.[46]

There was trouble, too, about claims for compensation from the local commoners[47] and six months later the Reverend Gray was writing to Endymion asking him sometimes to think about Somercotes 'even though your wishes are that you had never known it' and where Endymion had 'done good to everyone but yourself'.[48] Finally, about 1642, the commoners seized the land and broke down the banks. In his statement to the Committee for Compounding seven years later, Endymion declared that he had never received a penny in compensation and that, until the banks were repaired, the land was not worth more than £40 a year.[49]

Endymion's troubles over Somercotes did not, however, deter him from venturing into other drainage schemes. About 1637, for instance, in partnership with Sir Edward Savage and Edmund Wyndham, whose lovely wife was lady nurse to Prince Charles, he was granted leave to drain tidal marsh lands on the River Shannon in Ireland.[50] There was trouble here, too, and in the autumn of 1641 Endymion was writing from Edinburgh a tactful letter to Secretary Nicholas to ask his help in getting the grant reaffirmed. He had, he said, spent money in finding the marsh for the King and was content to leave Nicholas to 'do in the business what justly you may'.[51] Wales was the scene of yet another drainage venture, when in 1638 Endymion entered into an agreement with two partners for draining marshes in Carmarthen, Pembroke and Glamorgan.[52] In the same year, he and Wyndham had been given the right to search for minerals in the county of Flint, where Endymion had previously been given leave to enclose a common.[53]

(v)

In addition to Endymion's shares in projects and in the rewards of discovering abuses, the royal favour made him the beneficiary of some important grants and patents. One profitable grant, acquired in 1631, was the farm of the customs on French wines entering Lancaster, Liverpool and other ports. At some point, Endymion sold this to Sir Thomas Aston.[54] In 1635, he also obtained the farm of wines at Chester. It must have been a profitable grant, as £1,100 a year was the price to the King for the farm. Endymion did not farm it himself, but leased his grant to a Cheshire knight.[55]

Endymion had continued to enjoy his share of the profits of the Irish customs. But, at the end of 1637, he seems to have sold his rights, since the Lord Deputy ordered him to be paid the large sum of £3,864 13s. 4d., due to him as the remainder of a composition for his share.[56] It is probable that he used some of this money at the end of 1638 to buy, for £3,000, the reversion of the office of Surveyor of the Petty Customs of the Port of London, after the death of the holder, Richard Carmarden. The office was worth £700 a year and Endymion's old city friend William Courten and another merchant were associated in the purchase and were to inherit the office successively after Endymion's death. Two years later, Carmarden wanted to buy the reversion back from Endymion, offering in exchange some land, which he would lease from Endymion at £400 a year. It was unfortunate that Endymion did not accept the offer, as Carmarden lived until the Civil War had put the reversion out of Endymion's reach.[57]

A potentially profitable patent which Endymion secured in 1640, when it was too late for much use to be made of it, was for the manufacture of white writing paper. Endymion and three partners 'having learned the art of making white writing paper and desiring to set the art on foot in the King's Dominions', petitioned for a monopoly for fifty-seven years, only those licensed by the patentees to be allowed to manufacture the product. The King was also asked to prohibit the export of linen rags, which were all to be sold to the patentees. The petition was granted for a term of fourteen years, after Attorney General Bankes had reported favourably on it to the King.[58]

Probably the most important grant which Endymion obtained was that of the Postmaster-General's patent. The inland postal service was still primarily for governmental use. It was a service on horseback, based on stages, ten to fifteen miles apart, on the main post roads from London. These were the north road to Berwick, the north-west road to Holyhead, the west road to Milford Haven via Bristol, the south-west road to Falmouth via Exeter, and the south-east road to Dover. A postmaster—often the inn-proprietor —was in charge of each stage. He had to keep horses, bags, horns and guides. Riding post, being the quickest method of travel (hence the expression post-haste) was not confined to government packets and officials. It was also much used by private travellers. All post-riders hired fresh horses at each stage and rode to the next stage accompanied by a guide who brought the horses back. Apart from their pay and allowances, the postmasters were allowed to charge threepence a mile for each horse.

The patent of Postmaster-General had long been held by the Stanhope family. It was a profitable one, its perquisites including a fee, a payment by each postmaster on his appointment—and post places were valued as high as £100—and a percentage of the postmasters' pay. As in the case of most creditors of the Crown, however, the postmasters' pay was sadly in arrears. It was in September 1635 that Stanhope deputed his patent to Endymion and his eldest son George. What consideration Endymion gave Stanhope is not known, but one reason for the latter's relinquishing his patent may have been that in July, under the aegis of Secretary Coke, the postmaster general for foreign parts—which was separate from the inland patent held by Stanhope—had been given the task of setting up a general inland postal service for private users, based on fixed charge per letter according to mileage. This postal plan failed, however, to be implemented, and by royal order in 1637 the posts were confined to governmental use.

Endymion seems to have had some trouble over getting his patent confirmed, as in April 1636 he addressed to Windebank the following letter, whose phrasing must surely have secured the writer's object.

'May it please your Honour,

You are best acquainted how long I followed the business of the Postmaster's place, as being one to whom it was referred for the ending and settling of it, and I have made bold to intimate unto his Majesty in an humble letter his former gracious intentions towards me in the said business, of which I have received so favourable an answer from his sacred mouth, as I assure your honour it hath much lessened my sickness; yet I fear by something his Majesty said, that he might imagine I was not willing to have the Lord Stanhope's patent made void; therefore I made choice of your honour to do me the favour as to let his Majesty know that I have no disposition nor thought to be averse to any intentions of his, and for this I will hope that his Majesty doth it for the good of me his poor servant and creature, and if I be thought worthy by his Majesty to have the office, I will make it such a one for his honour and profit, as his Majesty shall have no cause to think it ill-bestowed: but I refer all to his Majesty's gracious will, for he best knows at what time and with what place to gratify each servant.'

Whether Endymion and George were able to increase the King's 'honour and profit' is doubtful. In 1661, George declared that the postal revenue had only been worth £5,000 a year to Charles I, but that it was now farmed for £21,500 a year. His claim, however, that the improvement was due to his efforts is quite untenable. In fact,

Endymion and George transferred their rights in the patent in March 1642.[59]

Leases of land and reversions were also among Endymion's grants from the King. One lease was that of the Forest of Exmoor with rights of de-afforestation;[60] and there were reversions of the leases of Marsly Park in Denbighshire and Raby Park in Durham,[61] and of the keepership of Hartwell Park for his son Charles.[62] On his brother Tom's death, Endymion was allowed to inherit his £50 a year from Trinity House in respect of the ballasting monopoly,[63] but the most curious grant that Endymion received was that of the right to have the employment of convicts who had been reprieved from sentence of death.[64]

One major source of revenue to the Crown and of profit to courtiers was that of wardships. If a minor or a lunatic was left as heir, the administration of the estate fell to the Crown, which sold it to a guardian of its own selection. While the guardian chosen was often the nearest kinsman, the system afforded good opportunities to courtiers to obtain guardianships, from the administration of which handsome profits would accrue during the ward's minority, while the guardian could also get a good price for his ward in the marriage market.

In 1629, for instance, John Sackville wrote to Endymion that Sir John Tasborough, a Suffolk man, was dying. His son was a minor, and Sackville thought that if Endymion could get the wardship from the King, it might be worth £2,000.[65] One wardship that Endymion obtained, as the gift of Archbishop Laud, was the administration of the estate of a certain William Taylor during the minority of his only child Margaret.[66] But Endymion's chief interest in this field was a family one. On his father-in-law, Lord Boteler's, death in 1637, he and his brother-in-law Lord Dunsmore became guardians of Olive's idiot brother William and administrators of the Boteler estates. These included manors and lands in Bedfordshire as well as Woodhall and other manors in Hertfordshire. During his lifetime, Lord Boteler had conveyed the estates to Endymion and Dunsmore in trust, to pay his debts on his death, to give £1,000 each to Olive and her sister Jane and to use the rest of the income for William's maintenance. One of the Bedfordshire manors, Streatley, with other lands in the county, had been mortgaged by Lord Boteler. Endymion became the owner of half the Streatley property by redeeming part of the mortgage for £650 out of his own pocket. According to Endymion's own statement before the Committee for Compounding, the Boteler estates, apart from Streatley, were worth £550 a year.[67] A side line from the Boteler guardianship was a payment of £2,500 to Endymion and Dunsmore from John Belasyse, who had married a ward of the late Lord Boteler and who paid this sum to redeem his eighteen-year-old wife's wardship.[68]

Endymion was fortunate to find in Richard Harvey a responsible and able confidential servant to help him not only in his own multifarious business affairs, but also in the financial transactions which he carried out for the King. Harvey was introduced to him by a very old friend, none other than William Calley, the cloth merchant, who had been Endymion's master in Madrid over twenty years before. Calley had retired from business not long after he had returned to England with the proceeds of the settlement of his Spanish debt.[69] In 1619 he had bought Burderop Park, an estate in Wiltshire on the high ground south of Swindon. There, he had settled down to a country life, though he and his son William held the office of Receiver-General of the Crown rents for Oxfordshire, Buckinghamshire and the City of Oxford.[70] Richard Harvey, who came of puritan Somerset stock, served Calley as his house and estate steward.

It was in 1635 that Harvey first began to work for Endymion. Although he continued to act as London agent and correspondent for the Calleys, it was not long before he was fully taken into Endymion's service and established in an office in the Porter house in the Strand. By 1637, a cousin was writing to him to ask how he was getting on in his 'late change of life and sphere'.[71] In Sir William Calley's will drawn up in 1640, he left £6 to his late servant Richard Harvey, adding that 'had he not had so good a fortune fallen unto him since his leaving my service, his legacy from me should have been more'.[72]

Harvey deserved his good fortune and served Endymion faithfully as he had served Calley. After the outbreak of the Civil War, he seems to have returned to Burderop, where young William Calley had succeeded his father. In Harvey's will, drawn up in 1659, he is described as 'Richard Harvey, gentleman, of Burderop in the parish of Chisledon in the county of Wilts'. He made a charitable bequest of £100, the interest on which was to be divided annually between twenty poor people of his parish. His executor, William Calley, was to have the sole right of nominating the beneficiaries. Harvey lived to a very old age, dying in 1669.[73]

CHAPTER VIII

(i)

A<small>T</small> a rough estimate, Endymion's income in 1628 had
amounted to nearly £3,000 a year. During the next
twelve years it must have been considerably increased by
the profits from the numerous grants and patents that he
acquired. Moreover, Olive had received £1,000 on her
father's death as well as an interest in Woodhall during
the life of her brother.[1] Endymion's pension of £500 a year
seems to have been regularly paid[2] and, in 1635, he had
been given £2,000 by the King. Of his business projects,
his partnership in the Courten association must, for some
years at least, have been highly profitable, though it is
unlikely that he got more than his money back from his
share in the soap company.

By any contemporary standards, Endymion's income
during these years was, therefore, a very large one, exceptionally so for a commoner. Yet, by the time the Civil War
broke out, he was in financial difficulties. About 1639, he
mortgaged Alfarthing to Sir Thomas Davies for £4,000,[3]
and, in 1641, he pledged his half share of Streatley Manor
and the other Bedfordshire land for a loan of £2,500 from
Robert Cooke.[4] In March 1642, Endymion and George
parted with their Post Office appointment, and, in May,
Olive was raising a loan of £450 on some of her jewellery.[5]

Large as Endymion's income was, his expenditure was
to scale. There was first the heavy personal cost involved in
his attendance on the King, a cost which far exceeded his
official £500 a year salary and any special payments made
to him on account of oversea missions. His splendid embassy to Brussels in 1634, for instance, must have cost a

good deal more than the £1,000 subsequently given him on its account. A petty cash account, kept by his valet for a five-weeks period in August and September 1637 and preserved amongst Endymion's papers, gives a valuable clue to the size and character of his normal official expenses, since every item, however small, was faithfully recorded by the valet. The period included twenty-four days of travelling on a short Progress from Oatlands to Odiham, Andover, Salisbury, Alton and Lyndhurst, staying at country houses on the way.

Endymion travelled with his valet, his coachman and coach, three riding horses—a black and a grey gelding and a grey horse—and his two grooms, Cuthbert Lambe and Walter Buckannon and the stable boy, John Richardson. The grooms' board wages at 1/– a day each, with the boy's 3/6 a week, came to £3 for the twenty-four days on the road. Then there was the cost of stabling, fodder, shoeing, and some new harness, which amounted to over £12. Laundry was another expensive item, amounting to 31/10 for three weeks for Endymion and his valet. Endymion's own wardrobe also needed constant attention and replenishment. There were two pairs of new boots and a pair of shoes bought at Salisbury for 31/4; a pair of woollen stockings for 6/–; three pairs of stagskin gloves bought at Andover for 13/6; lengths of frieze Holland for trousers and twenty-four yards of fine Dutch fustian that cost £3 9s. 8d; six pairs of cuffs and six plain bands for £1 16s. 0d. besides a pair of boots for the valet at 10/–, and repairs to boots and to Endymion's scarlet coat—in all, a clothes bill of over £7.

A trim from a barber cost 5/–; attention from a corn cutter 10/–; 1 lb. of tobacco 12/–, and dinners at Lyndhurst and Alton 25/10. One of the heaviest items of expenditure was tips. At Mr. Oliver's house, Endymion's tips to the groom, butler, cook and a woman amounted, in all, to £1, and, at John Arundel's, he gave £1 12s. 6d. to the two butlers, two cooks, a groom, a wash maid and a chambermaid. There was besides a constant flow of tips to servants who brought Endymion gifts from their masters; 5/– for bringing a present of Venice glass; 10/– to one who brought a present of Spanish melons, and 1/– to the porter who helped unload them; 4/6 to Lord Holland's man for bringing a haunch of venison; 1/– for the bearer of a basket of trout, fresh caught in the Kennet by Endymion's cousin John Popham of Littlecote; and so on. In all, including sundry tips to ostlers and porters and 6d. to an Irish beggar woman met on the road, Endymion's total expenditure on gratuities in three weeks came to over £5.

Unlike some members of the Court, such as Sir John Suckling, the poet, or the Earl of Southampton who had to sell his racing stable and the timber off his estates to meet his losses in matches at Newmarket, Endymion does not seem to have been a gambler. But there were wagers to be won or lost at bowls and the petty cash account included two items, amounting to over £5, for money handed to Endymion at the bowling green.

The valet's total cash expenditure on Endymion's behalf in the five weeks amounted to £71 13s. 8d. Even deducting £15, which Endymion gave as a present to his sister Elinor Crane, it seems that the incidental expenses of Endymion's official duties must have amounted to well over £500 a year, a large sum in terms of the contemporary value of money.[6]

Then there was the cost of the household in the Strand. In 1630, the lease of the property had been renewed for thirty years at the slightly reduced rent of £70 a year, but in 1634 Endymion bought it outright for £1,000, paying the Earl of Bedford £3 a year for the lease of the little garden.[7] It was a large establishment, with Endymion's and Olive's ever growing family and their nurses and tutors, as well as Harvey's office and a retinue of servants. There would have been, too, constant entertaining of friends and relations, and, as the years went on and George and Charles grew up, the expense of sending them abroad with tutors and of furnishing them with the means of cutting their own figures in the fashionable world.

We know a few of the costs of the Strand household from random bills found amongst Endymion's papers. The cost of wood for fires in September 1638 was, for instance, £2 13s. 9d. and in October £3 0s. 8d. This would have risen in the winter months and, apart from coal at 10s. a sack, a winter's bill for wood must have been at least £25.[8] Lighting was also an expensive item. The bill for candles from May to September 1635 was £5 19s. 8d., and from October 1635 to March 1636 £23 1s. 0d., a total of nearly £30 for a year. Retail food prices seem very low on present-day standards, but consumption in such a household as Endymion's was no doubt generous. Eggs were three for 1d., best fresh butter 5d. to 6d. a lb., while a best turkey cock cost only 4/6, a fat goose 2/4, fat capons 2/6, hens 1/2, and rabbits 7d. or 8d. according to the season.[9]

There were substantial bills, too, for Olive's wardrobe. She bought the materials for her dresses separately—black satin was 14/- a yard and velvet 22/- a yard—but the bills from her dressmaker for making up and for the accessories such as buttons, hooks and eyes, whalebone stiffening, etc., came to nearly £10 a quarter. The chief items were petticoats and waistcoats costing between £1 10s. and £2 for making up. Olive had a new petticoat and waistcoat nearly every month, cloth of silver, tabby-rose coloured and sky-coloured silk, white taffeta, 'ezebelah' coloured satin, etc. There were suits, too, of satin or mohair, costing £1 16s. 4d. to make up, and Holland coats at £1 1s. 0d. for making up six. As always, growing children were heavy on shoes and in six months in 1637, Olive bought thirty-three pairs for the family at a cost of £5 2s. 8d.[10]

Endymion's wardrobe was also a large one. A list of November 1637 shows that his linen consisted of fifteen whole shirts and twelve half shirts, two laced collars, six needlework and eighteen plain bands, seven pairs of laced and seventeen pairs of plain cuffs, eight laced night ruffs, four pairs of linen trousers, fifteen laced handkerchiefs, eight pairs plain linen and four pairs of lace boot hose, and six laced linen night caps and four cut work caps, and thirteen pairs of linen socks. There were, too, nearly a dozen pairs of coloured and embroidered garters, and seven pairs of coloured silk stockings, together with seven pairs of woollen stockings. He had twelve pairs of white gloves, and nine pairs of riding and other gloves. There was a pair of white Spanish leather boots with silver and gold spurs, two pairs of thin waxed boots and four pairs of thick ones, two pairs of Spanish kid shoes and three pairs of riding spurs.[11]

There had also been Olive's jewels to be bought. One account has survived. It was from the goldsmith for £47 and included gold ear-rings, headpieces and bracelets.[12] The jewellery on which she raised £450 in 1642 consisted mainly of diamonds and included a pair of pendants set with great rose diamonds, a pendant set with a great table diamond, diamond ear-rings, a diamond hat band and a diamond and ruby necklace.[13]

One major form of expenditure must have been Endymion's purchases of pictures and *objets d'art*, both for his own collection and as presents to the King. Endymion's own collection was housed in his London home and at Woodhall. It seems likely that he spent some £2,000 on it, a big sum in days when even a full size Van Dyck cost only £100, and when a Titian could be bought for the same price and a picture by many a good old master for much less.[14]

Endymion had no large inherited or acquired capital resources, and the substantial sums which he had to lay out for his business transactions must have been found from income. Nor were his transactions always profitable. The £3,000 he paid for the reversion of the Petty customs office, for instance, produced no return at all during Endymion's lifetime, and there is no doubt that his Somercotes drainage venture, like so many other similar projects, strained his resources without any compensating return. Edmund Wyndham was another courtier, with financial

resources of much the same character as those of Endymion, whose fortune was engulfed in drainage. He and
Sir Edward Savage had leased the King's twelve thousand
acres of the Great Level for £4,300 a year. Though they
sub-let most of the land, their losses on the rest through
defective drainage and inundations were so heavy that
Savage estimated them at £10,000.[15] Nor is it likely that
the project for draining land in Ireland, in which Endymion
joined Wyndham and Savage, yielded anything but loss.

Endymion's income was also reduced in 1639 when Laud
and other Councillors, in the King's absence in York,
decided to revoke or suspend some twenty-six commissions
and patents. Amongst them was Endymion's grant of the
fines on Sheriffs and under Sheriffs. Endymion surrendered
his grant, although many of the other revoked patents
were still being operated a year later.[16] The final and
possibly the most important factor, however, in Endymion's financial difficulties was the loans that he made
to the King. Living in daily association with Charles to
whom he owed so much of his wealth, he was in no position
to respond other than freely to appeals such as the King
made in April 1639 for contributions towards the cost of
the Scottish expedition. But Endymion's outstanding trait
was loyalty to his masters, and he who was always the
first gratefully to acknowledge the sources of his good
fortune, whether Buckingham or Charles, would not have
hesitated to give all the material as well as personal help
in his power to his benefactor in his hour of need. According to Endymion's own statement to the Committee for
Compounding in 1649, the King owed him £10,000. Though
this sum would not have referred wholly to loans, there is
no doubt that Endymion lent substantial amounts to the
Crown, including a loan of £1,000 in 1640.[17]

(ii)

During these years, Endymion and Olive were much less frequently parted than in the early part of their married life. Although Endymion was in constant attendance on his master, Charles's restless movements from palace to palace were mainly confined to his residences in or near London. Except for his visit to Scotland to be crowned in 1633, the King did not go far afield, his journeys being mostly to Newmarket and to the New Forest for sport, and to such places as the Isle of Wight and Salisbury. Endymion was therefore able to spend much more of his time in his Court lodgings at Whitehall, Greenwich, Hampton Court, Windsor and Theobalds, or in his own home in the Strand, where Olive lived most of the year, visiting Woodhall and Aston much more seldom.

The only letters exchanged between Endymion and Olive that have survived from this decade tell of a quarrel in the summer of 1634. Endymion's curt letter was written from Welbeck to Olive in London, 'at his house in the Strand, over against Durham House Gate'.

'Olive,—I writt unto you a letter by this gentleman which it seems you take unkindly. As I hope for salvation I know no cause for it, but sure you are apt to mistake me and are fearful that I should oblige you overmuch to esteem me; wherein, though you show but little love, yet 'tis a sign of a good conscience. God continue it in you, and send me grace to mend my life as I will my manners, for I will trouble you with no more of my letters, nor with any design of mine, yet I will not despair of you as you do of me, for I hope that age and good considerations will make you know I am

Your best friend
Endymion Porter.

Commend me to the children and send this enclosed to D'avenant with all speed.'[18]

Olive's humble and touching little reply must have

brought the quarrel to an end. It shows that Olive was deeply in love with her husband, perhaps more so than when they had married nearly fifteen years before.

'Sweetheart,' she wrote, 'My brother tells me that you are very angry with me still. I did not think that you could have been so cruel to me to have stayed so long away and not to forgive that which you know was spoke in passion. I know not how to beg your pardon, because I have broken my word with you before; but if your good nature will forgive me, come home to her that will ever be,

Your loving and obedient wife,
Olive Porter.'[19]

Olive and Endymion's affection did not lack pledges in the way of children. In the ten years following Philip's birth in 1628, Olive bore four more sons and two daughters. All were born in the family home in the Strand. Little 'Mun' had died at the age of two. Another boy, William, was born in 1632, but died at birth. A second Endymion was born in 1634 and only lived for nine months. Finally there came Thomas and James, born in 1636 and 1638, who both grew up to manhood. The two daughters, Mary and Lettice, were probably born in 1629 and 1631. In all, Olive bore twelve children, of whom five died in infancy.

Endymion was not often able to visit Aston, but his mother, Angela, still made her home in the Manor House. The old lady was alive as late as Christmas 1637, when Sir William Calley, writing to Richard Harvey, asked to be remembered to 'good old Mrs. Porter'.[20] Her son-in-law and daughter, William and Mary Canning, still lived close by at Foxcote, and William's brother Richard had rented a house and land at Aston from Endymion.[21]

The plague in London was again bad in 1630, and, as in the earlier plague year of 1625, Olive and Endymion sent their children away with Mrs. Gibson their nurse to the good air of Aston. Their grandmother was delighted to welcome the three boys, George, now rising ten, Charles aged seven, and the two-year-old Philip. Part of the time, the children stayed with their uncle and aunt at Foxcote, whence William Canning wrote to Endymion in May that his pretty little ones should want nothing that this poor place could afford, and that they were all in good health, but Philip the best company, being 'so peart and merry a fellow'.[22]

Little Philip was also his grandmother's favourite. 'I know,' she wrote to Endymion in June, 'that I can send you no better news than that your dear children are well. Philip is as merry as possible and my great friend. When I take him to bed, he will not leave my arms until he has pulled all the pins out of my hair and my collar as well, and before we separate we have a dance. I have to do all that he tells me. There is not such a child in the world. Many a time, I wish that you and his mother could come to the door to see the play that we have at night before he goes to bed. . . . The Lord be praised for the birth of the Prince.* Mrs. Gibson says that if he is as pretty as Philip, all the poets in England will have to write about him. She asks me to give her respectful greetings to her mistress.'[23]

Although Endymion resided so little at Aston and was a Justice of the Peace for Middlesex and not for Gloucestershire, he was a local figure of some importance. Together with Sir Baptist Hicks and Sir Nicholas Overbury, he was, for instance, a trustee of Chipping Campden Grammar school. The trustees met once a year on the Friday before Michaelmas 'to examine the schoolmaster's faults'. They had been appointed in 1627, after it had come to light that the former trustees of the charity, on which both the school and the poor of the town depended, had 'pursed up a great sum of money for their own use'. Being 'subtil and worldly men', they had tricked an old blind man into parting with the deeds of the charity and had pocketed all the income except £13 6s. 8d. a year which they gave the schoolmaster, while the school buildings decayed and the poor of Chipping Campden went hungry. When Endymion and his fellow-

* Charles, Prince of Wales, born 29th May, 1630.
228

trustees took over, the school was repaired, the schoolmaster's salary raised and an assistant appointed. The necessities of the poor were also relieved and apprentices assisted.[24]

It was, however, Woodhall rather than Aston that Endymion and Olive used as their country residence after Olive, in 1637, inherited a life interest in the former estate. Francis Dorvan, the steward, was in charge at Woodhall and it was there that the younger children were now sent in the care of their tutor, James Gibbs, who was a Porter relative.

Writing to 'Honest Mr. Harvey' from Woodhall in October 1638, Dorvan tells of his 'frustation' at the expected visit from Endymion and Olive not materializing. The two youngest boys 'Mr. Thos.' and 'Mr. James', (aged two and one), were in very good health, but their sister 'Mrs. Mary' 'continues still in her quartan ague and is very desirous to go to London if my Lady will be pleased'. Dorvan added a message from John Aldridge, the gamekeeper, that if his master and his Lady wanted some does killed, 'it must be within this seven or eight days at the furthest, because this wet weather will make them fall away'.[25] A year later, James Gibbs the tutor wrote again from Woodhall to Harvey. 'Here we are all alone, and apply ourselves to our books diligently, and so much the better, by how much the less distraction we find, and further we are from London. I hope to make Mr. Philip my masterpiece, according as he proceeds with me and takes learning. I have already showed his father the profit he hath made to his great satisfaction and joy, of one that could scarce read a word of English when I first undertook him. This I speak without any exaggeration or desire to arrogate more to myself than many that know it will give me. His father told us we should shortly be going oversea, but I fear it will not be before next Spring. I should be very sorry to come to London to teach him in the interim, for the many occasions of divertment that daily present themselves. So that I mean to write to Mi Senor to know his intention shortly and if we go not away this winter that he would be pleased to let us live in the country.'[26]

It may well have been to show how well justified was Gibbs's praise of his nine-year-old pupil, that the following letter was written in French by Philip in September 1638 to his brother George.

'Mon tres cher Frere. Je suis fort joyeux d'entendre que vous avez perdu votre fievre. Je seray bien aise de vous voir icy ou a Londres. Ma Tante estoit malade hier, mais auiourdhuy elle se porte mieux. Tous se recommendent a vous et ie demeure

Votre tresaymé Frere

Philip Porter.'[27]

The tutor did, in fact, take Philip abroad in January 1640.[28] Gibbs intended to go on to Padua or Bologna to complete his 'studies in physic',[29] but he and Philip were back at Woodhall by the end of October, according to a letter from Dorvan to Harvey. Mary was there, too, and her aunt Lady Newport who was entertaining Sir Kenelm Digby.[30] A month later, Dorvan was dismissed from Woodhall. He wrote to Harvey that he had been 'most falsely accused'.[31]

Philip was not the only one of the children to show early promise with his studies. George, at the age of seven, had written his first Latin exercise and it was preserved among Endymion's papers. In a clear schoolboy's hand, George copied out his translation into Latin of 'the roote of learning is bitter, but the fruite is sweet, for learning is the way to vertue and vertue is everlasting honor'.[32] But Charles was no scholar. 'As for Mr. Charles,' wrote Gibbs, 'no great matter could be worked with him; wherefore I should urge some settled course should be thought on for him.'[33] In 1637, when he was fourteen, he was sent to Madrid, where he was in the charge of Olive's poor relation, Mr. Butler.[34] From Madrid, Charles wrote home in January 1638.

'Dear Mother.

I have received your letter in which I understand that my father and you are very angry with me, which hath not troubled me a little to think that I should deserve any anger at either of your [piece torn] . . . the ways that possibly can be to retain your loves will do my endeavour to amend any fault you accuse me of. Therefore I beseech you, sweet mother, not to let your anger continue, for it is the only thing I desire to shun in this world. I am extremely glad to hear that my little brother Tom proveth so fine a child and that my nurse and you are friends again; I pray you to let it last both with her and me.

Your dutiful and obedient son
Charles Porter.

I pray you remember my humble duty and service to my lady Duchess and my Lady of Arundel.'[35]

Endymion had to pay five shillings postage on the letter, but it must have placated his parents, as they sent Charles 'a pair of black silk laced garters and roses', costing eighteen shillings.[36]

A message to Endymion from Sir Arthur Hopton, the English Resident in Madrid in August 1638, told that Charles was 'very well and grows a gallant youth'.[37]

It was in 1637, too, that sixteen-year-old George went abroad. Lured by the prospect of adventure at the siege of Breda, he left London for Holland in June with his friend Rupert and the young Elector, in such a hurry that he took no clothes with him other than those he had on his back.[38] Many English volunteers were taking part with the Dutch forces in the siege, including young George Goring, George Porter's future brother-in-law, who was wounded in the leg. Rumour went round that he had been killed and D'avenant promptly wrote a long elegy in the form of a dialogue between Endymion and Jermyn lamenting their young friend's death. George Porter returned to England a year later, landing at Dover in July 1638 in company with his aunt, Lady Newport.[39] He had been in

Paris in April, whence the attendant whom Endymion had sent out to look after him reported to Harvey that the young esquire had been 'a little coltish'.[40]

Endymion's naval brother Tom had never married. Endymion had given him the reversion of Alfarthing Manor,[41] and had doubtless helped him to secure such pickings as a grant of £50 a year from Trinity House in connection with their monopoly of ballasting ships in the Thames,[42] and as the grant of two-thirds of the cargo of a Dutch ship abandoned and driven ashore in Essex.[43] In 1633, Tom had been made Captain of Camber Castle, near Rye,[44] and in 1635 he was promoted from the *Warspite* to command the *Henrietta Maria*.[45] In August of that year he took Ambassador Aston to Corunna in her, returning with a consignment of money from the King of Spain for transport to Dunkirk.[46]

Tom's professional reputation stood high. The next year a naval correspondent suggested to Secretary of the Admiralty Nicholas, that Tom would be the best choice for command of the force for the proposed attack on the Sallee pirates, 'both for language, valour and other respects.'[47] It is possible that, but for ill-health, it would have been Captain Porter, instead of Captain Rainsborough, who, in the summer of 1637, led the successful naval expedition to the Moorish Coasts. But, in September, when Rainsborough dropped anchor in the Thames on his return with over three hundred freed English captives, Tom lay dying in Endymion's house in the Strand.

Endymion and his brother had shared travels ever since their first boyhood journey to Spain, and Tom's death at the age of less than forty must have been a very sad blow, the more since, at the time, Endymion himself was ill with a fever.[48] Tom was buried by night in the chancel of St. Martin-in-the-Fields. Endymion paid the funeral expenses. They were £1 for a velvet pall; £1 7s. od. for nine metal escutcheons; and £11 5s. 4d. for the burial expenses in the church. There was also a bill for £3 4s. od. for sixteen

gallons of burnt claret for the mourners.[49] Endymion had
also lost another brother, Edmund. He had been employed
by a London merchant and died at the end of 1627, aged
only twenty-four.[50] Only one other brother, Giles, was now
living, together with Endymion's four married sisters, Mary
Canning, Elinor Crane, Jane Bartelete, and Margaret
Bolton. Mary Canning was the sister of whom Endymion
was fondest. Living at Foxcote, so close to Aston, she
helped to look after his mother as well as his children.
From Foxcote, Mary used to send up presents of food to
her brother in London, on one occasion two turkeys to eat
on Shrove Tuesday, a dozen black puddings, a ham and a
collar of brawn. In return, Endymion sent her wine and
herrings from London and helped her with money.[51] He
also gave money to Elinor, whose husband was a connection
of Lady Marie Crane who sent Olive and Endymion presents
of poultry and deer from Stoke Park.[52] Endymion does not,
however, seem to have been on very friendly terms with his
youngest sister Margaret and her husband Edmund Bolton.
Bolton was imprisoned for debt in 1628 and he and his wife
were importunate in their requests to Endymion to use his
influence on their behalf. Endymion once tore up a scroll
which his brother-in-law had sent him suggesting ways in
which Endymion's help could be used for his benefit.[53] On
Olive's side, her youngest sister Anne, Lady Newport, was
the relation of whom the Porters seem to have seen the
most.

There were, of course, many friends in the Porter circle.
One friendship, in particular, happens to have lived for us
in the letters that have survived. It is Endymion's friendship with the Calley family. The positions of both Endymion and of William Calley had greatly changed since the
days, twenty years before, when young Endymion had
taken service in Madrid with the rich and respected merchant. Sir William Calley—he was knighted in 1629—was
now well over sixty. He had long retired from business and
was leading the quiet life of a country gentleman at Bur-

derop with his wife and their son William. But the changes
in fortune which had brought Endymion to high position
in the inner Court circle, and Calley to rural domesticity in
Wiltshire, had made no difference to Endymion's loyal
affection for his old master, an affection which Calley
warmly returned.

There were visits by Endymion and Olive to Burderop
and by Calley to London; and the Calleys relied on letters
from Endymion and Harvey for news of current events in
which they took a lively interest, though when old Calley
thanked Harvey for reminding him to write to Endymion,
he remarked sadly that it was 'the weakness of old age to
dote and be forgetful'. The Calleys were generous with their
presents of country fare, which they sent up to Olive in
London by Smith, the wagoner from Swindon. Collars of
brawn were the most frequent gift, though on one occasion
the brawn was overboiled. Hogs' puddings, black and white,
came up too; and a pigeon pie as a 'token of love and badge
of their poor country housewifery'; and, for Christmas, a
fat young swan. Young William sent Olive 'a rundlet of
metheglin', with the advice to let it have time to settle.
In return, young Calley's fondness for venison was gratified
by Endymion's arranging for gifts of buck from one or
other of the royal forests. Back to Swindon from London
in Smith's wagon came the delicacies which the Calleys
ordered through Harvey and which they could not buy
locally—lump sugar, currants, Jordan almonds, pistachio
nuts, ginger, mace, cinnamon, musk, cloves, pepper, olives,
capers, salad oil, Dantzig sturgeon, claret and other wines.
From London, too, the Calleys ordered material for their
clothes; linen for handkerchiefs, socks and hose, a piece of
kersey 'of crimson and liver colour or a marble grey or rat
colour', and enough of the very best and richest black satin,
'yet fit for an ancient woman', to make a straight-bodied
gown for Lady Calley. They sent for clothes, as well; a
black satin gown and a white satin waistcoat for young
Mrs. Calley, and for her husband a pair of gold colour silk

stockings and two codpiece points of musk coloured silk. Suitable small change for paying country wages had to be sent down, too, in the form of £3 in single pence or two-pences.

Sir William died in January 1641, when he was seventy-six. In his will, drawn up the year before, he ordered that Lord Cottington, his 'noble friend Mr. Endymion Porter', and his cousin John Nicholas the elder, should each be given 'a ring of gold with a death's head set therein in remembrance of me, each ring to be of the value of £3'. Young William, who wrote to Harvey that he 'had rather much over-do than one jot under-do the will of such a father as mine', was so anxious to make sure that the rings were of the full value, that he returned to Harvey the first that were made, as they contained an insufficient weight of gold. When the new rings were finished, he came to London to present them in person to Cottington and Endymion.[54]

Endymion resembled the King in his love for his wife. He was now also to resemble his master in having a wife whose devotion to her religion caused embarrassment and harm to her husband. Olive had not only been one of the first of the Court ladies whom the Pope's legate, Con, with the Queen's protection and support, had converted to Catholicism; with all the zeal of the convert she had also become 'the soul of the proselytising movement' in the Court circle.[55] Naturally, she desired to make her husband follow her lead. Endymion certainly had no hostility to Rome, to which his sympathies were far more attracted than to the Puritans. But even if he felt no deep and con-vinced attachment to the Anglican Church, loyalty to his master, the King, as well as the strongest reasons of self-interest, forbade any departure from at least the outward profession of the Anglican faith. Olive and Con schemed for his conversion, Cardinal Barberini in Rome being consulted by Con as to whether Endymion could be received into the Catholic Church if he continued to accompany the King to

Anglican worship.[56] But Endymion was not to be shaken from continuing to give his master his loyal service in religious as in other matters.

Endymion's attitude failed to curb Olive's impetuous and self-willed character, and she soon had better fortune in another quarter. Her father was lying dangerously ill at Woodhall. Hastening down from London, Olive fetched the dying man back to her house, where Con was able to visit him daily and achieve a death-bed conversion. Her Protestant sister, Lady Newport, had gone to Woodhall to protect her father from Olive, but she had arrived too late.[57]

Olive next turned her attention to another dying relative, her brother-in-law Tom. He, too, was brought to the house in the Strand, and visited by Con. He died a Catholic, grasping Con's rosary.[58] Another object of Olive's zeal was her gentle and lovely cousin, Mary, Marchioness of Hamilton, who, in the summer of 1637, was wasting away with fever. Mary had been brought up as a strict Protestant by her father Lord Denbigh, whom Con described as 'a Puritan ass'. Aided by Con, Olive now set out to convert her, visiting her daily and plying her with Catholic books and tracts. To counteract Olive's influence, Lord Denbigh brought in the Bishop of Carlisle. When the Bishop assured the dying woman that he would be willing to pledge his soul for hers, Olive retorted, 'Little will it help you, my sister, that the soul of that old man shall be with you in the Devil's house.' But in spite of Con's and Olive's efforts, the Marchioness died without openly avowing conversion.[59]

It was not long, however, before Olive achieved her most spectacular success, no less than the conversion of her sister Lady Newport, whose Protestant husband was Master of the Ordnance and high in Charles's favour. One evening after Lady Newport had been to the play in Drury Lane, she drove with Olive to Somerset House, where one of the Queen's Capuchin priests received her into the Catholic Church. In a letter to Wentworth in Ireland,

Garrard described 'the horrible noise' that ensued. Lord Newport was furious and hurried to Lambeth to complain to Archbishop Laud, naming Con, Wat Montagu and Tobie Matthew as the parties responsible. Laud was equally angered. The next day, he went on his knees to the King, begging him to banish Montagu from the Court and to allow proceedings to be taken against Tobie Matthew in the High Commission. Charles was deeply offended at what had occurred and promised that he would have things remedied.[60] It seemed likely, indeed, that he would accede to Laud's demand that the Queen's chapel at Somerset House, as well as the Ambassadors' chapels, should be closed to English subjects. But, warned by Con, the Queen intervened, pitting her influence with Charles against that of Laud. So successful was she that, in the end, the King issued the mildest proclamation carrying a vague threat of punishment for those who persisted in converting the King's subjects and who gave scandal by celebrating mass. To the alarm and consternation of Protestants, the Queen showed her contempt for the proclamation by arranging for Lady Newport and other recent converts openly to celebrate Christmas mass in her chapel.

It was, as Garrard wrote, an open secret that Lady Newport's conversion was the work neither of Wat Montagu, nor of Tobie Matthew, but of Con, Olive and the Duchess of Buckingham.[61] Olive's activities, which had hitherto avoided open scandal, were now notorious. Inevitably, Endymion's name came to be coupled with that of his wife as the object of Puritan suspicions and fears.

CHAPTER IX

(i)

In 1636, after seven years of Charles's personal rule, there must have seemed to Endymion to be no reason why a Parliament should ever again be summoned. The King, his master, was in the prime of life, happy in his marriage, with two sons to secure the succession, and as attentive to business as he was devoted to open-air exercise. Charles's Government was simple. His Council took Parliament's place and the affairs of the kingdom were regulated by Acts of State instead of by Acts of Parliament. The King presided in person at all important meetings of the Council and controlled its decisions. Of his former chief parliamentary opponents, Eliot had died in the Tower, while Wentworth was now the King's most trusted servant and, with a combination of firmness and tact, had established order and prosperity in Ireland. The revenue, in aid of which Charles had formerly been compelled to summon his Parliaments, had been made sufficient for a modest and frugal régime. The vexed question of tonnage and poundage had been settled by the King's continuing to impose it and, in 1636, its yield had been improved by an adjustment of all the rates. The revenue had also been assisted by the revival of the Elizabethan tax of ship-money levied on the coastal counties and sea ports, and the extension of its scope in 1635 to the whole kingdom. Though arousing some strong and influential opposition, it had been pronounced legal by the judges and the tax was being, on the whole, successfully collected. The returns to the Crown from the Court of Wards had also been greatly increased, while the ingenious Noy's revenue-raising devices, such as the payments for knighthood, the revival of the forest laws and the grants of patents, were all helping to swell the Exchequer. If the shortage of revenue forbade foreign adventures and war, this was a condition of affairs agreeable to most of the King's subjects who, in contrast to the peoples of the war-ravaged Continent, lived in a land of peace and prosperity, where harvests were good, and where the arts flourished.

Yet the next year, 1637, was to see the beginning of the end of the pleasant world in which Endymion and his family enjoyed so seemingly secure a place. Even if they had been publicly silenced, the members of the 1628 Parliament who framed the Petition of Right and put forward the Remonstrance had not abandoned their fight for parliamentary rights against arbitrary royal authority in temporal and spiritual affairs. Beneath the surface memories were nourished and, in Pym, the opposition had a leader of consummate skill and resource.

Nor was there lacking widespread dissatisfaction for the opposition to exploit. In temporal matters, the constant and irritating interference with every-day life produced by Charles's revenue-raising devices was increasingly alienating many of his subjects. Nor had the declaration of the judges in favour of the legality of ship money silenced the opposition to the tax.

In spiritual affairs, Charles regarded the Anglican Church as the soul of the State. It was the duty of the Crown to uphold and extend the authority of the Church and the duty of the Church to sustain the authority of the Crown. For the enforcement of this compact, Charles had the perfect instrument in Archbishop Laud, as steadfast against Rome as he was bitter against Puritan heretics. Irritation at Laud's interference with old customs grew widespread, and each prosecution in his Court of High Commission provoked fresh opposition and fresh resentment, which found vent in grossly insulting pamphlets passed secretly from hand to hand. It was through uttering such popular sentiments that Archie the jester met his final downfall.

He got drunk in a tavern and called the Archbishop a monk, rogue and traitor. This was repeated to Laud, who complained to the King. Charles at once ordered Archie to be expelled from the Court. He was replaced by a fool called Muckle John.[1] But notwithstanding the prevailing discontent a peaceful and prosperous England, left to herself, was still unprepared for revolt. The impulse for open resistance came from without. It came from Scotland.

In pursuit of their ideals of uniformity of worship throughout the King's dominions, Charles and Laud had, in 1636, turned their attention to Scotland. They decided to promulgate new canons for Scottish church rule and a new Prayer Book for Scottish church worship. In the spring of 1637, the new Prayer Book reached Scotland with orders that every minister was to buy two copies. Rumours were already rife that the new book was full of popish rites and was to be the first step towards Rome. In any case it was an attempt to dictate to Scotland from Whitehall. Scottish puritanism and Scottish patriotism were equally aroused and the opposition found leadership in the Scottish nobles who feared the domination of the Bishops.

The introduction of the new Prayer Book at morning Service in St. Giles's Cathedral in Edinburgh was the signal for a premeditated demonstration. The congregation hurled stools at the Dean, while the crowd outside flung stones through the windows. The King's Council was powerless to preserve order and had no option but to suspend the new Prayer Book. Charles was deeply angered and demanded that the use of the new book should be resumed.

No representations had any effect on his obstinate conviction that severity would succeed in securing his object. When in February 1638 the Council issued the King's proclamation, censuring the Scottish nobility and demanding complete submission, the leaders of the revolt replied by drawing up the National Covenant, which defiantly vowed to maintain the faith. In a few weeks the Covenant was being signed by fervent congregations in every kirk in southern Scotland, and the Council could do nothing to check the storm.

Both sides now turned to military preparations. General Leslie, an experienced professional soldier from the continental wars, planned the organization of a Covenanting army, while Charles began to see to the defences of the North of England. Money was the first necessity and the exchequer was empty. Loyal subjects were asked for gifts to help fill it, and the Queen and Con collected money from the English Catholics. In the Court circle, the younger men such as George Goring and Harry Wilmot raised and equipped small bodies of cavalry. The troop raised by Suckling, the poet and gambler, was especially resplendent in plumes and armour. Endymion was not without some military training. He had been connected with the voluntary bands raised in London on the model of the Honourable Artillery Company, but his duties had been mainly of a ceremonial character. In May 1637, as 'Captain at the Military Company', he had attended the funeral of the renowned soldier, Lord Vere. Later that year, he had commanded the four hundred gentlemen of the 'military or trained bands' who furnished the escort for the 'most pompous audience' given by King Charles to the ambassador of the King of Morocco. Besides Endymion's escort, the ambassador on his way to Whitehall was accompanied by an Earl and others of the Court, as well as by his own colourful followers on horseback. The magnificent reception given to the ambassador both in the City and at Court was intended as an acknowledgement by the King of Morocco's generosity in releasing, without ransom, some '330 or 340 English, Scottish and Irish slaves', twenty of whom took part in the procession. The King of Morocco had also sent Charles 'a noble present' of four horses 'valued at four times as many hundred pounds', with rich saddles and golden bits, and stirrups, besides four hawks 'of excellent hope'.[2]

Now Endymion's duty was to attend the King. He must certainly, however, have contributed money. His friend, Sir William Calley, sent a gift of £50 up from Burderop to the King, and the wealthy merchant and jeweller Sir Paul Pindar advanced £100,000.

Almost everyone in England heartily disliked the prospect of war, and the troops which were gradually collected from the counties were as unwilling as they were ill-equipped. Desertion was common and there were some mutinies.[3] In Scotland, however, the Covenanters had quickly suppressed any opposition, except that of the Gordons in Aberdeen, while Leslie, assisted by many other professional Scottish soldiers back from Germany, had built up a well organized and trained force, whose recruits were eager and fervent in what they believed to be a holy and righteous cause.

Charles appointed Arundel as his nominal commander-in-chief, but gave the cavalry to the Earl of Holland as a semi-independent command. Hamilton, the King's cousin and close friend, was put in charge of the fleet. On March 27th the King, with Endymion in attendance, left London. They reached York three days later, but the Covenanters had already taken the initiative. They had seized Edinburgh Castle and Dumbarton, where the King's Irish troops were supposed to land, while Leslie and Montrose occupied Aberdeen, thus forestalling a landing there from Hamilton's ships.

York gave Charles a friendly reception. He and his immediate suite were lodged in the handsome residence which Wentworth had enlarged for his use as Lord President of the North. The time was spent in drilling and reviews. Endymion's protégé D'avenant was there, serving as paymaster with the King's ordnance under Olive's brother-in-law, the Earl of Newport. Before he left London, he had secured a patent from the King for the erection of a new playhouse in Fleet Street, but a hitch had developed, and on April 16th Endymion wrote from York to Harvey asking him to follow D'avenant's business up with the Duke of Lennox and Lord Keeper Coventry and to pay the charges for sealing the patent.[4]

On May 1st, the King moved north to Durham. Two days later Endymion wrote from there to Harvey:

'I thank you for remembering my gauntlets and I pray you see that they be finished with all the haste you can, and send them to me with the pistols, if Mr. Courten have as yet procured them; likewise I would have you furnish me with half a dozen quires of paper, for we can get none here, and all my store is spent. . . . These pernicious rebels are very insolent, but the English are not afeared of them and I have sent my wife a proclamation which the King hath now sent into Scotland. I would have you read it, and with my hearty commendation to you, I rest

Your true friend

Endymion Porter.'[5]

The proclamation, a copy of which Endymion sent to Olive, had been issued on May 1st, with orders that it was to be read at the Cross in Edinburgh and in every shire. It was a hectoring document, declaring that if the Covenanters' leaders, including Argyll, Montrose and Leslie, submitted within twenty-four hours their cases would receive favourable consideration. Otherwise, a price would be put on their heads. No Scot, however, could be found to read the proclamation.

Young Charles Porter had just returned from Spain and Endymion was anxious to know what his two-year sojourn in Madrid had done for him. So he added a postscript to his letter to Harvey. 'I pray you send me truly your opinion of Charles.'[6]

In spite of the failure of Hamilton's plan to take Leith and effect a landing, and of the poor condition of the royal troops, Charles now determined to advance to the Border. From Newcastle, on the way north, Endymion wrote again to Harvey, asking him to send up some fine calico and two pairs of leather breeches. He also sent instructions

about forwarding a gold watch which he was having made
for the King.[7]

On May 28th, Berwick was reached and the royal party
took up their quarters with the army under canvas. Having
received some reinforcements, Charles decided to take the
offensive, but the increase in his army only made its payment and maintenance more difficult. The Scots, too,
advanced and reached Kelso. The Earl of Holland was
ordered to drive them back, but when he saw the enemy
in front of him, he hastily retired over the Tweed, and
Leslie and his well supplied and disciplined main army
encamped a dozen miles from Berwick. The Scots were,
however, reluctant to risk rousing English national feelings by an invasion. Instead, they sent Commissioners to
open negotiations which Charles was in no position to
refuse, since his exchequer was empty and the City of
London had firmly refused him the £100,000 loan which
he had demanded. On June 18th, the King signed the
Treaty of Berwick. Endymion at once sent the good news
to Olive and to Harvey. 'The peace is now concluded,' he
wrote to the latter, 'and I have sent my wife the articles
and conditions which you may copy out and send to Sir
William Calley.' 'I pray you get my pension if you can,'
he added, 'for all my money is spent.'[8] The peace conditions were that the Scots undertook to disband their
army and return the royal castles to the King, while Charles
engaged to disperse his troops and to consent to the holding of a General Assembly, followed by a Parliament in
Edinburgh in August.

Neither side, however, had confidence in the other. Some
of the Covenanting Lords refused to come to Berwick to
meet the King, and Charles, in turn, refused to go to
Edinburgh to open the Parliament. By the beginning of
August Endymion was back in London with his master,
having sent his two trunks south by sea with Arundel's
baggage.[9] Before he left Berwick, the King took the fateful
step of summoning Wentworth from Ireland.

The Lord Deputy was no stranger to Endymion, who had written to him on a number of occasions during his years in Ireland. Endymion's letters were either to recommend some friend to Wentworth's good offices or were on the subject of his Irish mining interests or his Shannon drainage scheme.[10] Wentworth's arrival in London stiffened Charles's attitude. Traquair, who had succeeded Hamilton as Charles's Commissioner in Edinburgh, was ordered to prorogue the Scottish Parliament until next summer and preparations were begun for a renewal of the war. But money had to be found, and Wentworth, confident in his ability to manage an English Parliament as he had managed Irish ones, urged Charles to summon a Parliament to vote him the necessary supplies.

(ii)

The winter of 1639–40 was to be the Court's last season of that happy gaiety in which Endymion and Olive shared. Charles and Wentworth—whom the King created Earl of Strafford in January—looked forward with confidence to the meeting of the new Parliament in the spring. Strafford thought that he had the measure of his old colleagues, the surviving parliamentary leaders, and believed that he could organize a Court party which, with the co-operation of the King and the Council, would be too strong for the opposition. Meantime a Council of War, with Endymion's old friend Nicholas as its efficient secretary, went ahead with preparations for the Scottish campaign. Northumberland was appointed Lord General and Lord Conway Deputy General and General of the Horse.

The Queen's pregnancy was a cause of Court rejoicing and the masque produced in January was one of the finest ever staged. Once again, D'avenant wrote the libretto and Inigo Jones designed the scenery, costumes and gorgeous spectacles. The masque was called *Salmacida Spolia* and its comforting theme was the triumph of Charles, as 'Philo-

genes or the lover of his people', over discord and tumult.
At its climax the King himself appeared, surrounded by
Lennox and nine other noble masquers, clad in powder
blue, silver and gold, while, from the sky, a large
multicoloured cloud floated down, in the centre of
which sat the Queen with ten of her ladies garbed as
Amazons.[11]

In the country, however, discord was not so easily
routed as in D'avenant's masque. Led by the officers and
shareholders of the Providence Company—Pym, St. John,
Warwick, Saye, Hampden and their friends—the opposition proved much more successful than the Court party
in getting their candidates returned to the new Parliament,
which met on April 13th. Skilfully marshalled by Pym,
the King's critics at once attacked the royal policies and
demanded redress of grievances before voting supplies.
Ship-money, monopolies, breaches of privilege, and religion
were all to be reopened. Strafford vainly sought to promote
a breach between Lords and Commons. The deadlock between opposition and King was complete, and on May 5th
Charles dissolved the Short Parliament.

Firmness was now Charles's resolution. He remained
optimistic, believing that the Scottish army was in poor
condition and that there was dissension among the Covenanting Lords. There was some substance in this latter
belief, in that Montrose had been in correspondence with
the King and with friends at the Court. He was unhappy
at the complete flouting of the King's authority and had
openly quarrelled with Argyll. Nevertheless, he and his
men joined the Scots army on the Border. In England,
Charles arrested and imprisoned Warwick, Saye, Pym,
Hampden and other parliamentary leaders, while Laud,
regardless of the fierce opposition certain to be roused,
pushed boldly on with his Church reforms. May Day in
London was marked by riots, and in the country generally
the gentry were even more dilatory than the year before
in raising local levies of troops. When mustered, the levies

frequently rioted and deserted. In several cases, they even murdered Catholic officers.

Endymion spent part of the summer in attendance on the King at Oatlands, where, in July, the Queen gave birth to a boy, christened Henry and created Duke of Gloucester. There was an important event, too, this summer in Endymion's own family, when George got married. It was a Court affair, the bride, Diana, being the daughter of Lord Goring, a leader of the Court monopolists, who in 1644 was to be made Earl of Norwich. Diana was the young widow of Thomas Covert, a Sussex gentleman. George Porter was already a friend of his new brother-in-law, George Goring, a brilliant but spendthrift and utterly unscrupulous young courtier, who had been wounded and lamed at Breda. Clarendon described George Goring in searing words. 'His ambition was unlimited and he was unrestrained by any respect to justice or good nature from pursuing the satisfaction thereof . . . and of all his quali-fications, dissimulation was his masterpiece.'[12] George Porter had inherited some of the charm and much of the instability of the Villiers blood, and George Goring's influ-ence on his young brother-in-law was to be disastrous.

Endymion had procured commissions in the royal army for both his elder sons. George became one of the King's Trumpeters and, through the Earl of Pembroke, was given the captaincy of a troop of horse under Conway's com-mand.[13] Charles was made a cornet of horse, serving with his uncle Lord Newport.[14] In April, George received orders from Conway to proceed to Newcastle with his troop. He was commanded to pay for everything on the way and to take special precautions against his men committing any disorderly or oppressive acts.[15] In spite of these instructions, George and his troop were soon in trouble. A furious com-plaint, witnessed by two local constables and the post-master's brother-in-law, came from Darlington that George's lieutenant and cornet had stolen a horse from the house in which they were billeted, had beaten up the owner of the house and his wife and children and would have killed the constable if he had not fled.[16]

George Butler, who had brought Charles Porter back from Spain, accompanied him as far as York on his way to join the army at Newcastle. From York, Butler wrote to Conway commending the young cornet to his care.[17] Charles was just seventeen. On May 20th, he sent a letter full of boyish enthusiasm to his father in London. It was the last that his parents were to get from him.

'Dear Sir,' he wrote, 'This is only to let you know how unwilling I am and have been since my coming hither to let slip any occasion of writing to you, for yesterday I did present my duty to you and to my mother in another packet, which I sent by the post, and knowing for certain that this will be safely delivered, I will give you an account of those things which I wrote in the other packet, for we hear say that all the letters that come from hence are broken open. My Lord uses me extremely kindly, for which I must entreat you to give him my thanks, and this last week he saw me exercise the troop, and was very well pleased with me. I hear, Sir, that you have received the trunk and swords out of Spain. Pray, Sir, if you please, make that sword of Luis de Ayala to be put into such a hilt as my brother's black one, and let it be deep enough that I might thrust both my fingers into it, for I like a good sword extremely. I have not had the happiness to hear from you since I came from London but once, which hath not troubled me a little, therefore I beseech you to let me hear from you as soon as you can, for there is nothing can be so welcome to

Your dutiful and obedient son
Charles Porter.

Pray, Sir, remember my most humble duty to my mother.'[18]

Lord Conway, at Newcastle, had been contemptuous of the Scottish army; but in the middle of August he wrote to London that he was expecting an immediate attack and could not hold Newcastle, whose fortifications were still unfinished. The King at once determined to go north to join his army and on August 20th he left London for York. Endymion was in attendance on his master, and Strafford, though worn with illness, followed.

On the same day as Charles left London the Scots crossed the Tweed, Montrose wading the river at the head of the army. By the time the King arrived in York, the Scots had reached the Tyne. Strafford was most dissatisfied with Conway's conduct. At a conference at York on August 29th he asked why Conway had not completed the fortifications of Newcastle, for which there had been ample time. Colonel Arthur Aston, who had come from Conway, replied that there had been no orders from the King to do so. Strafford then demanded why Conway had not engaged the Scots with his cavalry; to which Aston answered that if he had done so, the cavalry would have run away in face of the Scots artillery. Hamilton and other courtiers joined in Strafford's criticisms, but Endymion, who was present, supported Aston and fetched the King to the meeting. When the King came Aston repeated his rebuttal of the charges.[19]

The same day the King advanced with his troops to Northallerton to reinforce Conway. It was too late. The day before, Friday, August 28th, Conway had marched out of Newcastle with two thousand horse and three thousand foot to bar the crossing of the Tyne at the ford by the village of Newburn, six miles west of Newcastle. They found the Scots army of four thousand horse and two thousand three hundred foot approaching the village on the north bank. Conway hastily threw up and manned two earthworks to command the ford. About four in the afternoon, after a few musket shots had been exchanged, Leslie mounted one of his cannon on the tower of Newburn Church. From this dominating eminence he so battered the English earthworks that, when the Scots started to cross the river, the garrison of one fled and that of the other made little resistance. A gallant cavalry charge led by young Harry Wilmot temporarily checked the advance, but the Scottish cannon fire was too hot for the raw English troops and when the Scots came on again they swept over the English foot, and the English horse fled in panic.

The English casualties were very few, but amongst them was Charles Porter. Young Charles, Spanish sword in hand, had charged with Wilmot, only to be killed. 'There fell Endymion Porter's second son,' wrote a witness, 'a youth as much pitied as famed for his brave carriage and valiantness.'[20] Abandoning Newcastle, which the Scots entered the next day, Conway fell back on Durham, while the King returned to York. The death of the King's godson, the golden-haired youth of so fair a promise, was widely lamented. 'I have no words to express my sorrow for that brave young cavalier of so great expectations,' wrote a friend to Harvey.[21] It had fallen to Endymion and Olive to make the first great personal sacrifice in King Charles's cause.

Neither Strafford nor the King was disposed to accept the defeat at Newburn as final. Hopes were still placed on the possibility of landing some of Strafford's Irish army in Scotland with the co-operation of Hamilton and the fleet. But in London, Pym and his friends, released from imprisonment, were again active and the capital was seething with discontent and rumours. Hysterical fear of Rome prompted the wildest stories. Antrim's boastings and the existence of Strafford's well trained Irish troops lent colour to beliefs in an Irish plot to destroy the Protestant religion in England. Endymion's name was involved in some of the rumours. A political satire, classing Endymion with Tobie Matthew and Kenelm Digby as 'birds of a feather', declared that they were 'blowing the coals of dissension' against the Scots because they were not idolatrous and would have no mass.[22]

But a much more serious tale now inculpated Endymion, who was still at York with the King. In the middle of

September Charles received a most urgent and secret letter from Laud in London. The Archbishop was almost hysterical with anxiety. It was, he wrote, 'the greatest business that was ever put to me' and it had made him fall into 'an extreme faint sweat'. The cause was a letter that had just reached him from Sir William Boswell, the Ambassador at The Hague. In it Boswell, enjoining great secrecy, had told him of a plot against the lives of the King and the Archbishop, with the intent to destroy the Protestant religion. News of the plot had been revealed to Boswell by one Andreas ab Habernfeld, reputed to be a chaplain to the Queen of Bohemia, who said that he had the story from one of the conspirators turned informer. Boswell urged Laud to give him authority to make further investigations and to offer a reward to the informer for the full story.

Charles took Laud's letter calmly. Laud had written that 'this information is either true or there is some mistake in it', on which Charles's dry marginal comment was 'it is an unanswerable dilemma!' But he replied, in secret as Laud had urged, authorising him to tell Boswell to make full inquiries.

In the middle of October, Boswell sent Laud 'the large particulars' of the plot. The informer, who still refused to give his name, was apparently an English clergyman who had been persuaded by Con to become a papist and join the conspiracy on the promise of great promotion. The plot was a Jesuit one, with Con at its head, abetted by a number of people close to the King, namely Arundel and his wife, 'she champion of the popish religion'; Gage, who was alleged to maintain a nunnery in his house which was full of 'lascivious pictures'; a Scottish captain called Read, 'a secular Jesuit'; Tobie Matthew, who 'neither day nor night spareth his machinations', and—Endymion Porter. The informer described Endymion as 'Master Porter of the King's Bedchamber, most addicted to the Popish religion, is a bitter enemy of the King. He reveals all his greatest secrets to the Pope's legate. Although he very rarely meets with him, yet his wife meets him so much the oftener, who, being informed by her husband, conveys secrets to the Legate. In all his actions, he is nothing inferior to Tobie Matthew; it cannot be uttered how diligently he watcheth all the business. His sons are secretly instructed in the Popish religion, openly they profess the Reformed. The eldest is now to receive his father's office under the King which shall be. A cardinal's hat is provided for the other, if the Design shall succeed well. Above three years past, the said Master Porter was to be sent away by the King to Morocco, but he was prohibited by the Society, lest the business should suffer delay thereby. He is a patron of the Jesuits, for whom for the exercise of religion, he provides chapels both at home and abroad.'

Con, reported the informer, kept 'an Indian nut, stuffed with most sharp poison' ready to kill the King, and it was the conspirators who had provoked the Scottish war in order to bring about the King's downfall. The story was further embellished with all the trappings of mysterious weekly meetings and disguises.

It is difficult to imagine how Boswell could have placed any credence in such an obviously trumped up tale. But the Parliamentary leaders seem generally to have believed that such plots were being hatched by the Catholics, and some colour seemed to be given to their fears by the favour shown to Catholics at the Court, by Charles's friendship with the Papal agents and, above all, by the activities of intriguers in the Queen's household. That Endymion should have been named as one of the chief conspirators was a measure of the harm that Olive's conduct had done to his reputation outside the Court.

Fortunately, Charles knew how fantastic the story was and dismissed it with the contempt it deserved. Three years later, however, Prynne found the correspondence among Laud's papers and had it published, by order of Parliament, as a pamphlet entitled 'Rome's Masterpiece.'

It confirmed Parliament's view of Endymion as being beyond pardon.[23]

George was still on service with his troop of cavalry on the Durham–Yorkshire border. His father wrote several letters to him from York, sending him clothes and gloves. George had been ill, so Endymion despatched some medicines which had cured Endymion's brother Giles, as well as 'two pasties of venison, the overcast one if you heat it in the oven will be excellent hot, the upright one is to eat cold'. George's hounds, which were with his father at York, were also sent up to him. With Charles dead, Endymion and Olive were doubly anxious about George, the more since he neglected to write to them. Olive asked the Queen to use her influence with the King to get George sent home, and Endymion, signing his letters 'your truest friend and most loving father', urged his son 'to keep a careful watch, for therein consists your safety; sleep in the day and watch the nights.' But stories of George's wild behaviour reached them and his father wrote again, 'Though you take your pleasure in the day, yet see you be vigilant in the night . . . this I charge you now to look to, and see that you obey me in something, for your own good and your honour.'[24] Olive's letter from London, written with a heart aching from the loss of Charles, was much sharper.

'George,' she wrote, 'I am very sorry that you continue still your disorder without having any sense of Almighty God that hath preserved you from so many dangers, and if that would not move you, if you had any good nature or sense of the affliction your father and I suffer, you would not do it, you knowing that I love you more than my soul. Dear child, do not add to my affliction, for if I fail of having comfort in thee there is nought for me in this life. Farewell, my heart, and make haste home.

Your most affectionate Mother.'[25]

All attention was now focused on the elections for the new Parliament. The King's friends worked hard to increase

the return of his supporters and Endymion was nominated
as one of the candidates for Droitwich in Worcestershire.
It was a Borough, returning two members, where the
franchise was limited to the mayor, aldermen and a few
burgesses. In the Short Parliament, Droitwich had been
represented by Sandys, a royalist and head of a prominent
Worcestershire family, and by Wilde, a lawyer, who had
represented the Borough in earlier Parliaments and was
known as an outspoken critic of the King's domestic and
foreign policies. Wilde had, however, become Recorder of
Worcester and was a candidate for one of the Worcester
City seats, so that his place at Droitwich was now vacant.[26]

Endymion had no territorial connections with Worcestershire, although Aston was only just across the Gloucestershire border, but he may have been favourably known
locally through taking an interest in a scheme for making
navigable the River Salwarpe on which Droitwich stands,
and which, if successful, would have considerably cheap-
ened the transport of Droitwich salt.[27] He probably owed
his nomination, however, to the Windsor family who had
important local landed interests. Endymion had long known
the 6th Baron Windsor, who had been second-in-command
of the fleet that brought Prince Charles and Endymion
back from Spain in 1623. No doubt, too, the burgesses had
hopes of rewards from one so well-placed in the King's
favour as Endymion. In the wider franchise of the counties,
the forty-shilling freeholders came in thousands to the
county towns to be entertained by the candidates before
the noisy and turbulent poll. But in the close Borough of
Droitwich, Endymion and Sandys were elected without a
contest.

CHAPTER X

(i)

ON November 3rd 1640, the King, omitting most of the customary pageantry, went by water from Whitehall to Westminster to open the new Parliament, in which Endymion took his seat. The great majority of the four hundred and ninety-three members were firmly convinced that the King's policies and Government had been wholly bad and that 'they must not only sweep the house clean below, but must pull down all the cobwebs which hung in the top and corners, that they might not breed dust and so make a foul house hereafter'.[1] Their first object must be to apply the traditional remedy of getting rid of the King's Ministers, headed by Strafford and Laud. There was also a strong element, led by Pym and Hampden in the Commons, who believed that much more than a change of Ministers was needed, and that the only safeguard against despotism in Church and State was the transfer of effective power from the King to Parliament. Those, like Endymion, who could be counted upon to support the King were a small minority, and, as allies, the King's critics had the formidable support of the disciplined Scottish Army, still occupying the North of England.

The King's opening speech, in which he referred to the Scots as rebels, was coolly received. For the first week, Endymion listened to member after member presenting petitions and complaints against abuses—ship-money, monopolies, innovations in religion, Star Chamber sentences and other invasions of the liberty of the subject. Pym's tactics were to let the full weight of the recital of these grievances sink in before launching his attack on Strafford. But the latter's arrival in London forced Pym's hand. He had to strike before Strafford could launch his counter-stroke of accusing the Parliamentary leaders of treasonable correspondence with the Scots. On November 11th, Strafford took his seat in the Lords. In the Commons, behind locked doors, articles of impeachment against Strafford were hastily drawn up with the full agreement of such a majority as Endymion and his fellow supporters of the King were powerless to obstruct. Late in the afternoon, Pym, followed by three hundred members, went to the Lords to demand that Strafford should be imprisoned on the Commons' charge of high treason. Hearing the news, Strafford re-entered the Lords, but was ordered to withdraw by his fellow peers who, as a body, were as hostile to him as were the Commons. In his absence, they agreed to the Commons' request and he was only recalled to be made to kneel and hear their sentence of custody. Within a few weeks, Laud had also been impeached and was in the Tower, while Secretary Windebank and Lord Keeper Finch had fled the country.

The local levies in the English Army had gone home, but the cavalry and some of the specially raised infantry were still in Yorkshire. Amongst them was George Porter and his troop. Like the rest of the Army, they were grumbling at their arrears of pay, especially since any money that Parliament could find was being sent to support the Scots. George was also complaining about the way he was being treated by his commanding officer. Matters were not improved by an order that each Captain was to make good his troop's deficiencies in horses and weapons out of his own pocket. In George's troop of fifty, fourteen men had no horses, while fifteen carbines, eight cases of pistols and some headpieces and back and breast plates were missing. George was also in trouble when a number of his men broke into a house near Doncaster and made off with what they could find. George succeeded in getting a £10 advance of pay, but soon afterwards he resigned his commission and was back with the family in London by the end of the year.[2]

The dissatisfaction among the troops at their neglect was brought to a head early in March next year, when the Commons took £10,000 which had been assigned to the English Army and transferred it to help increase their contributions towards the pay of the Scots. Led by Henry Percy, Northumberland's brother, a group of the King's supporters in the Commons planned to get the Army officers to sign a declaration that they would stand by the King if Parliament tried to compel him to exclude the Bishops from the Lords or to disband the Irish Army before the Scots forces were disbanded. Endymion was a party to their plans, which had the King's approval. With the Queen's encouragement, however, Jermyn, the Master of her Horse, abetted by the irresponsible poets Suckling and D'avenant, were already planning much more drastic action. Their scheme was to replace Northumberland by Newcastle as the head of the Army and to appoint the ambitious and unscrupulous George Goring, George Porter's brother-in-law, as Lieutenant General, under whose command the Army would then march to London and seize the Tower. Matters were hastened towards the end of March by the arrival from Yorkshire of Captain Chudleigh, who brought with him a letter from the Army officers to Northumberland setting out their grievances. At a meeting with Jermyn and Goring, Percy and his friends refused to have anything to do with the plan to make Goring Lieutenant General and to bring the Army to London. When the dispute was referred to the King, he had no hesitation in siding with Percy. Seeing his ambitions thus dashed, Goring decided to curry favour with Parliament by betraying his friends. He warned Newport of the conspiracy and Newport, in turn, told Bedford and Pym. They decided to keep their knowledge to themselves for the moment and to let Goring go back to his post at Portsmouth.

The Queen and Jermyn, ignoring the King's refusal of support, now sent Chudleigh back to Yorkshire with instructions to urge the Army to accept Goring as their General and to be ready to move south. At a meeting at Boroughbridge on April 3rd, the Army officers agreed to give Chudleigh a letter to Goring 'heartily embracing him' as their Lieutenant General. Chudleigh was also given a letter to Endymion signed by Lieutenant Colonels Vavasour and Fielding to ask him to assure the King of their fidelity and of their acceptance of Goring. When Chudleigh reached London, however, he was intercepted by Suckling who took the letter, telling Chudleigh that Endymion was a 'stranger to the business' and knew nothing of the King's intentions.[3] It is clear that Endymion, though aware of Jermyn's, Suckling's and D'avenant's rash plans, had no part in the Queen's and Jermyn's disloyalty in disregarding the King's decision to reject them. In intercepting the letter to Endymion, Suckling was concerned to keep the King in the dark as to how far the conspirators had gone.

Meantime, all eyes had been turned to Westminster Hall, where Strafford's trial opened on March 22nd. From Burderop, William Calley wrote to ask Harvey to be sure to get him a cheap book of Strafford's trial and defence.[4] Wooden scaffolding supporting tiers of benches had been erected in the Hall to accommodate the numbers who wished to hear the impeachment. From one of these benches Endymion and members of the Commons watched the proceedings. Charles and the Queen also came every day, sitting in a special box. Pym opened the case for the prosecution, starting with Strafford's administration in Ireland and leading up to Article 23, the accusation that he had threatened to employ the Irish Army against England. In support of this grave and treasonable charge, Pym had, up his sleeve, a copy of Secretary Vane's notes of a Council meeting, held a year before. These notes had surreptitiously been copied by Vane's son and shown to Pym who had made a copy of young Vane's copy. According to the notes, Strafford had spoken to the King of 'an Army in Ireland you may employ here to reduce this kingdom'. Pym now called Secretary Vane to bear witness that Strafford had advised Charles to use the Irish Army to put down the opposition in England. Strafford's masterly and vigorous defence had already disposed of Pym's earlier charges. In reply to Vane, he called other members of the Council who testified that the Council had been considering ways of reducing Scotland, not England, and that Strafford had never contemplated using the Irish troops anywhere but in Scotland. When, on April 10th, Pym demanded the right to produce new evidence in the shape of young Vane's notes, Strafford also claimed the right to summon new witnesses for the defence. The Lords decided in Strafford's favour, and the Commons, with angry shouts, withdrew from the Hall. The King was seen to be laughing. It was clear that the attempt at impeachment had failed to convict Strafford of anything that could be called treason under the existing laws.

From the start, however, Pym had been convinced that nothing short of Strafford's death would prevent his future return to power, when Pym and his friends would suffer the same fate as had overtaken Eliot. That afternoon, in the Commons, he launched his second attack. If the legal process of impeachment had failed, he would proceed by Bill of Attainder, by which a majority in Parliament could pass an Act that Strafford was guilty of treason and should be executed. Strafford's final speech to the Lords on the impeachment charge appealed to their sense of law and justice, and he was heard with sympathy. But in the Commons, Pym pressed on with the Bill of Attainder. On April 21st, the vote was taken. Two hundred and four members voted for passing the Bill and only fifty-nine against. Endymion was, of course, among the fifty-nine. Such was the temper of the Commons that a list of the names of those who had voted against the Bill was posted up in Old Palace Yard. The persons named were labelled 'Straffordians, betrayers of their country'. As was intended, this unprecedented procedure roused the fury of the mob against those who had voted for Strafford's acquittal.[5]

All now turned on whether the Lords would pass the Bill of Attainder. Charles had some confidence that they would refuse to do so.

But London was full of wild rumours of plots, and crowds were besieging Westminster. It was in this atmosphere already so heavily charged with fear and suspicion that Pym now revealed to the Commons the Army plot that Goring had betrayed to him. The courtiers concerned fled. Percy, Jermyn and Suckling succeeded in reaching France, but D'avenant, conspicuous from lack of a nose, was apprehended at Faversham and brought back to London. Crowds, shouting for justice, surrounded the House of Lords. Only forty-eight peers were in their seats when the vote on the Bill of Attainder was taken, and only eleven voted against it.

Strafford had nobly written to the King from the Tower to release him from his promise to save him, but Charles's agony of mind, which Endymion must have shared, was only relieved by Bishop Williams's advice to separate his public from his private conscience. On May 10th, two days after the Lords had passed the Bill of Attainder, Charles brought himself to give it his assent. At the same time he passed Pym's bill prohibiting the dissolution of the present Parliament without its own consent. The next day, torn by conscience, Charles sent the eleven-year-old Prince of Wales to the Lords to appeal for mercy. It was in vain. Twenty-four hours later, before an immense throng of spectators, Strafford, unflinching, met his end on the scaffold.

Charles was now forced to promise to disband the Irish Army. He told the Spanish Ambassador that some of the soldiers would be available for service under the King of Spain for his war with Portugal. George Porter was one of four officers who were given the rank of colonel and ordered each to raise a regiment of one thousand men from the Irish forces and take them to Spain. In June, George went to

Dublin, bearing a letter from the King to the Earl of Ormonde, who had been given charge of the Irish Army when Wentworth came to England.

'Ormonde,' Charles wrote, 'I have taken this occasion by the recommending the son of one of my faithful servants to assure you that I very much esteem you and that I do but seek an occasion to show it you by more than words, as I commanded the Vice-Treasurer to tell you more fully, and in particular concerning the Blue Riband of which you may be confident, only I desire you not to take notice of it until I shall think it fit. The particular for this bearer, George Porter, is to permit him to make up a Regiment of the Disbanded Army, if he can do it by permission to carry them out of the country for the King of Spain's service. This is all, so I rest

Your assured friend

Charles R.

Whitehall, 19 June. 1641.'[6]

George, however, never sailed for Spain with his Irish troops. There were delays and objections on the part of some members of the Irish Parliament. Finally, in August, the English House of Commons refused to allow any Irish troops to be used in Spain. Events were very shortly to show how unfortunate this decision was.

(ii)

It was on Scotland rather than on Ireland that Charles's first hopes were pinned. Although the terms of a peace treaty had been settled, there was a growing coolness between the Scottish Commissioners and the English Parliament, and in Scotland, a moderate party seemed to be forming. Hamilton had been wooing Argyll, while Montrose, jealous of Argyll and looking to the Crown as a balance against the factious Scottish nobility, had been in private correspondence with Charles, but had been imprisoned when the King's reply was intercepted. In the belief that he could win the Covenanters to his side and bring Scottish influence to bear on England, Charles resolved to open the Parliament in Edinburgh in person.

On August 10th he set out for Scotland, accompanied by Hamilton, Lennox and the Elector Palatine, for whose service Scottish military aid was ostensibly to be enlisted. Endymion went with his master, having obtained leave of absence from the House of Commons.[7] The Queen stayed behind at Oatlands, and Olive and her children removed to Woodhall from the plague-infested capital. The King left Endymion's friend Nicholas to act as his watchdog in London and report to him. At Newcastle, Charles and his suite were entertained by General Leslie, and the King reviewed the Scottish Army which was on the eve of disbandment. On August 14th, the royal party rode into Edinburgh. Pursuing his policy of ingratiating himself with his Scottish subjects, the King attended Presbyterian Church services and ratified all the legislation passed by the last Scottish Parliament. He received Argyll warmly and ignored Montrose, who was still a prisoner in Edinburgh Castle. Charles was magnificently entertained amid scenes of loyal rejoicing and wrote to Nicholas that all difficulties had been overcome.

In fact, however, Argyll's determination to be master of Scotland was in no way altered. He had already won Hamilton over, and he was willing to show goodwill to Charles only in so far as the King's subservience strengthened his hands against those nobles, such as Montrose, who had no wish to exchange Charles's rule for that of Argyll. Endymion had no share in his master's facile optimism. He could see how Argyll, making full use of his influence with Hamilton, was merely taking advantage of Charles's conciliatory tactics for his own ends, and he was under no illusion that Charles, by giving in to Argyll, was succeeding in winning Scotland to his side against the opposition in England.

'Much honoured friend,' Endymion wrote to Nicholas on

September 7th. 'We have no certainty of our return, for
his Majesty's business runs in the wonted channels, subtle
designs of gaining the popular opinion and weak executions
for the upholding of monarchy. The King is yet persuaded
to hold out, but within two or three days must yield to
all; and here are legislators that know how to handle him,
for they have his bosom friend* sure, and play the game as
he directs them, that sees both. Traquair dares not appear
and though Montrose be in hold, he is so gallant a gentleman and so well-beloved as they will be fearful to meddle
with him, but will keep him up so long as the King is
here, for they imagine he would turn Caesarian. I take
the boldness to mention you now and then to his Majesty,
and he speaks most graciously of you. I pray God bless
him and send him quickly and safe into England, where I
am sure they desire him heartily at this time.

Your faithful friend and humble servant

Endymion Porter.[8]

Four days later, Endymion wrote again to Nicholas. His
first letter had shown his good judgement. In this second
letter, the honesty of his character also emerged, despising
appeasement at the expense of loyal friends, and steadfast
in his own duty, in spite of the disasters that he saw looming ahead.

'Since my last unto you,' Endymion wrote, 'there is
nothing of news, but one and the same delay to bring the
King to be weary of staying here and so to yield to all
their desire (which he is most apt to do) and so to streighten
time, as he must leave all such as have appeared contrary
to the humours of the Covenanters to be judged by them,
which may cost some of them dear. And they that scape
best will repent that they ever showed themselves for the
King; for the public applause opposes monarchy and I
fear this Island before it be long will be a theatre of dis-
tractions. God Almighty send you much happiness and
give every true-hearted Englishman a right judgement

* Hamilton.

to study the preservation of our nation, for we are like to see lamentable times; but if there be a fate in it, we cannot discern the secrets of heaven, but must submit to all. I am sure I am and ever will be

Your most affectionate friend and humble servant
Endymion Porter.'[9]

Charles's honeymoon with Argyll was short-lived. When it came to appointing the Officers of State, the King was forced to discard his choice and accept Argyll's nominees, while Leslie's troops, some of whom he had hoped would be placed at his disposal, were all sent home. But Argyll's enemies were also active. Early in October, a group of hard-drinking royalist soldiers of fortune, headed by the Catholic Earl of Crawford, plotted to seize Argyll and Hamilton when they visited Charles's lodgings in Holyroodhouse. Will Murray, Endymion's fellow groom of the Bedchamber, was deep in the plot and was to admit them. As in the case of the Army plot in England, one of the conspirators turned informer. Neither Charles nor Endymion was implicated, but the consequences were gravely damaging to Charles's position in Scotland. He was refused the public inquiry that he demanded and his protestations of innocence failed to dispel general suspicion and mistrust.

On October 27th, while Charles was playing golf, momentous news reached him from Ireland. The King's plans for winning over the Covenanters had been accompanied by the hope of also gaining support for the royal cause from the Catholic Lords in Ireland. During the summer, Charles had been in correspondence with the Protestant Ormonde and with the Catholic Lord Antrim. While the King was not responsible for what followed, his intrigue with the Irish Catholic Lords helped to spark off a situation which was, in itself, highly explosive. The whole of native Ireland was in a desperate mood. During the last thirty years, plantations of English and Scottish settlers had evicted the Irish from the richest lands in Ulster and elsewhere. Further evictions were threatened. The Irish also feared, not without cause, that their religion, long persecuted, would soon be extirpated by a Puritan-dominated English Parliament. A proud and warlike people were bound, sooner or later, to resort to armed rebellion in defence of their lands, their religion and their liberty. And now, Strafford's firm hand had been replaced by the feeble grasp of two Lords Justices, while Strafford's Irish Army, instead of being sent overseas, had been disbanded to scatter armed and trained men all over Ireland.

The news that reached Charles in Edinburgh on October 27th was that a rebellion had begun, but that, by good fortune, information of what was afoot had come in time to save Dublin, although in Ulster, the Irish chieftain, Sir Phelim O'Neill, was carrying all before him. Apart from sharing his master's anxiety over the effect of the rebellion on the possibility of Irish support, Endymion had his own special concern about the fate of his drainage venture and other financial interests in Ireland. He had, too, good friends there, such as Sir William St. Leger, the President of Munster, whose lives might be in danger. Two days later he sent a letter to Ormonde.

'My most honoured Lord,' he wrote, 'I would I had as much power and worth in me to serve your Lordship as I have ambition to be known to you; then I am sure the obligations I owe you should not be long unrequited nor I fail in that I so much desire. But your Lordship hath a gallant disposition that looks upon truth and goodwill with equal eyes; and therein my condition may be compared with the best, for no man can love your Lordship better nor honour him more than I do.

This gentleman will acquaint your Lordship how the affairs do stand here, which rather recoil than advance to his Majesty's service. But what fate it is that rules us, I know not; sure it must be an untoward one that hath put three kingdoms into such a tottering disease, as at this day the King himself cannot say he is absolute over either of them. And if the news that is brought hither

of a revolt there be true, unless his Majesty make use
instantly of your Lordship's wisdom and courage to save
Ireland, it will quite be lost at once, while the other two
moulder away. But I am no statesman; my course is in a
lower sphere. I can wish well, and pray for his Majesty;
and whensoever your Lordship shall be pleased to command
me,

    I am, by conquest and free will
        Your Lordship's most devoted humble servant
                Endymion Porter.

Edinburgh, this 29th October, 1641.'[10]

The full tale of what was happening in Ireland did not
immediately reach Edinburgh or London. Then report
after shocking report filled England with shuddering horror
and alarm. The forces of savagery had been released. All
over Northern Ireland, English clergy and officials were
being hanged or stabbed to death. The English settlers and
their families were fortunate if they were merely beaten
and stripped of their clothes and driven naked to die of
hunger and cold in the bogs or on the hill-sides. Many
were tortured with the kind of bestiality made familiar
to the present age by Mau Mau, while their cattle hobbled
to death with their legs cut off. Women great with child
were ripped open and their unborn babies thrown to pigs
and dogs; men, women and children were slashed and
mangled so as to die a lingering death. It was said, too,
that, like Mau Mau, the leaders encouraged these atrocities
so as to put their followers beyond the hope of pardon.[11]
Some fifteen thousand English were probably killed in the
first weeks of the rebellion, though rumours greatly exaggerated this figure.

It was not long before the names of the King and of
Endymion were implicated in the rebellion. Sir Phelim
O'Neill boasted that he was acting on Charles's orders and
produced a Commission under the Great Seal of Scotland
dated October 1st, in which the King empowered his
Catholic subjects to rise, to capture all forts and castles

and 'to seize the goods, estates and persons of all English Protestants'.[12] All evidence shows that the Commission was a forgery, a fact confirmed by O'Neill when he was on trial for his life twelve years later. Even when offered a pardon if he would admit that the Commission was genuine, he maintained that he had forged it himself. But the story of O'Neill's Commission was none the less damaging to the King. According to one common rumour, which was later printed in a pamphlet, the Great Seal of Scotland, during a vacancy in the Lord Chancellor's office, had been entrusted to the keeping of Master Endymion Porter, who had clandestinely affixed it to the Commission.[13]

(iii)

Charles and Endymion left Edinburgh for London on November 18th. The King departed in an atmosphere of goodwill. Argyll was made a Marquis, and Leslie an Earl. In England, a reaction in the King's favour had set in during his absence. For this, the zeal of the Presbyterians in the House of Commons was largely responsible. Their attacks on the bishops and the organized Church had opened a breach between the Commons and the Lords. London, too, was full of religious fanatics, self-appointed prophets from the humblest walks of life, breaking into churches and preaching against their betters. The wealthy aldermen of the City took alarm and elected a royalist as the new Lord Mayor. In Parliament, moderate members, once Strafford had fallen and the King had conceded so much, had no wish to go to the extreme of completely overthrowing the royal power. Pym fought hard to rally his forces against this reaction. His chief weapon was a Grand Remonstrance, designed finally to discredit the King by recalling every grievance throughout his reign. The debate on the Remonstrance took place on November 22nd, while Charles and Endymion were on their way to

London. Not only the King's supporters, but former opposition leaders such as Hyde and Falkland objected to flouting the King's concessions and his apparently conciliatory attitude by raking up and publishing his past errors. Only fifty-nine members had voted against Strafford's attainder; now, one hundred and forty-eight voted against Pym's Grand Remonstrance, which was only carried by eleven votes amid scenes of angry tumult. Two days later, the Queen came out to meet Charles at Theobalds and Olive must certainly have joined her from near-by Woodhall to greet Endymion. The next day the King re-entered his capital to be magnificently welcomed by the City at a banquet in the Guildhall.

Charles's hopes that he had London on his side were soon shattered. The Lord Mayor and Aldermen might support him, but the new elections to the Common Council went strongly in favour of the Puritan opposition, and the city mobs showed their feelings in frequent rioting. In Parliament, and outside, the horrors of the Irish rebellion formed a dark background to men's thoughts this unhappy Christmas of 1641. At the end of December a letter to Endymion, dated December 3rd, from a friend in Dublin, Thomas Whyte, was read aloud in the Commons. It painted a gloomy picture. Ulster was completely lost. In Leinster and Connaught, most of the septs had risen and the English were besieged in their fortified places. Only in Munster were conditions better, thanks to the influence of Ormonde and St. Leger.[14]

If the King could have remained patiently on the defensive, taking his stand on the preservation of Church and constitution, Pym's attacks might well have alienated all moderate opinion. But Charles's hand was now forced. As the new year opened, he heard that the Parliament leaders had secretly determined to impeach the Queen. Charles was prepared to go to any lengths to avert such insult and danger from his loved wife. He agreed to follow her advice to strike first by impeaching her would-be impeachers. Pym, Hampden and three other members of the Commons were selected as the key offenders.

Endymion would have been in Charles's confidence when, after the Queen had called him a coward, the King finally resolved to go to the House of Commons in person to secure the arrest of the five members. But the secret of Charles's intentions was betrayed. Endymion was probably in his seat in the silent Commons that afternoon and witnessed his master's discomfiture when the King found that 'his birds were flown', and when Speaker Lenthall returned his historic answer to Charles's question where they were.

After the fiasco in the Commons and when threatening mobs were crowding round Whitehall and Westminster, Charles realized that the game was lost. His first thought was to get the Queen safely away from the country and out of the reach of her enemies. On January 10th, taking the Queen and the royal children with him, he hurriedly left Whitehall for Hampton Court. The next day, the five members triumphantly returned to Westminster by river, surrounded by gaily dressed boats, while the City trained bands marched on shore. At Hampton Court, no preparations had been made to receive the royal party and the King and Queen had to sleep in one room with their eldest children. On the 13th, the King and his family moved to Windsor. Endymion, in attendance on Charles, had left London equally hurriedly, while Olive and the children stayed at home in the Strand. She sent a message after him, asking for money and wondering whether she and the family should go for safety to Woodhall. Endymion had written to her as soon as he reached Hampton Court, but his servant Nick, to whom he entrusted the letter, had disappeared on a drunken spree. From Windsor, on the 14th, he sent Olive another letter.

'My dearest love,' he wrote, 'as for monies, I wonder you can imagine that I should help you, but you always look for impossibilities from me, and I wish it were a time of miracles, for then we might hope for a good success in everything. . . . I could wish you and your children in a safe place, but why Woodhall shall not be so I cannot yet tell; I could likewise wish my cabinets and all my other things were at Mr. Courten's, but if a very discreet man be not there and take the advice of the joiner to convey them thither, they will be as much spoiled in the carriage as with the rabble; dearest love, to serve God well is the way to everything that will lead us to a happy end, for then He will bless us and deliver us out of all troubles; I pray you have a care of yourself and make much of your children and I presume we shall be merry and enjoy one another long. . . . I will give you leave to kiss Mrs. Marie* for me; I wish sweet Tom† with me, for the King and Queen are forced to lie with their children now, and I envy their happiness. I pray you let this bearer come to me again when you hear where we rest, and so good night sweet Noll.

Your true friend and most loving husband
Endymion Porter.'[15]

The King was not to re-enter Whitehall until the day of his execution, and when Endymion, after his master was dead, next saw his London home, it was an uninhabitable ruin. Soldiers had been billeted in it, the doors were gone and even some of the walls pulled down.[16] Nor was Endymion ever again to enjoy any of the pictures and other treasures which he had so devotedly collected. Olive had adopted his suggestion and his valuables were moved to his friend Courten's house at Clapham, but eighteen months later, on the information of a servant, Parliament sent a search party to seize them, and Courten vainly tried to save them by saying that Endymion had given them to him in payment of a debt.[17]

It was at this crisis in his fortunes, with his comfortable world falling round his ears and with the future looming

* His elder daughter, Mary.
† His son Tom, aged six.

perilously black and uncertain, that Endymion reaffirmed to Olive the principle that guided all his conduct. 'Whither we go,' he wrote to her from Windsor, 'and what we are to do, I know not, for I am none of the Council; my duty and loyalty have taught me to follow my King and Master, and by the Grace of God, nothing shall divert me from it.'[18]

CHAPTER XI

(i)

ENDYMION followed the King and Queen from Windsor to Greenwich, where preparations were made for the Queen to leave for Holland, taking with her Princess Mary to rejoin her fifteen-year-old husband, the son of the Prince of Orange. The Queen also arranged to take her own and the Crown Jewels. It seems probable that Endymion's daughter Marie, who had just entered her teens, accompanied the Queen as one of her maids of honour. They all left Greenwich early in February. After spending three days in Canterbury, the Queen and her party embarked at Dover. Charles went down to the shore to say farewell. It was a tearful parting and the King could hardly tear himself away from his wife. The weather, too, was unkind. In a stormy passage one of the ships foundered with the loss of all the ornaments from the Queen's chapel, including a piece of the true cross, but the Queen and her ladies and the jewels reached The Hague safely.[1]

Charles and Endymion rode sadly back to Greenwich. Although the Commons begged the King to return to Whitehall, Charles was resolved to go north to York, where he believed he could rally his supporters and reassert his authority. Early in March he left Greenwich for Theobalds and Newmarket. Endymion was in attendance and the Prince of Wales was with them. At Newmarket, a parliamentary delegation waited on the King. Convinced that Parliament intended to strip him of his lawful authority in order to destroy the Church, Charles would not listen to the deputation and rejected out of hand the request to place the militia under parliamentary control. Accommodation between King and Parliament was, in fact, no longer possible.

On March 19th, the King and his party rode into York. At the end of January, Parliament had appointed a Committee to consider the removal from attendance on the King of those whom they suspected of exercising a malign influence. On February 15th the Commons resolved, though only by a majority of three, that amongst others 'Endymion Porter of the Bedchamber should be removed from the persons and courts of the King and Queen as one that is conceived to give dangerous counsel'. Endymion was also removed from his position as captain of the trained band company of Westminster.[2] Neither the King nor Endymion took any notice of the Commons' resolution, but two months later the Commons ordered that Endymion and his fellow member of Parliament, John Ashburnham, groom of the Prince of Wales's bedchamber, should be forthwith summoned to attend the House.[3] Endymion, safely in York, wrote to Speaker Lenthall excusing his non-attendance on the grounds that the King refused him leave of absence.[4] Charles sent a warrant to the Speaker ordering him to read a message to the House in which he stated that he had commanded Endymion and Ashburnham to stay with him for the performance of their duties and that he had no doubt but that this just excuse would be acceptable.[5] So far, however, was this from being the case, that the Commons resolved that if Endymion and Ashburnham were not in their places by May 16th they would be proceeded against for contempt.[6]

All that spring and summer of 1642 England was moving steadily, if most reluctantly, towards the inevitable clash of arms. A stream of members of Parliament came to join Charles at York, headed by Lord Keeper Lyttleton, bringing the Great Seal; and thirty-five peers signed a declaration that the King stood for the 'true Protestant religion, the just privileges of Parliament, the liberty of the subject, and the law, peace and prosperity of the Kingdom'.[7] This was a belief which Endymion shared with a growing number of his countrymen.

Olive seems to have joined Endymion at York in May, when the steward at Woodhall arranged for their younger daughter, Lettice, to be sent up north by wagon.[8] George was also in York with his father. All through July, Endymion was in attendance on the King as he rode round the northern Midlands, recruiting the gentry to his cause. On August 9th, the King proclaimed Essex and his officers traitors, to which Parliament retaliated by denouncing as traitors all who helped the King. Endymion was with his master at Nottingham on August 22nd, when his old acquaintance of Madrid days, Sir Edmund Verney, the Knight Marshal, bore the Royal Standard out from the Castle. There, too, were the young Prince of Wales and Duke of York, and Endymion's friend Rupert with his brother Maurice, who had both recently landed in Newcastle. Parliament's declaration that the King's followers were delinquents, liable to death and confiscation of their property, converted many a lukewarm royalist into a whole-hearted supporter of the King's cause. Recruits flowed in and the royal army grew to a force of ten thousand. But all the South and East of England—the richest and most populous part of the country—were now under Parliament's control, and Pym and his friends were confident of a swift and victorious end to the war when Essex took command of the Parliamentary army, twenty thousand strong, at Northampton.

On September 13th Charles with his army left Nottingham to march via Derby and Stafford to Shrewsbury and Chester, so as to be joined by reinforcements from Wales and the North-West. Two days later an unfortunate adventure befell Endymion and his son George. The King's Derbyshire adherents had stored arms and ammunition in the Grange, the house of a Catholic gentleman near West Hallam, six miles from Derby. The Parliamentarian Mayor of Derby got to hear of this store. Secretly collecting three troops of horse, he rode out from Derby on the night of September 15th and surrounded the Grange. When the

Parliamentary force broke open the door and entered the house, they found Endymion and George there. Their search also revealed a secret passage and a hiding place where they discovered a Jesuit priest disguised as a serving man. Fortunately almost all the arms had already been sent to Nottingham. The Mayor did not dare to arrest Endymion or George, but the unfortunate priest was removed to Derby to be sent on to London.[9]

It was as well that Endymion escaped arrest. Parliament had sent instructions to Essex to proclaim a pardon to all who would abandon the King's cause within ten days. Eleven persons were, however, specifically exempted from any pardon. They were Bristol, Newcastle, Falkland and five other peers, together with Nicholas, Hyde and Endymion Porter.[10] Endymion was the only one of the eleven not on the Council or in high office, but Olive's fervent Catholicism and Endymion's own Spanish connections and position of close confidence with the King had evidently rendered him the object of Parliament's particular suspicion.

(ii)

Endymion, thirteen years older than his master, was fifty-five at the start of the Civil War. In it, he held no combatant command. He was, it is true, made Colonel of the 7th Regiment of Foot, but the appointment was an honorary one and the regiment was commanded in the field by its Lieutenant Colonel, Vavasour.[11] Endymion's place was with the King, and throughout the next three years he remained at his master's side.

Not that such service was free from danger or physical hardship, especially for an ageing man, accustomed to the comfortable life of London and the Court. There were many weary months in the saddle, accompanying Charles when he rode at the head of his army from Shrewsbury to Edgehill and on to the outskirts of London in the opening campaign in the autumn of 1642, or a year later in the

campaign of Gloucester and Newbury; or in the long pursuit
of Essex to Cornwall in 1644; or in 1645, in the marches
and countermarches that ended at Naseby and the retreat
to Wales.

Endymion, too, was at Charles's side in battle, at Edgehill, at both battles of Newbury, at Cropredy Bridge and
at Naseby, sharing the risks that the King, heedless of
personal danger, faced with his soldiers.

At Edgehill, Endymion had as a companion Dr. William
Harvey, the great anatomist, who was put in charge of the
young Prince of Wales and his brother, the Duke of York.
After the King, attired in a black velvet coat, lined with
ermine, and wearing a velvet-covered steel cap on his head,
had ridden right round his army, speaking words of encouragement to his cheering soldiers, he was with great difficulty persuaded to abandon his intention of advancing at
the head of his troops. Instead, the royal party stationed
themselves on some rising ground to the rear of the right
wing. There Dr. Harvey sat under a hedge, reading a
book to the young Princes. Presently, as the royal army
advanced, Essex's cannon began to fire. The balls passed
harmlessly over the heads of the soldiers, but a number
came plunging down near the King and his party, causing
Dr. Harvey to shut his book and make a hurried move.
From their point of vantage, Endymion and his master
saw Rupert and his horsemen on the right and Wilmot
on the left shatter the opposing cavalry and vanish in
pursuit into the distance, accompanied by the royal reserve
of horse, including the King's bodyguard, who could not
be restrained from joining in the chase. But the royal
infantry in the centre, fighting the stubborn Parliamentary
foot, had been left without cavalry protection—and no foot-
soldiers of the day were a match for cavalry in the open.
In their wild charge and pursuit, the Royalist horse had
overlooked the Parliamentary reserve of cavalry, stationed
in broken ground to one side. These were now the only
horsemen left on the field. They broke into the left of the

royal infantry and, with the Parliamentary foot, overwhelmed the centre. The King's footguards, the old Earl of
Lindsey at their head, fought with fury before being
destroyed. Lindsey was captured, mortally wounded.
Verney was killed and the Royal Standard taken with
eleven out of the footguards' thirteen colours. Endymion's
own seventh regiment was broken and its Lieutenant-
Colonel, Vavasour, taken prisoner.

Seeing the disaster overtaking his infantry, Charles and
his attendants rode forward to encourage the wavering
two regiments who were still putting up a fight. The royal
party were in grave peril as Essex prepared for his final
advance. At that moment Rupert reappeared on the field.
After plundering Essex's baggage he had met Hampden
with a strong Parliamentary force marching from Warwick
to reinforce Essex and had, most fortunately, been turned
back. But night was beginning to fall and Rupert's horse
were too disorganized to attempt a further attack. In the
gathering darkness a brave deed did something to redeem
an afternoon when the King's great chance of ending the
war at one stroke had been thrown away by the inexperi-
ence and lack of discipline of the royal cavalry. A Captain
rode into the enemy's lines, seized the captured Royal
Standard and brought it safely back. The King knighted
him on the spot.

As soon as it was dark the King's forces withdrew to
the slopes of Edgehill. The late October night was bitterly
cold and Endymion lay with the King and his other attendants on the bare hill-side, clustering round a little brush-
wood fire. When morning broke, Essex's army was seen
still to be in position in front of Kineton, but early the
next day it withdrew to Warwick and the King and his
army resumed their march towards London.[12]

Only once again were the King and Endymion in such
personal danger as at Edgehill. Nearly three years later,
in the last great battle of the war, Charles and his attendants
were with the royal army's reserves a little to the rear as

Rupert advanced to the attack on Fairfax's and Cromwell's army, strongly positioned in front of the village of Naseby and outnumbering the royal forces by nearly two to one. The King and Endymion saw Rupert, on the right of the royal army, break Ireton's cavalry, some of whom fled as far as Northampton. The royalist infantry then closed with the enemy foot. But, on the other wing, Cromwell, with his first line of horse, forced the royal cavalry under Langdale to give ground. Seeing this, the King was about to advance the support of his infantry, when the Scottish Earl of Carnwarth, fearing for Charles's person, seized his horse's bridle. Someone gave the command to wheel right and the Royalist reserve, bearing Charles and Endymion with them, rode hurriedly back for a quarter of a mile before again halting. In the meantime, Cromwell had finally routed Langdale's horsemen. His Ironsides then turned on the exposed flank of the King's infantry and overwhelmed them, almost all being killed or taken prisoner. Rupert, returning to their help, was attacked by those of Ireton's horse who had been brought back into the fight. Reforming his line, Fairfax advanced with horse, foot and artillery. Charles tried to rally his army, calling out 'One charge more and we recover the day'. But Rupert knew that it was hopeless to attack Fairfax's complete army with the remains of the royal cavalry and that retreat was the only course. Closely pursued by Fairfax's troopers, the retreat soon turned into a rout, which did not stop until Leicester was reached, fourteen miles away. In the rout, the King lost his baggage wagons with his cabinet of papers and letters and all his and his attendants' personal effects. Some of the royal household were taken prisoner, including four of the King's footmen, one of his pages, his chamber keeper, his confectioner and his victualler. Endymion's own personal servant, Nicholas Johnstone, was among the captives.[13]

(iii)

If Endymion was too old to play a fighting role, the war brought full opportunity for military advancement to his twenty-two-year-old eldest son. Apart from having Endymion's influence to assist him, George Porter was an old friend of Rupert, while his brother-in-law George Goring was now back in favour. With characteristic duplicity Goring had again changed sides. As Governor of Portsmouth he had persuaded Parliament to send him £3,000 as well as arms and munitions for the defence of this important stronghold. Once in receipt of these, he had declared for the King, and when Waller recaptured Portsmouth for Parliament, Goring escaped to join the Queen in Holland.[14]

On the outbreak of war, George became a colonel of horse under Rupert and probably fought at Edgehill. A year later, at the end of 1643, he left Rupert's command to go to York as Commissary General in the Earl of Newcastle's army.[15] He departed under a cloud. In a letter to Rupert from York on December 20th, he wrote of the frown that Rupert had cast on him at his leaving and how his only thought was to regain Rupert's favour 'which I so undeservedly lost'.[16] His opportunity came in March 1644. The invasion of England by Parliament's new allies, the Scots, had placed Newcastle between two enemy forces and when he called for help, Rupert set out to relieve Newark which was closely besieged. George joined Rupert outside Newark and helped in the rout of the Parliamentary forces. He was then sent to occupy Lincoln, whence he wrote to Rupert on March 24th that he had captured some cannon there and that the townspeople had told him of the terror which Rupert's name had inspired in the enemy.[17] On March 28th, George was back in Newark after occupying Gainsborough, but he had again offended Rupert by not reporting to him and was quarrelling with Colonel Hunks, under whose command Rupert had placed him. Newcastle, however, ordered George to return to Yorkshire in order to

meet a threat from Sir Thomas Fairfax. Although George
wrote to Rupert pleading to be allowed to stay in Lincolnshire, he had to return north.[18] He was a thoroughly irresponsible and unsatisfactory subordinate and his dilatori-
ness in obeying Newcastle's instructions allowed Sir Thomas
Fairfax to join forces with his father and capture Selby
with three thousand prisoners, while Newcastle shut himself up in York. In spite of this failure, Major-General
George Porter, a few months later, was one of the commanders of Newcastle's main body of infantry in the centre
of the line at Marston Moor. In the desperate and disastrous
struggle which destroyed Newcastle's army and lost the
North to the King, George was wounded and taken prisoner.[19] He was sent to the Tower, but negotiations for
his exchange were soon on foot. Both Rupert and Goring
wrote to him promising him an exchange and, on October
10th, the Commons ordered that Major-General Porter
should be exchanged for Major Kerr. Waller, however,
wanted another Parliamentary officer exchanged in Kerr's
place, and it was not until December 2nd that the Commons, after a long debate, agreed that Essex should arrange
the exchange as he thought fit.[20]

George Goring was now commanding an army in the
West and, after his release, George Porter joined his
brother-in-law as second in command. They spent the early
months of 1645 in Exeter, their troops living off the country
and creating a reign of terror among the inhabitants.
Utterly unscrupulous and profligate as Goring was, he had
ability, courage and great resource in emergency. But the
influence of his strong personality brought out all the
worst in George Porter's spoiled and weak character—his
quarrelsome vanity and his addiction to loose and easy
living. George, only too readily, fed Goring's 'wild humour
and debauch' and made him 'turn his wantonness into riot
and his riot into madness'. Lacking Goring's courage and
skill as a soldier, George Porter was, in his brother-in-law's
words, 'the best company, but the worst officer, that ever

served the King'.[21] Goring's opinion of George's military qualities was strikingly endorsed at the battle of Langport in July 1645, when Goring was trying to prevent Fairfax and Cromwell from relieving Taunton. The day before the battle, Goring detached George and three brigades of horse and sent them across the River Yeo. At midday George 'being then in his utmost debauches with some of his officers' was completely surprised by Massey and fled with his men. Goring, coming up, checked the enemy, saying to one of his officers that George 'deserved to be pistolled for his negligence and cowardice'. The next day, Fairfax and Cromwell broke through Goring's lines, the Royalists flying in disorder and losing most of their infantry and many prisoners. George managed to escape, other officers making way for him to cross the bridges over the dykes in the marshy valley.[22]

(iv)

It was in Oxford that Endymion made his home with the Court between November 1642 and May 1645. Even before the Royal Standard had been raised at Nottingham, the University had shown its loyalty to the King by sending him £10,000, while dons and undergraduates had enthusiastically offered their services to the royal cause. Collecting what arms they could find, they exercised in the college quadrangles under the eye of Dr. Pink, the pro-vice-chancellor. Dons in holy orders were seen drilling with pikes, while undergraduates carried stones to the top of Magdalen Tower to drop on the enemy.

The townsmen, being mostly in sympathy with Parliament, took no part in these martial proceedings. The first soldiers to enter Oxford had, however, been a party of Royalist horse; but they had soon left and the city had been occupied by Lord Saye with a considerable Parliamentary force. Saye had the scholars disarmed, but refrained from seizing the college plate other than some belonging to Christ Church which had been hidden in a cellar. A bonfire was, however, made of 'Popish books and pictures' and the soldiers shot at and damaged statues of the Virgin and Child over college gates. The Parliamentary forces had left three weeks before Edgehill.[23]

A week after the battle, Endymion was riding into Oxford with his master at the head of the royal infantry, amid the heartfelt cheers of the University and the less willing plaudits of the townsmen. But there was only time to bestow the degree of Master of Arts on the Prince of Wales and the Duke of York, before the King and his suite were on their way to Reading; and it was not until the end of November that Endymion was back at Oxford with the King.[24]

Oxford now became the King's headquarters. The city was fortified with trenches and earthworks. The artillery was parked in the grounds of Magdalen, with the ammunition stored in New College cloisters; while the law and logic schools were turned into granaries and the music and astronomy schools into clothing depots. A mint was also established and the colleges gave their plate to be melted down and turned into coin.[25]

The King took up his residence at Christ Church where Endymion would have lodged with him. Olive was still in York and the Queen still in Holland, but in February (1643) the good news came that the Queen had arrived in England. She landed at Bridlington on the afternoon of February 22nd, bringing with her a good supply of arms and ammunition as well as a large sum of money, the proceeds of the jewels. A Parliamentary squadron, under Captain Batten, was on the watch to intercept her ships with their Dutch escort. At four o'clock next morning, the Queen, asleep in a house facing the pier, was awakened by a cannonade from Batten's ships, for whose guns her house seemed to be the chosen target. With the cannon balls crashing into the roof, the Queen hurried out into the street, but found that Mitte, her old and ugly but much loved dog, had been left behind. She insisted on going back for Mitte before finding refuge in a ditch outside the town, where she lay for two hours, while a sergeant was killed by a cannon ball only twenty paces away and one of her maids of honour was driven out of her mind by terror.[26] Only the falling tide and the threat of intervention from the Admiral commanding the Dutch escort finally made Batten sail off.

Olive was at York to greet the Queen and, probably, her maid-of-honour daughter, Marie Porter. On March 2nd, Endymion wrote from Oxford to Olive and to the Earl of Newcastle. 'I beseech your Lordship,' ran his letter to Newcastle, 'not to wonder at this tattered Mercury, as we have had such luck in our cavaliers as we thought this way the best to secure letters. I am extreme glad that the Queen is safe arrived at York and now I hope your Lordship will not suffer Tadcaster to be fortified nor the rebels to domineer as they have done. I have long wished to place my wife in the Queen's Bedchamber. I beseech your Lordship to do in it as you shall think best and oblige me according to your accustomed goodness. I have sent your Lordship the Queen's letter herein enclosed and, with it, a copy of excellent verses.'[27]

The 'tattered Mercury' was the messenger in disguise to whom Endymion's letters were entrusted, together with a letter from Charles to the Queen. Unfortunately, the messenger was intercepted in Coventry and the letters he carried were sent to London. On March 10th, they were read aloud in the Commons. The 'excellent verses'—perhaps they were the work of John Cleveland—seem to have been a lampoon on Parliament and this 'libel' was also read out. The Commons ordered the messenger to be kept a prisoner at Coventry and resolved that 'Mr. Endymion Porter be disabled from sitting or continuing any longer a member of this House during the Parliament'.[28]

Endymion's official expulsion from Parliament would have left him unmoved, but from York came news of a grievous personal loss. On March 15th, Marie Porter was buried in York Minster. If, as seems likely, she had been with the Queen at her landing at Bridlington, she may well have been the little maid of honour for whose youth the terrors and exposure of that night proved too much.

(v)

Charles and Endymion rode out to Edgehill to meet their wives and escort them back to Oxford. The arrival of the Queen and the Court ladies added colour and gaiety to the Oxford scene. The King still made Christ Church his headquarters. The Queen lodged at Merton. The other colleges were filled with officers of the army and their wives, and the ladies and gentlemen of the Court. The gardens of Trinity were a favourite meeting place. There Endymion and Olive would walk with their friends, among them the beautiful Lady Isabella Thynne, who was frequently to be seen in the gardens playing her lute. She and her friend, Mrs. Fenshawe, used to attend morning chapel in Trinity 'half-dressed like angels'. It was all too much for the octogenarian Dr. Kettell, Trinity's eccentric and tyrannical President. Accustomed to be absolute ruler of his domain, he now found himself plagued by frolicsome ladies and insulted by rude soldiers. Such unwonted indignities finished the old gentleman off.[29]

The Court was still the cultural centre of England and some of the old life blossomed once more at Oxford. There, Endymion again had the company of men of learning, of poets and playwrights. For a year, until he sought and found death on the battlefield, there was Lord Falkland, the Secretary of State, a poet himself and the friend of all learned men; and his most intimate companion, Dr. Chillingworth, the Anglican divine. There was the great little Dr. Harvey, whom Charles made Warden of Merton. Scientifically curious as ever, Harvey used to come to Trinity to study pre-natal growth by daily opening the eggs of a hen which a friend kept in his rooms. There was

7   Endymion Porter, by William Dobson

Sir John Birkenhead, poet and fellow of All Souls, who was chosen to write the Royalist weekly journal, *Mercurius Aulicus*. There was William Cartwright, renowned among his Oxford contemporaries for his learning and eloquence and famous in the world outside as the author of the tragi-comedy *The Royal Slave*. When he died of fever at the age of thirty-two, the King shed tears and went into mourning. There was John Cleveland, the satirist and wit, whose barbed partisan verses delighted the Royalists as much as they infuriated Parliament. He had been turned out of his Cambridge college for malignancy and when he came to Oxford he was made much of by the Court.[30] Endymion's own protégé, D'avenant, the poet laureate, was in Oxford from time to time. He had managed to escape to Holland in the summer of 1642 and the Queen had there employed him as a messenger to the Earl of Newcastle. The Earl, who had 'the misfortune to have something of the poet in him',[31] made D'avenant Lieutenant-General of Ordnance in his army and Charles knighted him. Above all, there was painting for Endymion to see and enjoy in the work of William Dobson, whom Aubrey described as 'the most excellent painter that England hath yet bred'.[32] Dobson's father, 'a very ingeniose person', came from St. Albans and was Lord Chancellor Bacon's right-hand man in build-ing Verulam House. But he spent all his money on women, and necessity forced young Dobson to take up painting.[33] There is a story that Van Dyck saw a copy of one of his pictures in a shop, found Dobson, its painter, at work in a garret and introduced him to Charles. At any rate, Dobson was made Sergeant Painter to the King after Van Dyck's death and, at the end of 1642, joined the Court at Oxford. He was then thirty-one years old.

All Dobson's work that has survived was crowded into the four years at Oxford before the surrender of the city. His studio was in the High Street. To it came the King's officers to sit for their portraits when they returned from the field. The Prince of Wales was painted, and Rupert with two of his officers, and Byron and Northampton and many others. Dobson's time was so much in demand that, in order to check the flow of sitters, he made them pay half the price of the portrait in advance.[34] He also seems to have employed pupils, since Aubrey's first antiquarian effort, as a young undergraduate, was to get 'Mr. Hesketh, Mr. Dobson's man, a priest, to draw the ruins of Osney, two or three ways before 'twas pulled down'.[35]

One of Dobson's finest pictures is of Endymion.* The portrait, now in the Tate Gallery, shows the sitter as if he had just returned from shooting Cotswold hares at Aston. His gun is in his hand and a boy holds a dead hare at which a spaniel is sniffing. Endymion's left arm rests on an urn on whose sides are figures representing the arts, while a classical bust—possibly of Apollo—stands on a pedestal in the background.

Unfortunately Dobson inherited his father's weaknesses. Extravagant living plunged him heavily into debt and his brief day was ended when the King left Oxford. Moving to London, Dobson was imprisoned by his creditors and was only released in time to die in October 1646, in his thirty-sixth year.

(vi)

Between campaigns, Endymion and Olive were able to resume some family life in Oxford. Their three younger boys, Philip, Thomas and James, were with them and their daughter Lettice. Two of Olive's sisters, Lady Newport and Lady Dunsmore, with their husbands, were also in Oxford and Endymion's youngest brother Giles, who was serving in the King's army, must sometimes have joined the family circle. A Porter cousin, too, was a fellow of Exeter College. Woodhall lay in enemy territory and was inaccessible, but Aston was within easy reach, and Endy-

* A portrait in the National Portrait Gallery, catalogued as being of Endymion Porter by Dobson, represents some other sitter.

mion, no doubt, rode across the Cotswolds to his manor, when opportunity offered, to see his sister Mary Canning and her husband and to discuss the crops and rents with Richard Bee, the steward.

Although Endymion and Olive had raised a considerable sum of money shortly before the war by the sale of some of Olive's jewels and by borrowing £2,500 on the security of his share of the Streatley lands, the Porter finances were as straitened as were those of the King and almost all the Court. Endymion's income from grants, patents and business enterprises had vanished; Olive's Woodhall and Bedfordshire rents could not be collected, while Aston rents were falling to less than half their pre-war level.[36] Luckily, Endymion's £500 a year pension was still being paid, and, in the autumn of 1644 during the King's campaign in the West, Endymion received a welcome windfall when he and Hopton were allowed to take the customs duties on wines in West Country ports for 1643 and 1644, worth between £400 and £500.[37]

The strain of campaigning was telling on Endymion's health. In the spring of 1644, his cousin of Exeter College wrote to a friend that his 'dearest Endymion labours from an ague' though he hoped to shake his illness off.[38] But Endymion was, at least, spared the cruel anxiety and parting which his master had to suffer that year because of the Queen's health. She was again expecting a child, and the King decided that Oxford no longer offered her a safe home. Instead, Exeter was chosen as the best place of refuge. In April (1644) Charles accompanied his wife as far as Abingdon, where they parted. They never met again. The Queen reached Exeter safely, but she was wretchedly ill and wrote to her doctor, Mayerne, in London begging him to come to her. Charles also sent him a message, 'Mayerne, for the love of me, go to my wife.'

The baby, a girl baptised Henrietta, was born in June. But the Queen's health grew worse. In heartbreaking letters to Charles she wrote that she was in great pain, with her legs paralysed and 'colder than ice'. She believed that she was dying. 'Adieu, my dear heart,' she ended a letter, 'if I die, believe that you will lose a person who has never been other than entirely yours.'[39]

When Essex refused the Queen a safe conduct to Bath, she resolved to escape to France. In July, she managed to reach Falmouth where she embarked on a Dutch ship. She left the infant princess behind in Exeter, in the devoted care of Lady Dalkeith, who had been born Anne Villiers. She was Olive's cousin and the daughter of Endymion's first master, Edward Villiers.

(vii)

Endymion was, of course, among the one hundred and seventy-five members of the House of Commons who obeyed the King's summons to join his rival Parliament which met at Oxford at the beginning of 1644. His name was among the signatories which this futile Oxford Parliament sent to Essex asking him to help bring about peace. Needless to say, Essex refused to present the letter to the Parliament at Westminster.[40]

One new friend whom Endymion made about this time was Montrose. Since early in 1643 Montrose had vainly been trying to persuade first the Queen in York and then the King to authorise him to lead the Scottish Royalist sympathisers in an attack on the Marquis of Argyll. Now that Argyll and the English Parliament had become allies and a Scots army was across the border, Montrose, who had come to Oxford, was at last able to secure the King's Commission as his Lieutenant-General in Scotland. Armed with the Commission, he hastened to York to borrow a few men from Newcastle's army with whom to invade Scotland. Endymion must have been one of those who had backed his ideas, and Montrose had evidently taken a liking to the courtier whose influence with the King was used on his behalf. Writing from York to Spottiswoode, the acting Secretary of State in Oxford, Montrose ended his letter, 'Let this, I pray, remember me to all my friends; and I intreat you will keep particular good intelligence with them all, and chiefly Mr. Porter.'[41]

While at Oxford, Endymion again became involved in a secret Irish venture. Ever since the start of the war, Charles had been hoping for armed aid from Ireland. But all through 1642 and most of 1643, the war of skirmishes and sieges had continued with horrible brutality on both sides between the Irish Catholic rebels and the Protestant English and Scottish settlers, reinforced by English troops. On the whole, the advantage had been with the rebels, with whom on Charles's orders, Ormonde had begun negotiations early in 1643. But in was impossible to accept their terms whereby, in return for complete liberty for the Catholic Church in Ireland and an independent Irish parliament, they would send an army of ten thousand to England to fight for the King. Nevertheless, Charles eagerly listened to the grandiose plans secretly unfolded to him by the Catholic Earl of Glamorgan, the Marquis of Worcester's son. Glamorgan's schemes were not confined to the use of an Irish army of ten thousand men. He was also to raise a force in South Wales and to recruit a further army of six thousand men in the Low Countries. The large sums of money needed to meet the cost of the scheme were to be obtained from the Pope, from Catholic princes and from the sale of titles and wardships. All this had to be kept a close secret, and the Commissions giving Glamorgan authority to command the several armies, to sell peerages, baronetages and wardships and to have a Dukedom for himself, and the King's daughter Elizabeth as a bride for his son, could not be witnessed and sealed in the normal way. Charles was not even prepared to let the Lord Keeper into the secret. Only Endymion seems to have been taken fully into Charles's confidence. As Glamorgan wrote to Clarendon, 'In like manner, did I not stick upon having the Commission inrolled or assented to by the King's counsel, nor indeed the seal to be put unto it in an ordinary manner, but as Mr. Endymion Porter and I could perform it, with rollers and no screw press.'[42] It was not, however, until March 1645 that Charles ordered Glamorgan to proceed to Ireland, armed with further wide Commissions of authority. Glamorgan's ship was wrecked off the Lancashire coast and he did not finally land in Dublin until August.

By that time, Endymion had left England. In May 1645, he rode out of Oxford with the King at the start of the Naseby campaign, taking his last view of the city that had sheltered him for two and a half years and where Olive and the children were to remain for nearly a year longer. Moving north-west by Stow-on-the-Wold, the King came to Chipping Campden, and Endymion was able, for the last time, to ride down the hill to his lovely little house at Aston. That day saw the needless destruction of a near-by house with which Endymion had long been familiar. Lest it should give shelter to the enemy, Rupert put fire to the great mansion at Chipping Campden which Endymion's friend and neighbour, Sir Baptist Hicks, the first Lord Campden, had built thirty years before at a cost of £30,000.[43]

Endymion rode with Charles into Wales after Naseby, the fatal battle that proved 'the entire ruin of all the King's affairs'.[44] The end had now come to Endymion's twenty-five years of faithful royal service. Some time in July, he was ordered by the King to carry letters to the Queen in Paris. Digby also entrusted him with letters to Jermyn, the Queen's Minister, in which he made plain the desperate state of the King's affairs and the need for help, above all for money.[45] It was probably in a South Wales port that Endymion, all his personal effects lost with his servant in the Naseby rout, found a ship to carry him to France.

CHAPTER XII

QUEEN Henrietta Maria had already been in France for more than a year by the time Endymion reached Paris with the letters he carried to her. She had landed at Brest after a hazardous voyage in the course of which her ship, chased by a Parliamentary squadron from Torbay, had been in such danger of capture that the Queen had ordered the Captain to blow the ship up rather than let her fall into her enemies' hands.[1] But she had been received in France with all the honour due to the aunt of the boy King, Louis XIV, and the sister-in-law of the Regent, Anne of Austria, who, with Cardinal Mazarin, ruled France. The English Queen had been given rooms in the Louvre and had been allotted the palace of St. Germain, thirteen miles out of Paris. There she had set up her Court, with Henry Jermyn, her old favourite and adviser, as her Minister. Thanks to a generous pension from the Regent she was able, at first, to live in considerable splendour, but her style of living declined as she stripped herself of money and jewels to send help to her husband.[2]

Most that is known of Endymion's stay in France derives from a long letter, written eighteen months after his arrival to his old friend Edward Nicholas, when the latter, also an exile, was living at Caen in Normandy.[3] Endymion found some friends in Paris, such as the Marquis of Newcastle, who was occupying his time by training horses in dressage; and Sir Richard Browne, Charles's resident at the French Court. D'avenant was there too. But no warm welcome awaited Endymion from the Queen and her advisers. As a protégé of Buckingham and as a constant supporter of the Spanish interest, he was not likely ever

to have been in the Queen's special favour, in spite of
Olive's conversion to Catholicism. It was to Charles that
Endymion's service and devotion had always exclusively
been given. Now that he no longer had his master to attend,
his usefulness had gone. He was, in any case, nearly sixty
years old, suffering from bouts of ague and unfit for the
arduous work of messenger such as the Queen gave to his
fellow groom of the bedchamber, Will Murray, who was
thirteen years younger. He found himself, too, completely
out of sympathy with the Queen and Jermyn's policies.
His experience and judgement would not allow him to
subscribe to their wild and unrealistic projects for restoring
the King's fortunes. 'Here in our Court,' he wrote to
Nicholas, 'no man looks on me, and the Queen thinks I
lost my estates from want of wit rather than from my
loyalty to my master.'[4] When in November, Newcastle
asked Margaret Lucas, one of the Queen's maids of honour
and soon to become Newcastle's second wife, to pay some
attention to Endymion, she coldly replied from St. Germain, 'As for Mr. Porter, he was a stranger to me, for
before I came to France I never saw him or at least knew
him to be Mr. Porter or my Lord Newcastle's friend. I
never speak to any man,' she primly added, 'before they
address themselves to me, nor look so much in their face
as to invite their discourse.'[5]

It was at St. Germain that Endymion found lodgings,
writing to Nicholas that 'I am so retired into the skirts of
a suburb that I scarce know what they do at the Louvre,
and I want clothes for a Court, having but that poor
riding suit I came out of England in, which shows I am
constant in my apparel as I am in respects to your Honour,
and I am confident that when your Honour shall take a
survey of all my actions you will find I never altered, nor
was fantastical in seeking after new friendships.'[6] Like
Nicholas, Endymion was in desperate need of money.
'I am a sad man,' he wrote, 'to hear your Honour is reduced
to want; but it is all our cases, for I am in so much necessity,

8   Medallion of Endymion Porter
by Warin, 1635

that were it not for an Irish barber that was once my servant, I might have starved for want of bread. He hath lent me some moneys that will last me for a fortnight longer, then I shall be as much subject to misery as I was before.'[7] But in spite of the Queen's neglect and his penniless condition, Endymion's faith remained unshaken. 'God be thanked,' he told Nicholas, 'I know my own heart, and am satisfied in my conscience, and were it to do again I would as freely sacrifice all without hope of reward, as I have done this.'[8]

The news that came from England brought no comfort to the exiles. Rupert had surrendered Bristol in September 1645, and before the winter was out all the West was lost, the Prince of Wales flying first to Scilly and then to Jersey. In Scotland, the defeat at Philiphaugh had ended Montrose's astonishing run of victories. In Ireland, Glamorgan, going beyond any authority given him by Charles, had signed a secret treaty with the Catholics, granting them religious freedom. But as soon as the secret leaked out, Glamorgan had been arrested by Ormonde, whom he had not consulted, and was disavowed by the King. Charles himself had spent the winter in Oxford, where Montreuil, Mazarin's agent, was appealing to him to come to terms with the Scots. It was Mazarin's interest to keep England weak and divided and, for this purpose, to strengthen the power of the Scots as a check to the English New Model army.

The Queen and Jermyn also urged a Scottish alliance on Charles, even at the cost of making religious concessions to the Presbyterians. But Endymion was under no illusions as to French intentions. He wrote to Nicholas, when the latter was still in Oxford with the King, that he was to expect nothing from France, though 'they made believe here that we should have ten thousand men presently'. In regard to an understanding with the Scots Endymion saw that Montreuil was acting in the interests of the French rather than of the King and that 'when we fall out among ourselves, the Scots and French will fall upon us and divide us'.[9]

But the hardest news that Endymion had to bear was that of the treachery of his son George. After the rout at Langport and the loss of Bridgwater, Goring and George had again retired to Exeter. Goring was ill with gout, and George was mainly occupied in trying to extract a satisfactory apology from a Colonel Tuke who had written him an insulting letter after George had recommended another officer for the vacant post of Major-General of Horse. George had wanted to fight a duel with Tuke, but had been stopped by Goring's intervention. Tuke's letter, while absolving George from cowardice since he had killed a colonel in a duel, was brutally frank about the rest of George's character, his falsity, his ridicule of the Bible and his 'great and constant debaucheries, with many other vices not fit to be named'.[10] Goring's army was, in fact, little better than a mob and, towards the end of November, Goring himself embarked at Dartmouth for France, excusing his departure on the grounds of ill-health. George had no more wish to continue fighting than had his brother-in-law. For some time there had been rumours about his loyalty. He was believed to be in correspondence with the enemy and not only because his wife, Diana, was living among them, probably at Woodhall.[11] The rumours proved to be true. On November 26th, after receiving Fairfax's safe conduct, George crossed the lines and rode to London, Goring, before he went to France, having conveniently signed a warrant for £200 for his expenses.[12] Two months later, in February 1646, George appeared before the Committee for Compounding. He pleaded that he had deserted places of honour and profit in the King's service and that his estates in Kent and Sussex were only held during the lifetime of his wife. His fine was fixed at £1,000, but it was remitted by the Commons in March, and, in April, an ordinance was passed for the pardon of his delinquency.[13]

More fortunate than his master, Endymion was reunited

with his wife in May. Leaving Oxford, Olive had come to London through the Parliamentary lines. On April 6th, the Speaker's pass for her to leave England was handed to the Serjeant-at-Arms, who was ordered to appoint one of his servants to escort her, at her own expense, to Dover or Rye and to see her on board ship. When, a fortnight later, she was still in England, the Commons ordered her to leave the country by May 1st or to be proceeded against as a spy.[14]

Just as Olive was leaving England, the King had ridden out of Oxford, accompanied by only two attendants, and had put himself in the hands of the Scottish Army near Newark. The Scots took him, a prisoner, to Newcastle, where they proceeded to make every effort to induce him to accept the Presbyterian Covenant. In July, the English Parliament sent their own propositions to Newcastle. The King was to take the Covenant and abolish the episcopal church, while the militia and navy were to be placed in Parliament's hands for twenty years. Once again, the King's chief supporters, Endymion's name among them, were to be excluded from pardon. Both the English and Scottish Commissioners begged the King to accept. The Queen, from Paris, exerted all her personal influence on him to do so. But Charles would not thus abandon his power, his church and his friends. If, however, the King refused to comply with the Scots' wishes, they were not prepared to give him a refuge in Scotland, thereby risking a revival of Scottish royalism as well as a quarrel with the English Parliament. After much bargaining, they agreed to withdraw their forces from England for a payment of £400,000, half to be paid before they left. By early in 1647, the last Scottish soldier had crossed the Tweed. The King, under the escort of Commissioners from Parliament, was taken from Newcastle to Holmby House in Northamptonshire. His hope now lay in the rivalry, in England itself, between the Presbyterian majority in Parliament who wished to disband the army, and the

Independents, with Cromwell and his Ironsides, whose leading spirits refused to accept the fetters of a Presbyterian rule.

Watching these events from St. Germain, Endymion had no sympathy with the Queen's efforts to get the King to accept Presbyterianism, albeit only as a temporary expedient to retrieve his fortunes. 'It seems your Honour's friends, the Scots,' he wrote to Nicholas, 'have sold him and yet they are his white boys. And our grandees lay the fault at his not taking the Covenant and signing the propositions; yet I am of opinion they would have done like Scots had he done all the unworthy acts they could have desired of him.' He ended his letter with a postscript quoting 'an epigram' which had been sent him from London.

> 'The Scots must have two hundred thousand pound
> To sell the King and quit our English ground;
> And, Judas like, I hope 'twill be their lots
> To hang themselves—so farewell lousy Scots.'[15]

Nor was Endymion sanguine that Charles would be able successfully to play the Independents off against the Presbyterians. 'If the Independents,' he wrote, 'would but alter their opinions a little and say they would have a King, I would go to them presently and kiss their feet, for that were the right way to despatch the business; but a pox upon the Presbyterians and them too; they will not fall out till it be too late to do our master good or to save our nation from a general ruin, which I am afraid will be the end.'[16]

Endymion was also corresponding with James Howell, his old friend of Madrid days, who was in the Fleet prison in London. 'We are now Scot free,' wrote Howell in February 1647, and went on to comment on the number of bastards the Scots had left behind them. He shared Endymion's views about France and the pleasure that the French Government would be taking at England's calamities, and how Scotland 'always served France for a brand to set England on fire for their own ends'.[17]

Endymion's health had been growing worse. He had complained to Howell about it and, in September 1646, D'avenant wrote from St. Germain to a friend to say how he had been hoping to visit him in Paris, but 'I am likewise void of that happiness by Mr. Porter's indisposition of body'.[18] D'avenant was one friend who remained loyal to his old patron. Ill, penniless and, above all, frustrated in his desire to be of some service to his master's cause, Endymion now determined to leave the air of Paris which agreed with him so little either physically or mentally. He foresaw, too, the troubles that a year later, in the outbreak of the Fronde rebellion, were to bring war to Paris and destitution to the English Queen. 'Those that have fomented all the uproars of Christendom,' he wrote, 'may by the Tyler's law be paid in their own kind, for in this country there is as much combustible matter to take fire as in any place of the world, the whole kingdom being discontented.'[19] 'So soon as I can get a small sum to carry me into Flanders,' he told Nicholas, 'I resolve to go thither, and I shall not starve there; beside I may be able to do my Master some service in those parts, and when I go I will advertise your Honour of my departure, for by your Honour's good advice I may do something for our King's good and that I will study all the days of my life, whether I be commanded to do it or no.'[20]

Some time in the early months of 1647, Endymion and Olive left the tawdry atmosphere of the exile-Court in Paris and went to Brussels. Endymion was on familiar ground in Spanish Flanders, among people who would not have forgotten the man who, only twelve years before, had led the English King's mission to the Infante. Brussels and Antwerp friends seem to have given him credit, so that he and Olive were comfortably lodged and no longer in any want. The few letters that have survived from the two years that Endymion spent in Brussels show him in a much more cheerful and resigned mood. One letter,[21] written in November 1647, was to Sir Richard Browne in Paris. It enclosed letters to 'my most sweet Marquis of Newcastle' and to 'my Lord Marquis of Montrose'. Montrose had come to Paris early in 1647. He was splendidly received by the French Court, but found himself as much out of sympathy with the English Queen and her entourage as Endymion had been. Browne was the son of Christopher Browne of Sayes Court, Deptford. His wife Elizabeth was the daughter of one of Endymion's Gloucestershire neighbours and their daughter Mary was married to John Evelyn, the diarist.

'Most honoured Sir,' Endymion began his letter to Browne, 'I write not often to you for fear of troubling you. But I wish myself often in your company, because I love it as you do pie, and God send me but good news next week of our poor Master's safe delivery from his enemies, the Agitators, and I will be merry with you in my next. Was there ever so crossed a nation as we are, that must be thought murderers for a company of fellows that are possessed with legions of devils and would make us believe they have the Holy Ghost. I hope the Lord will serve them, one of these days, as he did those whom he sent a-fishing in the swine! For unless there be some such course taken with them we shall never live at quiet. I beseech you buss my sweet country-woman for my sake, with such a buss as made the lass turn nun. Come, Sir Richard, if our Gloucestershire mistress were out of the verge of wife, she is worth one thousand drabs that make you believe the moon is made of green cheese. I thank God I am now past these things, paternoster and good wine are the pastime of the aged. Present my humble service to Mrs. Evelyn and to the sweet Lazala of Deptford and be pleased to assure yourself that

I am, honoured Sir

Your most affectionate humble servant,

Endymion Porter.'

'Agitators' was the name that had been given to the representatives or agents, elected by the regiments of the Army. In June 1647, on Cromwell's and Ireton's orders, the King had been carried off by Cornet Joyce and his troopers from the guardianship of the Parliamentary Commissioners at Holmby House. He had been taken first to Newmarket and, finally, to Hampton Court. That summer, Cromwell and Ireton had almost reached a settlement with the King, based on religious and political compromises, which England as a whole would have welcomed. But Charles was never fully sincere in his dealings with the Army leaders. He was still hoping to play off the three sides—Parliament, the Scots and the Army—against one another, and although the Army had seized London, Cromwell had to deal with the republican radicals in the Army's ranks—the Levellers—who preached what we today might call Socialism or Communism, but what Cromwell called Anarchy. In November, the clash between Cromwell and Ireton and the new Agitators came to a head. Cromwell openly declared against the Levellers, but it was believed that they might assassinate the King if he fell into their hands. The way was accordingly left open for the King to remove himself from danger and on November 11th he left Hampton Court and found a refuge, though still as a prisoner, at Carisbrooke Castle in the Isle of Wight. Four days later, Cromwell crushed the Army revolt.

In another letter to Browne, sent in May of the next year (1648) Endymion wrote that he hoped that Sir William Fleming and Will Murray would be bringing back 'chirping news' and that Browne would give Will Murray 'a rouse at the Spread Eagle and not forget me, but dash me in one glass as you do an orange peel and I believe William will not like the wine the worse'.[22] Fleming and Murray had been sent from Scotland to The Hague by Hamilton and other Scots Lords on May 1st to invite the Prince of Wales to come to Scotland. A strong reaction in favour

of the King and against the tyranny of the Army had
set in during the early months of 1648. There were riots
in many parts of England and, in Scotland, an army
under Hamilton's command was preparing to cross the
border. But the second civil war was short lived. The
Royalists were too disorganised and too scattered to resist
the swift and disciplined moves of Cromwell and his
soldiers. The old Earl of Norwich, George's father-in-law,
was defeated by Fairfax at Maidstone and surrendered
Colchester after a siege, while Cromwell, after putting
down the rising in Wales, marched north and destroyed
the invading Scots at Preston. Before the end of the
summer Cromwell and the Army were complete masters of
England.

In the meantime, Olive had gone to England at the end
of 1647 to try to obtain permission for Endymion to return
home and compound for his delinquency. The conditions
for compounding were that a delinquent had to furnish,
on oath, an inventory of all his possessions, to admit his
fault and to pledge himself to accept the new order. Olive
may also have been concerned to try to salvage something
out of her Woodhall inheritance. Her idiot brother, to
whom Olive was co-heir, died in 1647, but, the year before,
Parliament had removed Endymion and his brother-in-
law Lord Dunsmore from their guardianship, and had replaced them by another brother-in-law, Lord Howard of
Escrick, who had taken the Parliamentary side.[23] On
January 5th, 1648, Olive was granted leave by Parliament
to stay in London to pursue the question of her husband's
composition, but her leave was revoked on January 17th
and she had to return to Brussels without achieving her
object, although in March the Lords sent Endymion's
petition to the Commons.[24]

In August of 1648, the Marquis of Newcastle joined
Endymion in Flanders. He arrived in Antwerp so impoverished that he was forced to take lodgings in a public
inn until Endymion, 'one of his friends who had a great

love and respect for him', insisted on the Marquis sharing his house in Brussels. Endymion was also probably instrumental in obtaining for Newcastle the lease of a house in Antwerp belonging to Rubens's widow.[25] Newcastle's immediate financial needs were relieved by a loan from William Aylesbury, who had come to Antwerp on behalf of the Duke of Buckingham in order to sell or pledge for credit a large consignment of pictures and other valuables from York House. It was £200 of Buckingham's money thus raised that Aylesbury lent to Newcastle.[26] Aylesbury was Hyde's brother-in-law and was known to Endymion, who seems to have had a hand in the loan. From Brussels, on August 19th, he wrote to Aylesbury in Antwerp that illness had prevented his waiting on him, but since Aylesbury wanted to see him concerning some business of Newcastle's, he would be ready to show all the love and duty that his heart could afford. He could not, however, meet Aylesbury for a few days as he had promised to accompany his wife on a short journey which she wished to make.[27] Aylesbury's timely loan enabled Newcastle to get sufficient credit to take and furnish Rubens's widow's house, where he was soon once more happily occupied in training his horses.[28]

In November, Parliament, still hoping to win the King over to its side and to resist the Army's demand to bring the King to trial, tried to make some concessions to Charles by only condemning to banishment seven leaders of the second civil war and only naming seven others of the King's chief supporters as being absolutely excepted from pardon. In this more favourable atmosphere, the Commons finally acceded to Endymion's petition to be allowed to return to attend the Committee for Compounding.[29]

On December 1st, when the King was carried off by the Army from Carisbrooke Castle and lodged in the dark and desolate fortress of Hurst Castle, the last act of his tragedy began. The date of Endymion's leaving Brussels is not known, nor whether he was in London on January 29th,

standing among the great crowd in Whitehall, whose horror
and revulsion at their King's execution broke out in a
groan of agony. Wherever he was, Endymion must have
felt that the death of his master, to whom he had given his
full devotion for so many years, was the end of everything. He was certainly back in London by the spring of
1649 and, in April, he appeared before the Committee for
Compounding at Goldsmiths Hall.

In his humble petition to the Committee Endymion
declared that 'your petitioner being a servant in ordinary
to the late King, was by the commands of his said Majesty
required to attend his person in the duty of his place
during the late troubles both at Oxford and other places
whilst they were holden as garrisons against the Parliament. That during such attendance he did adhere unto
the said King when he was engaged against the Parliament
but never took upon him any commands or did bear arms
in the said war. That his estate being sequestrated for his
said delinquency, he humbly prays that he may be admitted
to a moderate and favourable composition for his estate'.
The very shaky signature that he appended is that of an
old and sick man.

His inventory of his possessions was based on the current
depreciated values. He showed the rental value of his
Aston and Mickleton estate as only £154 a year and his
Somercotes investment at only £40 a year. Most of his
income from landed property was shown as deriving from
his guardianship of Olive's brother and from Olive's share
of Woodhall. £650 of the total of £850 a year came from
these sources. Apart from this, the assets he showed were
only on paper. There was the £500 pension for his and
Olive's lives, but this was already a year in arrears. Including the £500 arrears of pension, he claimed that the King
owed him £10,000. There was the £500 a year rental value
of Alfarthing Manor, but this had been mortgaged for
£4,000, and when Endymion failed to pay the mortgage
interest the mortgagee had sold the estate. There were

other debts owing to him of £1,600. There was, too, the office of Surveyor of the Petty Customs of the Port of London, the reversion of which Endymion had bought from Carmarden for £3,000. This should have fallen to Endymion on Carmarden's death, but he had been unable to obtain it. Finally, there were his pictures, furniture and valuables which had been in the Strand house and at Woodhall, but which had been seized. He valued them at £2,000. As against such paper assets he owed £3,000, his chief creditor being Robert Cooke who had lent him £2,500 in 1641 on the security of the Streatley lands and had been paid no interest since 1643. Cooke put in a special claim to the Committee on account of this debt.

The Committee took a merciful view of the wreck of his fortunes which Endymion's inventory had disclosed. At the end of June, they assessed his fine at only £222 10s. 0d. A few days later, he applied again to the Committee for authority to seize any of his goods that had been stolen by private persons and not taken and sold by Parliament. He reported that he had already discovered some of his property to the value of £100. The Committee granted his request.[30] Perhaps it was in search of some of his own treasures that, in May, he had gone to look at the collection of pictures in the London house of Geldorp, the painter and dealer. There John Evelyn the diarist found him.[31]

Endymion did not live to see his fine paid and his estate discharged. He was in his sixty-third year and his health had been steadily failing. He died only a few weeks after his last appearance before the Committee and, on August 20th, he was buried in the church of St. Martin's-in-the-Fields, his London parish. Endymion's will has disappeared; it is said to have been drawn up in 1639, and one of his descendants[32] preserved an extract from it. After commending his wife and children to the good and gracious care of the King, he ended by charging all his sons, upon his blessing, 'that they, leaving the like charges to their posterity, do all of them observe and respect the children and family of my Lord Duke of Buckingham, deceased, to whom I owe all the happiness I had in the world'. It was a fitting valediction from a man whose outstanding trait was loyalty and gratitude to his friends.

EPILOGUE

(i)

OLIVE'S and George's first task was to pay the fine imposed by the Committee for Compounding and to obtain the discharge of Endymion's estate. This they succeeded in doing in May of the next year (1650).[1] As soon as the estate was in their hands, Olive and George, with the three executors of the will, Lord Lumley, Sir William Russell and Edward Cooke, sold the Aston and Mickleton Manors, for which they obtained £2,320.[2] They had, however, no immediate success in their efforts to regain any rights in Alfarthing Manor.[3] Olive and George seem to have made the Strand House inhabitable again and it remained the family home until 1667, when George sold it for £1,450.[4]

The Porters' existence, like that of most Royalists, was a precarious one during the Commonwealth. Nor was it made less so by the behaviour of George, Philip and Thomas. George continued as ready as ever to pick a quarrel. In August 1652 he was concerned in a dispute with Lord Montague and was ordered to be apprehended and brought before the Council. He found himself again imprisoned in the Tower, although he was soon discharged.[5] Imprisonment did nothing to mend his ways and a warrant was out two years later to arrest him and the Earl of Oxford to prevent their fighting a duel.[6] Philip's conduct was much worse. He was only twenty-one when his father died. From the age of sixteen he had known little or no home life or parental discipline and his tutor's 'masterpiece' had grown into a young ruffian. In the summer of 1652 he was threatening his mother with violence after a quarrel with her, and was bound over by the magistrates to appear at the next sessions in the Old Bailey. Not only did Philip not appear, but he again threatened Olive. 'In a very rude and unnatural manner and with wicked oaths before her door, he did disturb and threaten her and some of her friends.' When Philip was found, he was committed to Newgate prison, 'there to remain till he be discharged by due cause of law'.[7] Only a year later, having been released from prison, Philip was in trouble again. He and five friends, including Lord Mohun, had challenged some Roundheads to a fight and a warrant was issued to apprehend them and bring them before the Council.[8] The next year, Philip was arrested on a more serious charge. He and three friends were committed to the Tower accused of High Treason. They were released on bail five months later, but Philip did not long enjoy his freedom. His short and wasted life came to an end in 1655.[9]

Even Tom, young as he was, added to poor Olive's troubles. In February 1655, when he was barely nineteen, he ran off with his eighteen-year-old cousin Anne Blount, the Earl of Newport's daughter. He abducted her from her father's house in St. Martin's-in-the-Fields, taking her to an inn at Southwark. There, in a local church, they went through a form of marriage. Old Newport was furious and took steps to have Tom arrested and imprisoned and the marriage declared invalid on the grounds that the bride was a minor and that neither party had any residential qualification in Southwark. He also took legal proceedings against Olive. But a reconciliation and a valid marriage later took place.[10] Nor was this Tom's only crime. Only a month after he had abducted Anne, he fought a duel in Covent Garden and mortally wounded his opponent. Pleading guilty of manslaughter but not guilty of murder, he was sentenced to be burned in the hand.[11]

Better times returned for the Porters with the Restoration. Charles II had barely landed before George, ignoring his past apostasy, was presenting a certificate to affirm that he had forsaken a good estate to serve the late King,

that he had twice had to buy back his sequestered property and that, during the Commonwealth, he had been
engaged in the loyal cause.[12] He was soon in receipt of a
pension of £500 a year 'for good and faithful services',[13]
and in 1663, he became a Gentleman of the Privy Chamber
to Queen Henrietta Maria.[14] Tom and James received
Commissions as Captains in Lord Gerard's regiment of
horse.[15] Olive herself was given the office of Surveyor of
the Petty Customs, the reversion of which Endymion had
been unable to inherit.[16] She did not long enjoy it. In
December 1663 she died and was buried beside Endymion
in St. Martin's-in-the-Fields.

George was still 'the best company', and his social gifts
made him a favourite at Charles II's Court. Perhaps it
was the Villiers blood exercising its charms on King James's
grandson. In the summer of 1665, Charles sent him to
Paris, with £200 for his expenses,[17] to carry messages to
Charles's favourite sister, Henrietta, the baby princess
born in Exeter during the war, who had been smuggled
out of England by the faithful Lady Dalkeith and who
was now Duchess of Orleans. Her mother-in-law, Anne of
Austria, was dying. 'I send this bearer, George Porter,'
wrote Charles, 'with no other errand than upon the subject
of the Queen Mother's indisposition, who I fear, by the
nature of her disease, and what I find by the letters from
thence, will not long be in a position to receive any compliments. This bearer will tell you of our fleet being gone
to seek out the Dutch, and you know him so well as I
need say nothing more to you. He will play his own part,
and make you laugh before he returns, which is all the
business he has there, except it be to assure you with how
much kindness I am yours'.[18]

The next Christmas, George was taking part in 'warm
country dances with the Duke of Monmouth and the Duke
of Buckingham'.[19] In 1676, he was made a groom of
Charles's bedchamber at £500 a year. He had also succeeded
to Olive's office of Surveyor of the Petty Customs and

enjoyed several other profitable royal grants.[20] George and his wife Diana had several children. Their eldest son, George, was made one of the Gentlemen Ushers to the new Queen in 1663, while a younger son, Aubrey, became a page of honour to the King.[21] In 1664 their eldest daughter, Mary, married the second Lord Strangford as his second wife. It is from this marriage that descendants of Endymion are living today. George died in 1683, two years before the death of the King.

Tom inherited his father's literary tastes and turned playwright. D'avenant had remained the Porters' loyal and grateful friend and, in 1661, had given to Olive half of one of his ten shares in his new theatrical company and playhouse. It was a generous gift, for half of a share was worth £900. He also allowed George to buy another half share in this highly profitable venture which gave a very handsome return to the shareholders. In 1662, D'avenant requited Endymion's goodness to him still further by staging Tom Porter's first play, a tragedy called *The Villain* and by writing an epilogue to it.[22] Pepys's friends were so enthusiastic in their praise of the play that Pepys took his wife to see it on its second night. He did not enjoy it, partly because he was expecting too much and partly because his conscience was nagging him for breaking his vow and going to the theatre.[23] A few years later D'avenant produced another successful play written by Tom called *A Witty Combat or the Female Victor*. Tom shared his elder brother George's readiness to pick a quarrel with the sword. D'avenant, in his epilogue to *The Villain*, referred amusingly to his reputation in this respect. In 1667, Tom fought a duel with his greatest friend, Sir Henry Bellasyse. Pepys described at length how the two friends, who had both drunk too much, got involved in a ridiculous argument as to which was the first to draw his sword in a quarrel. Bellasyse boxed Tom's ear, and knowing that when sober next day they would make it up, Tom insisted on fighting that night. Both were wounded, Bellasyse so severely that, believing he was dying, he kissed Tom and begged him to fly and escape the consequences.[24] But both recovered and Tom wrote several more plays before he died in 1680.

James, the youngest boy, was the only one to inherit his father's loyal and honourable character. He became a groom of the bedchamber to the Duke of York, and when his master came to the throne he was made Vice-Chamberlain of the Household. He also commanded a troop of horse in Monmouth's rebellion. When King James lost his throne, James Porter followed him into exile and officiated as Chamberlain at the Court of St. Germain until the King died in 1701.[25]

(ii)

Future generations in England, to the country's tragic and incalculable loss, were only to enjoy a meagre portion of the fruits of the love, skill and money which Charles had lavished on his pictures, in whose collection Endymion had played his useful part.

The Puritan attitude to the arts had long been made clear. It was strictly utilitarian. In pictures, only portraits were tolerable. Most subject pictures were considered to be lascivious, while religious pictures excited special aversion as being superstitious.

The Civil War gave militant Puritanism the opportunity of putting its ideas into practice. Not only did its armies wantonly pillage churches, but special committees of Parliament were set up to destroy all kinds of idolatrous or superstitious monuments. It was by orders, for instance, of a parliamentary committee that a Rubens altarpiece in the chapel of Somerset House was hurled into the Thames.

Finally, only two months after the King's execution, Parliament resolved to have all the personal effects of the royal family inventoried, appraised and sold except what should be reserved for the use of the State. Even if Parliament's immediate reasons were the wish to prevent theft, to repay loyal Parliamentary supporters owed money by the late King, and to raise funds for the new régime's urgent needs (the first £30,000 realised was to be lent to the Navy), it was Puritan indifference to or active dislike of the arts that encouraged the decision.

In July 1649, Parliament passed the act for the sale. Trustees, of whom Belcamp seems to have been the only picture expert, were appointed to make the inventory and valuation of all the goods. Ten thousand pounds worth, initially, and subsequently another ten thousand pounds worth, were to be reserved for the Council's own use.

In Whitehall, St. James's, Somerset House, Hampton Court, Greenwich, Oatlands, Nonesuch, Wimbledon and the other royal residences, everything was meticulously listed and appraised for sale, from the crown jewels and regalia to the blankets and kitchen utensils, from a Raphael Madonna to 'a small bed, very old. £2'.[26]

The inventory shows Charles's incomparable collection in its full glory. The pictures numbered nearly one thousand four hundred, headed by the Titians of which there were some twenty-three major examples. The Italian Schools were represented by some of the greatest works of the masters, works by Raphael, Leonardo da Vinci, Correggio, Andrèa del Sarto, Mantegna, Giulio Romano, Veronese, Tintoretto, Giorgione, Caravaggio, Bassano, Palma Vecchio and others. Peter and Jan Breughel, Mabuse, Mor, and others represented the Flemish school. There were, too, the Dürers, Rembrandts, Holbeins and Hilliards, while the superb Rubens and Van Dycks headed the long list of works by contemporary artists. Such was the treasure which Parliament so callously dispersed.

The disposal of this huge catalogue took a number of years. The inventory value of the pictures came to over £30,000, a great sum for those days. Its measure, in our modern eyes, may be gauged by the individual valuations, which, for instance, set Titians at from £500 to £100, Raphael's St. George at £150, and Holbeins from £200 downwards. Most of the pictures were sold at their valuation price or a few pounds over.

In order that the best prices should be secured, special facilities were given to oversea buyers. In this way, most of the finest pieces left England, including almost the whole collection of Titians. The chief foreign purchases were on behalf of the Archduke Leopold Wilhelm, the King of Spain, Cardinal Mazarin of France and the Queen of Sweden. Mazarin, amongst other treasures, secured two Correggios valued at £1,000 apiece and Titian's Venus of the Pardo, valued at £500. The King of Spain's purchases were so extensive that eighteen mules were needed to transport them to Madrid from Corunna, to which port they had been shipped.[27]

Fortunately, there were some pictures amongst the goods kept for the use of the Council. The Raphael cartoons, for instance, were reserved for Cromwell himself. The Council's reservations were, however, mostly for furniture, tapestries and household goods for the State offices. There were, too, a number of English buyers such as Colonels Webb and Hutchinson, and Gerbier, Lanier and Lely, whose purchases remained at home.

Endymion's own collection was entirely dispersed. Only one of his pictures remains in the hands of his descendants. It is the big picture that Van Dyck painted in 1633 of Endymion, Olive and the three elder boys. Lely acquired it and it was while it was in his possession in 1672 that Mary Beale, perhaps the first professional English woman painter, borrowed it to make a miniature copy which Lely commended as the best copy of a Van Dyck he had ever seen. He also very much liked two full-size copies which Mary Beale made of Philip in the picture.[28] The original picture was in the sale of Lely's superb collection, which took place shortly after his death in 1680. It was bought by the Earl of Mulgrave for £155.[29] Mulgrave was created

Duke of Buckingham and Normanby in 1703, and when he died in 1721, Buckingham House and its contents were left to his widow. On her death twenty years later, the house came into the possession of the Duke's illegitimate son Sir Charles Sheffield. The picture hung in the salon at Buckingham House, and during this time it was copied by Jervas, George II's court painter.[30]

In 1751, the connoisseur George Vertue inspected the picture when it had been taken down and sent to be repaired and cleaned. 'Upon a strict review,' Vertue recorded in his notebook, 'the picture is much decayed and damaged—examining the lady's picture her face and neck almost changed and painted over—Sr Endymion—soft muddled laboured face—as a copy—the two eldest boys the best and most free and genteel—and shows the spirit and pencil of Van Dyke, the little boy at his mother's knee standing the face sprightly and lively.' Vertue made a little sketch of the picture in his notebook and added, 'when it is repaired and cleaned see it then if I can.'[31]

In 1763, the contents of Buckingham House were auctioned in London. In the catalogue was listed 'the remarkable fine picture of Endymion Porter's family by Van Dyke'. It was sold for £67 4s. od.[32] Its damaged condition would account for the low price, but the buyer is unknown, although a note by Dallaway in his 1827 edition of Walpole's *Anecdotes of Painting* states that it was bought 'for the late King'.[33] There is no trace of such a purchase in the royal archives, but some forty years later the picture was acquired by Endymion's descendant, the sixth Lord Strangford, who was Ambassador in Lisbon, Constantinople and St. Petersburg. From Lord Strangford it has come down into the possession of the present owner, his great-great-granddaughter. Today it hangs in a Cotswold house, not so far from Endymion's own home at Aston. The damage that Vertue described is plain to see, but Endymion's grave and kindly face looks proudly down on his wife and his three boys to remind his descendants of that happy time when, in the Duchess of Newcastle's words, 'Mr. Endymion Porter who was Groom of the Bedchamber to his Majesty King Charles the First,' held 'a place not only honourable, but very profitable.'[34]

REFERENCES

CHAPTER I

1. There are no parish registers extant for Mickleton for these years, but the year of Endymion Porter's birth can be established from the medallion portrait executed by Warin. It is dated 1635 and its inscription states that Endymion was then aged 48.
2. Charity Commissioners' Report, Gloucestershire, 1824–68. p. 477.
3. J. Burke, *Genealogical and Heraldic History of the Commons*. London, 1836. III, p. 577.
4. Calendar State Papers Domestic, 1591/4. pp. 12, 134.
5. Miss Hamilton's Papers.
6. Calendar State Papers Domestic, 1581/91. p. 567.
7. Calendar State Papers Domestic, 1595/7. p. 259.
8. Calendar State Papers Spain, 1580/86. p. 456; Calendar State Papers Domestic, 1629/31. p. 395.
9. State Papers Spain, 17/38.
10. Calendar State Papers Domestic. 1611/18. p. 109.
11. Calendar State Papers Domestic, 1581/91. pp. 500, 557.
12. Mickleton Parish Papers, Gloucestershire County Records Office. P.216/IN/3/14.
13. Calendar State Papers Domestic, 1595/97. p. 259.
14. Calendar State Papers Domestic, 1603/10. pp. 234, 268, 301.
15. Calendar State Papers Domestic, 1611/18. p. 167; Addenda, 1625/49. p. 468.
16. Treswell, 'Relation of the Earl of Nottingham's Journey to Spain', *Harleian Miscellany*. III, pp. 425–48.
17. Many contemporary sources attest that Endymion and Tom Porter spent part of their youth in Spain. It is very unlikely that they would have been sent there before peace was negotiated in 1604. It seems, therefore, a safe assumption that the occasion of their going was their grandfather's appointment to Nottingham's mission and the renewal of his Spanish connections.
18. Except where otherwise noted the particulars of Nottingham's journey are drawn from Treswell, op. cit.

REFERENCES

19. R. Winwood, *Memorials of Affairs of State in the Reigns of Queen Elizabeth and King James I*. London, 1725. II, p. 67.
20. S. de Madariaga, *The Fall of the Spanish American Empire*. London, 1947. pp. 180, 181.
21. Ibid.
22. Winwood. II, p. 75.
23. Winwood. II, p. 73.
24. Winwood. II, p. 71.
25. State Papers Spain, 11/45.
26. Winwood. II, p. 76.
27. Ibid.
28. Winwood. II, p. 69.
29. Cecil MSS., quoted by David Mathew, *The Jacobean Age*. London, 1941. p. 40 footnote.
30. State Papers Spain, 13/142; J. Howell, *Epistolae Ho-Elianae*, ed. Jacobs. London, 1892. I, p. 56.
31. G. Maranon, *El Conde-Duque de Olivares*. Madrid, 1952. pp. 12–30.
32. State Papers Spain, 34/150.
33. Francisco de Jesus, *Narrative of the Spanish Marriage Treaty*, ed. Gardiner. Camden Society, London, 1869. p. 183.
34. State Papers Spain, 16/239.
35. Winwood. II, p. 327.
36. State Papers Spain, 13/142.
37. Ibid.
38. State Papers Spain, 17/7.
39. Historical Manuscripts Commission, Downshire MSS. III, p. 111.
40. Downshire MSS. III, p. 140.
41. Downshire MSS. III, p. 261.
42. Sherborne MSS. Public Records Office. 31/8/198.
43. Winwood. II, pp. 149, 150.
44. Downshire MSS. III, p. 261.
45. Downshire MSS. II, p. 464.
46. Downshire MSS. II, pp. 27, 76.
47. Winwood. II, p. 465.
48. Downshire MSS. II, p. 320.
49. Downshire MSS. III, p. 111.
50. Downshire MSS. III, p. 247.
51. Downshire MSS. III, p. 245.
52. Downshire MSS. III, p. 366.
53. Downshire MSS. III, pp. 234, 262.
54. Downshire MSS. III, p. 302. This date for Endymion's return to England would agree with Arthur Wilson's statement of

ENDYMION PORTER

the date of his entering Edward Villiers' employment, viz. 'before either the Marquis or his Master were acceptable at Whitehall'.

55. Downshire MSS. III, pp. 431, 438.

CHAPTER II

1. Downshire MSS. II, p. 404.
2. Arthur Wilson, *Life and Reign of King James I* (A complete History of England to the death of King William III). London, 1719. p. 763.
3. *A Royalist's Notebook, the Commonplace Book of Sir John Oglander*, ed. Bamford. London, 1936. p. 41.
4. Bishop Goodman, *Court of King James I*, ed. Brewer. London, 1839. I, pp. 225, 226.
5. Oglander. p. 196.
6. Clarendon, *History of the Rebellion*. Oxford, 1826. I, p. 18.
7. Sir Henry Wotton, *Reliquiae Wottoniana, Life and Death of the Duke of Buckingham*. London, 1685. p. 210.
8. T. Birch, *Court and Times of James I*. London, 1849. II, pp. 78, 79.
9. B. Gerbier, *To all men that love Truth*. 1646. Quoted by H. Ross-Williamson, *Four Stuart Portraits*. London, 1949. p. 29.
10. Goodman. II, pp. 326–44.
11. Birch. II, pp. 69, 70.
12. Clarendon. I, p. 18.
13. J. Halliwell, *Letters of the Kings of England*. London, 1846. II, p. 153.
14. Downshire MSS. III, p. 192.
15. Calendar State Papers Domestic, 1619/23. pp. 15, 255, 307; Addenda, 1580/1625. p. 631.
16. Calendar State Papers Venice, 1621/23. p. 439.
17. Scudamore Papers, C115/N4/8607.
18. Calendar State Papers Domestic, 1611/18. p. 605; 1619/23. p. 78.
19. Calendar State Papers Domestic, 1619/23. p. 95.
20. Calendar State Papers Venice, 1621/23. p. 439.
21. Miss Hamilton's Papers.
22. Birch. II, p. 167.
23. Calendar State Papers Domestic, 1619/23. p. 47.
24. Goodman. I, p. 182.
25. Birch. II, p. 70.

REFERENCES

26. Goodman. I, p. 182 footnote.
27. Birch. II, pp. 59–79.
28. R. Chester Waters, *Genealogical Memoirs of the Chesters of Chichely*. London, 1878. I, pp. 137–60, from which the particulars of the Boteler family have been drawn.
29. Calendar State Papers Domestic, Addenda, 1603/25. p. 557.
30. Calendar Committee for Compounding, p. 1804.
31. Calendar State Papers Domestic, 1637. p. 556.
32. Birch. II, p. 12.
33. Clarendon. II, p. 15.
34. Calendar State Papers Domestic, 1625/6. p. 76.
35. Calendar State Papers Venice, 1621/23. p. 439.
36. The Court's movements have been drawn from J. Nichols, *The Progresses etc of King James I*. London, 1828. III and IV.
37. Birch. II, p. 198.
38. Birch. II, p. 209.
39. Nichols. IV, p. 614.
40. Birch. II, p. 207.
41. Calendar State Papers Domestic, 1619/23. p. 332.
42. Ibid.
43. Ibid.
44. Ibid.
45. Calendar State Papers Domestic, Addenda, 1625/49. p. 559.
46. Calendar State Papers Domestic, Addenda, 1625/49. p. 60.
47. Ibid.
48. Calendar State Papers Domestic, 1619/23. p. 332.
49. Ibid.
50. Ibid.
51. Ibid.
52. *Historical Account of Thomas Howard, Earl of Arundel, by his son Viscount Stafford*. Quoted by M. Hervey, *Life of Thomas Howard, Earl of Arundel*. Cambridge, 1921. p. 465.
53. Calendar State Papers Venice, 1610/13. p. 106.
54. Nichols. II, p. 489 footnote.
55. Birch. II, p. 207.
56. Hervey. pp. 131, 256.
57. W. N. Sainsbury, *Original Papers illustrative of the life of Sir Peter Paul Rubens*. London, 1859. pp. 60, 61.
58. Calendar State Papers Venice, 1621/23. p. 451.
59. I. A. Philip, *Burlington Magazine*. May 1957.
60. Goodman. II, pp. 369, 370.
61. P. Oppé, 'Sir Anthony Van Dyck in England,' *Burlington Magazine*. 1941.
62. Calendar State Papers Domestic, Addenda, 1580/1625. p. 631.

63. O. Millar, *Burlington Magazine*. April 1951.
64. *Dekker his Dreame*. London, 1620.
65. Calendar State Papers Venice, 1621/23. pp. 450–53.
66. Ibid.
67. Ibid.
68. *Autobiography of Sir Simonds D'Ewes*. London, 1845. I, p. 170.
69. Arthur Wilson. p. 734.
70. Nichols. IV, pp. 673–709.
71. Calendar State Papers Domestic, 1619/23. p. 283.
72. H.M.C. *IX Report*. Part II. Appendix. p. 440.

CHAPTER III

1. J. R. Green, *Short History of the English People*. London, 1893. III, p. 1013.
2. Calendar State Papers Domestic, 1625/26. p. 350.
3. Sherborne MSS. P.R.O. 31/8/198; S.R. Gardiner, *History of England from the accession of James I to the outbreak of the Civil War*. London, 1884. IV, p. 370.
4. State Papers Spain 27/59 (Sir Tobie Matthew's description of the Infanta); Howell. I, pp. 155, 238.
5. Sherborne MSS.
6. Howell. I, pp. 110, 111.
7. Birch. II, p. 344.
8. Calendar State Papers Venice, 1621/23. p. 485.
9. Calendar State Papers Domestic, 1619/23. p. 453.
10. E. de Fonblanque, *Lives of the Lords Strangford*. London, 1877. p. 24.
11. State Papers Spain, 25/297.
12. State Papers Spain, 25/295.
13. State Papers Spain, 25/297.
14. Calendar State Papers Domestic, 1625/26. p. 350.
15. State Papers Spain, 25/302; H.M.C. Buccleugh MSS. I, p. 211.
16. Calendar State Papers Venice, 1623/25. p. 243.
17. Gardiner. III, p. 390.
18. State Papers Spain, 25/302.
19. Calendar State Papers Venice, 1621/23. p. 502.
20. Birch. II, p. 353.
21. London County Council Records. B.R.A. 723/8, 9, 10.
22. Calendar State Papers Domestic, 1625/26. p. 350; J. Rushworth, *Historical Collections*. London, 1721. I, p. 120.
23. Rushworth. Ibid.
24. Clarendon. I, pp. 20–32.

REFERENCES

25. Calendar State Papers Domestic, 1619/23. p. 503.
26. Halliwell. II, p. 166.
27. Calendar State Papers Venice. 1621/23. p. 635.
28. Calendar State Papers Venice, 1621/23. p. 454.
29. Calendar State Papers Domestic, 1629/31. p. 21.
30. Calendar State Papers Domestic, 1619/23. pp. 495, 497, 502, 503; Wotton. pp. 212–17; Nichols. IV, pp. 807, 808.
31. Calendar State Papers Venice, 1621/23. pp. 585, 586; Wotton. p. 214.
32. Halliwell. II, p. 163.
33. Fonblanque. p. 27.
34. Wotton. p. 216; Wilson. pp. 763, 764; Calendar State Papers Domestic, 1619/23. p. 533.
35. Halliwell. II, p. 173.

CHAPTER IV

1. Howell. I, pp. 164, 165; Birch. II, pp. 366, 367; Calendar State Papers Domestic, 1619/23. p. 502.
2. H.M.C. Mar and Kellie MSS. *Supplementary Report*. p. 152.
3. Calendar State Papers Domestic, 1619/23. p. 503.
4. Calendar State Papers Venice, 1621/23. p. 581.
5. D. Neal, *History of the Puritans*. London, 1822. II, p. 122.
6. Calendar State Papers Domestic, 1619/23. pp. 520–43 *passim*.
7. Calendar State Papers Domestic, 1619/23. p. 533; Halliwell. II, p. 172.
8. Calendar State Papers Domestic, 1619/23. p. 554; Birch. II, pp. 378–82; Halliwell. II, p. 174.
9. Calendar State Papers Domestic, 1619/23. p. 520.
10. State Papers Spain, 26/118; Halliwell. II, p. 183.
11. Halliwell, ibid.
12. Calendar State Papers Venice, 1621/23. p. 611; Sherborne MSS.
13. Nichols. IV, p. 847; Birch. II, p. 410.
14. Gardiner. V, pp. 14–24; Halliwell. II, p. 189.
15. Calendar State Papers Venice, 1621/23. p. 638.
16. State Papers Spain, 26/151.
17. Calendar State Papers Domestic, 1619/23. p. 554.
18. Gardiner. V, pp. 26–52; Calendar State Papers Venice, 1621/23. p. 639.
19. Halliwell. II, pp. 206, 207.
20. Howell. I, p. 174.
21. Birch. II, pp. 399, 400.

22. Howell. I, p. 169.
23. Ibid.
24. H.M.C. Mar and Kellie MSS. *Supplementary Report.* p. 170; Howell. I, p. 172.
25. Calendar State Papers Venice, 1623/25. p. 21.
26. National Library of Scotland. Miscellaneous MSS. 1879.
27. J. Pope Hennessy, *The Raphael Cartoons.* H. M. Stationery Office, 1950.
28. Calendar State Papers Domestic, 1623/25. p. 69.
29. State Papers Spain, 34/226.
30. Calendar State Papers Domestic, 1619/23. pp. 585, 590.
31. Howell. I, pp. 169, 170; Francisco de Jesus, p. 252; Birch. II, pp. 423, 424; Calendar State Papers Domestic, 1623/25. p. 110.
32. M. Whinney and O. Millar, *English Art 1625–1714.* Oxford, 1957. p. 27.
33. Halliwell. II, pp. 207, 208.
34. Calendar State Papers Domestic, 1623/25. p. 21.
35. Halliwell. II, p. 220.
36. Halliwell. II, pp. 213, 218.
37. Calendar State Papers Domestic, 1623/25. p. 37.
38. Calendar State Papers Domestic, Addenda, 1580–1625. p. 657.
39. Halliwell. II, p. 218.
40. Gardiner. V, pp. 89–96, 105, 106, 111, 112.
41. Halliwell. II, p. 226.
42. Calendar State Papers Domestic, 1623/25. p. 69.
43. Ibid.
44. Howell. I, p. 172; Hardwicke Miscellaneous State Papers. London, 1778. I, pp. 477, 478.
45. Calendar State Papers Venice, 1623/25. p. 47.
46. Nichols. IV, pp. 909, 910.
47. National Library of Scotland. Miscellaneous MSS. 1879.
48. Calendar State Papers Domestic, 1623/25. p. 69.
49. National Library of Scotland. Miscellaneous MSS. 1879.
50. Francisco Pacheco, *Arte de la Pintura*, ed. F. J. Sanchez Canton. Madrid, 1956. I, p. 156.
51. Nichols. IV, pp. 921, 922; Birch. II, p. 419; Sherborne MSS.
52. Calendar State Papers Venice, 1623/25. p. 134.
53. Gardiner. V, pp. 118–19.
54. Nichols. IV, pp. 925, 926; Sherborne MSS.
55. Nichols. IV, pp. 927–30; Birch. II, pp. 420, 422, 423.
56. Birch. II, pp. 426, 427.
57. Rushworth. I, p. 105.
58. Howell. I, pp. 184–89; Gardiner. V, pp. 145–56.

REFERENCES

59. T. Birch, *Court and Times of Charles I.* London, 1849. II, p. 104; Calendar State Papers Domestic, 1623/25. p. 113.

CHAPTER V

1. Calendar State Papers Domestic, 1623/25. p. 110.
2. Fonblanque. p. 45.
3. Calendar State Papers Domestic, 1619/23. p. 473.
4. Birch. II, p. 474.
5. Calendar State Papers Domestic, 1623/25. p. 326.
6. *Dictionary of National Biography.*
7. Calendar State Papers Domestic, 1623/25. p. 359.
8. Birch. II, p. 488.
9. Calendar State Papers Domestic, 1623/25. p. 453.
10. Birch. II, p. 490.
11. Calendar State Papers Domestic, 1625/26. p. 197.
12. Birch. II, p. 506.
13. T. Birch, *Court and Times of Charles I.* London, 1849. I, p. 5.
14. Birch. I, p. 3.
15. Birch. I, p. 22.
16. Nichols. IV, pp. 1037–49.
17. Calendar State Papers Domestic, 1625/26. pp. 23, 528.
18. Calendar State Papers Domestic, 1625/26. pp. 210, 255.
19. E. Chambers, *The Elizabethan Stage.* Oxford, 1923. I, pp. 27–70.
20. Calendar State Papers Domestic, 1625/26. pp. 23, 528.
21. C. Pitcairn, *History of the Fifeshire Pitcairns.* Edinburgh, 1905. pp. 337–40; Calendar State Papers Domestic, 1625/26. p. 544.
22. *Dictionary of National Biography; G.E.C.'s Complete Peerage.*
23. *Dictionary of National Biography.*
24. Lord Chamberlain's Registers. P.R.O. LC3/1.
25. Pipe Office declared accounts, Treasurer of the Chamber, P.R.O. E351/544; Lord Chamberlain's Registers P.R.O. LC3/1; Calendar State Papers Domestic, 1629/31. p. 140.
26. Lord Chamberlain's Miscellanea. P.R.O. LC5/180.
27. Sainsbury. p. 68; C. R. Cammell, *Great Duke of Buckingham.* London, 1939. pp. 374–6.
28. Birch. I, pp. 30, 31.
29. Calendar State Papers Domestic, 1625/26. p. 43.
30. Calendar State Papers Domestic. 1625/26. p. 45.
31. Birch. I, pp. 28, 37.
32. Calendar State Papers Domestic, 1648/49. p. 432.
33. Calendar State Papers Domestic, 1637/38. p. 492.

34. Ibid.
35. Miss Hamilton's Papers.
36. Calendar State Papers Domestic, 1637/38. p. 482.
37. Anthony Wood. *Athenae Oxonienses.* London, 1820, p. 222.
38. Ibid.
39. Ibid.
40. Ibid.
41. *Annalia Dubrensia;* Bristol and Gloucestershire Archæological Society, Vol. XIII, pp. 103–17; *Works of Sir William D'avenant.* London, 1673. p. 236.
42. L. Hotson, *I, William Shakespeare.* London, 1937. pp. 51, 267; Calendar State Papers Domestic, 1629/31. p. 254.
43. Fonblanque. pp. 48, 49.
44. Birch. I, p. 39.
45. Birch. I, p. 48.
46. Birch. I, pp. 50, 52.
47. Calendar State Papers Domestic, 1625/26. pp. 154, 553.
48. H. Walpole, *Anecdotes of Painting in England,* ed. Dallaway. London, 1828. II, p. 391.
49. Sainsbury. p. 65.
50. Sainsbury. pp. 256, 257.
51. Walpole. II, p. 16.
52. Sainsbury. pp. 310–16.
53. *Robert Herrick's Poetical Works,* ed. Martin. Oxford, 1956. Introduction, p. XIII.
54. Herrick. p. 41.
55. Herrick. p. 324.
56. Herrick. p. 72.
57. Herrick. p. 183.
58. Herrick. p. 229.
59. Birch. I, p. 78.
60. Birch. I, p. 98.
61. H.M.C. *XI Report.* Appendix, I. pp. 66, 67.
62. Ibid.
63. Birch. I, p. 101.
64. Ibid.
65. Calendar State Papers Domestic, 1625/26. p. 350.
66. *House of Lords Journals.* p. 1672.
67. Sherborne MSS. P.R.O. 31/8/148.
68. Birch. I, p. 112.
69. Ibid.
70. Birch. I, p. 113.
71. Birch. I, p. 121.
72. Ibid.

73. Ibid.
74. Birch. I, p. 138.
75. Birch. I, p. 119.
76. Birch. I, p. 120.
77. Birch. I, p. 228.
78. Oglander. p. 27.
79. Birch. I, pp. 241, 247.
80. Birch. I, p. 240.
81. Herrick. Introduction, p. XIII.
82. Calendar State Papers Domestic, 1627/28. p. 415.
83. Calendar State Papers Domestic, 1627/28. p. 414.
84. Birch. I, pp. 287–90.
85. Birch. I, p. 291.
86. Birch. I, p. 286.
87. Sainsbury. p. 324.
88. Sainsbury. pp. 325, 326.
89. Sainsbury. p. 325.
90. Sainsbury. p. 327.
91. G. Vertue, *Note Books*. Walpole Society, London, 1930. I, p. 112. (Richard Symonds' Note Book.)
92. Sainsbury. pp. 326, 328.
93. Sainsbury. p. 328.
94. Sainsbury. p. 323.
95. Sainsbury. pp. 330–37.
96. Ibid.
97. I. A. Philip, *Burlington Magazine*. May, 1957.
98. Calendar State Papers Domestic, 1635/36. p. 76.
99. Calendar State Papers Domestic, 1627/8. p. 577.
100. Calendar State Papers Domestic, 1627/8. p. 585.
101. Birch. I, p. 362.
102. Birch. I, p. 364.
103. Calendar State Papers Venice, 1628/29. p. 312.
104. Calendar State Papers Domestic, 1628/29. p. 219.
105. Calendar State Papers Domestic, 1628/29. p. 199; 1633/34. p. 331.
106. Calendar State Papers Domestic, 1628/29. p. 169; 1637. p. 457; 1637/8. p. 492; 1639. p. 38.
107. Calendar State Papers Ireland, 1625/32. pp. 255, 377, 439.
108. Calendar State Papers Ireland, Addenda, 1625/60. p. 90; 1633/47. p. 106.
109. Calendar State Papers Ireland, 1625/32. p. 294.
110. Calendar State Papers Domestic, 1625/26. p. 581.
111. Calendar State Papers Domestic, 1628/9. p. 125.
112. Calendar State Papers Ireland, 1625/32. p. 294.

113. Calendar State Papers Venice, 1628/29. pp. 187, 188; H.M.C. *XI Report*. Appendix I. p. 156–65.
114. Calendar State Papers Domestic, 1627/28. pp. 2, 144.
115. Calendar State Papers Venice, 1628/29. pp. 252, 312.
116. Calendar State Papers Domestic, 1629/31. p. 216; Addenda, 1625/29. p. 732; W. H. Carpenter, *Memoir of Sir Antony van Dyck*. London, 1844. p. 25.
117. Calendar State Papers Venice, 1628/29. pp. 312, 361; H.M.C. *XI Report*. Appendix. I, p. 165.
118. Calendar State Papers Domestic, 1628/29. p. 241.
119. Oglander. pp. 38, 39.
120. Calendar State Papers Venice, 1628/29. pp. 447, 459; Calendar State Papers Domestic, 1628/29. p. 395.
121. State Papers Spain, 34/37.
122. Calendar State Papers Domestic, 1628/29. pp. 443, 444, 453; 1629/31. p. 168; Calendar State Papers Venice, 1628/29. pp. 466, 492, 515; Birch II, p. 4.
123. Birch. I, p. 430.
124. State Papers Spain, 34/128.
125. Aubrey, *Brief Lives*, ed. Lawson Dick. London, 1949.

CHAPTER VI

1. Lord Chamberlain's Miscellanea. P.R.O. LC5/180.
2. Birch. II, p. 208.
3. Vertue. I, p. 114.
4. Calendar State Papers Ireland, 1625/32. p. 294.
5. Calendar State Papers Venice, 1621/23. p. 452.
6. Calendar State Papers Domestic, 1629/31. p. 138; 1631/33. pp. 230, 256; *Sir Thomas Herbert's Memoirs*. London, 1711. p. 130.
7. Walpole. II, p. 93.
8. Lord Chamberlain's Registers. P.R.O. LC3/1.
9. *Dramatic Records of Sir Henry Herbert*, ed. Adams. New Haven, 1917. pp. 60, 65.
10. Howell. I, pp. 317, 318.
11. Sainsbury. p. 323.
12. T. May, *The Tragedy of Antigone*. London, 1631.
13. J. Suckling, Poems. *English Poets*, ed. Chalmers. London, 1810. VI, pp. 491, 492.
14. Aubrey. p. 85.
15. D'avenant. p. 235.
16. D'avenant. p. 223.

17. D'avenant. p. 217.
18. D'avenant. p. 237.
19. D'avenant. p. 215.
20. D'avenant. p. 320.
21. D'avenant. p. 229.
22. Aubrey. p. 86.
23. D'avenant. pp. 234, 235.
24. Herbert, ed. Adams. pp. 22, 35, 54.
25. D'avenant. p. 235.
26. D'avenant. p. 165.
27. *S. Pepys's Diary.* August 15th, 16th, 23rd, 1661.
28. Herbert, ed. Adams. p. 55.
29. Herbert, ed. Adams. p. 56.
30. Calendar State Papers Domestic, 1637. p. 71.
31. G. Bromley, *A Collection of Royal Letters.* London, 1787. p. 86.
32. Calendar State Papers Venice, 1636/39. p. 184.
33. Calendar State Papers Venice, 1636/39. p. 188.
34. D'avenant. p. 200.
35. Calendar State Papers Domestic, 1636/37. pp. 505, 559.
36. Calendar State Papers Venice, 1636/39. pp. 184, 185.
37. M. Green, *Lives of the Princesses of England.* London, 1849. V, pp. 540, 541.
38. Calendar State Papers Domestic, 1637. p. 82.
39. D'avenant. p. 200.
40. D'avenant. p. 201.
41. *Dictionary of National Biography.*
42. Walpole. II, pp. 93, 94.
43. Sainsbury. p. 323.
44. Calendar State Papers Domestic, 1631/32. pp. 38, 39.
45. B. Reade, *Burlington Magazine.* March 1947; H. M. Ogden, *Burlington Magazine.* September 1947.
46. Whinney and Millar. p. 4.
47. 'Catalogue of the Contents of the Cabinet Room', MSS. in Royal Library. Folio 35.
48. Royal Library, folios 13, 27; Bodleian MSS. Ashmole 1514. Folios 60, 66, 80, 92, 94.
49. Whinney and Millar. p. 4, note 3.
50. W. Sanderson, *Graphice.* London, 1658. pp. 20–24; Vertue. IV, p. 31.
51. Knowler, *Earl of Strafford's Letters and Despatches.* London, 1739. II, p. 1.
52. Whinney and Millar. p. 4, note 3.
53. P.R.O. Roman Transcripts, Panzani to Barberini. Jan. 30, 1636.

54. Gordon Albion, *Charles I and the Court of Rome*. London, 1935. Appendix I. pp. 397, 400.
55. Sainsbury. pp. 280–90.
56. Sainsbury. pp. 352, 353.
57. Walpole. II, p. 94.
58. Sainsbury. p. 146.
59. Ibid.
60. Calendar State Papers Domestic, 1637. p. 548; 1637/8. pp. 434, 467; Sainsbury. pp. 191–205.
61. P.R.O. Exchequer Port Books, E/190/44/1, 1640/41.
62. Calendar State Papers Domestic, 1638/39. p. 196.
63. H.M.C. Portland MSS. II, p. 131.
64. Howell. I, p. 324.
65. Calendar State Papers Venice, 1632/36. p. 296.
66. Ibid; Calendar Clarendon State Papers. I, p. 53.
67. Fonblanque. pp. 60, 61.
68. Calendar State Papers Venice, 1632/36, p. 300.
69. Calendar State Papers Domestic, 1634/35, p. 461.
70. Calendar State Papers Venice, 1632/36, p. 403.
71. Calendar State Papers Venice, 1632/36. p. 319.
72. Ibid.
73. Calendar State Papers Domestic, 1635. p. 571.
74. Bodleian MSS. Ashmole, 1514. Folio 172; E. Croft Murray, *Burlington Magazine*. April, 1947.
75. Calendar State Papers Domestic, 1639/40. p. 22.
76. Calendar State Papers Domestic, 1639/40. p. 24.

CHAPTER VII

1. Calendar State Papers Domestic, 1625/6. p. 526; 1628/29. p. 544.
2. Calendar State Papers Domestic, 1627/28. p. 227.
3. Calendar State Papers Domestic, 1628/29. p. 585.
4. Calendar State Papers Domestic, 1629/31. p. 84.
5. Calendar State Papers Domestic, 1629/31. p. 124.
6. Calendar State Papers Domestic, 1625/26. p. 208.
7. Calendar State Papers Domestic, 1629/31. p. 258.
8. Calendar State Papers Domestic, 1628/29. p. 437.
9. Calendar State Papers Domestic, 1639. p. 268.
10. Calendar State Papers Domestic, 1635/36. pp. 2, 7.
11. Calendar State Papers Domestic, 1635/36. p. 429.
12. Calendar State Papers Domestic, 1635/36. p. 433.

REFERENCES

13. Calendar State Papers Domestic, 1631/33. p. 552.
14. Calendar State Papers Domestic, 1637/38. p. 255.
15. Calendar State Papers Domestic, 1639. p. 2.
16. Calendar State Papers Domestic, 1635/36. p. 182.
17. Calendar State Papers Domestic, 1631/33. p. 472.
18. Calendar State Papers Domestic, 1640/41. p. 355.
19. Calendar State Papers Ireland, 1625/32. p. 650; 1633/47. p. 67.
20. Calendar State Papers Domestic, 1631/33. p. 511.
21. J. R. Elder, *The Royal Fishery Companies of the 17th Century.* Edinburgh, 1912. pp. 35–84.
22. Calendar State Papers Domestic, 1637/38. pp. 17, 371.
23. Calendar State Papers Domestic, 1637/38. p. 147; Hughes, *Studies in Administration and Finance.* Manchester, 1934. pp. 88–115.
24. Knowler. I, pp. 176, 446; T. Rymer, *Foedera.* London, 1727. XIX, pp. 381, 504, 567, 592; Calendar State Papers Domestic, 1631/8 *passim.*
25. Except where otherwise noted, the account of the Courten Association is based on J. Bruce, *Annals of the East India Company,* 1600–1708. London, 1810. I, pp. 329–440.
26. *Dictionary of National Biography.*
27. Birch. II, p. 262.
28. Calendar State Papers Domestic, 1635. p. 96.
29. Calendar State Papers Domestic, 1634/35. pp. 573, 575.
30. Birch. II, pp. 261, 262.
31. Birch. II, pp. 268, 269.
32. Calendar State Papers Domestic, 1637. p. 82.
33. Calendar State Papers Domestic, 1637. p. 81.
34. Knowler. II, p. 117.
35. Rymer. XIX, pp. 146–156.
36. Calendar State Papers Domestic, 1631/33. p. 411; Calendar Committee Compounding, p. 1804.
37. Calendar State Papers Domestic, 1637. p. 548.
38. Calendar State Papers Domestic, 1634/35. p. 129.
39. Calendar State Papers Domestic, 1637/38. p. 374.
40. Calendar State Papers Domestic, 1638/39. p. 13.
41. Calendar State Papers Domestic, 1639. pp. 151, 152.
42. Calendar State Papers Domestic, 1648/49. p. 398.
43. Calendar State Papers Domestic, 1639. p. 316.
44. Calendar State Papers Domestic, 1639. p. 325.
45. Calendar State Papers Domestic, 1639. p. 497.
46. Calendar State Papers Domestic, 1639/40. p. 88.
47. Calendar State Papers Domestic, 1639/40. p. 364.
48. Calendar State Papers Domestic, 1639/40. p. 484.

49. Calendar Committee Compounding. p. 1804.
50. Calendar State Papers Ireland, Addenda, 1625/1660. p. 226.
51. *The Nicholas Papers*, ed. Warner. London, 1886. p. 45.
52. Calendar State Papers Domestic, 1637/38. p. 292.
53. H. A. Wyndham, *A Family History 1410–1688*. Oxford, 1939. pp. 181–83; P.R.O. T.56/8. p. 27.
54. Calendar State Papers Domestic, 1629/31. p. 554; 1660/61. p. 393.
55. Calendar State Papers Domestic, 1635. p. 78.
56. Calendar State Papers Ireland, 1633/47. p. 176.
57. Calendar State Papers Domestic, 1638/39. p. 191; 1640/41. p. 439; 1660/61. p. 313; Calendar Committee Compounding. p. 1804.
58. Calendar State Papers Domestic, 1640. p. 226.
59. Calendar State Papers Domestic, 1635/36. p. 355; 1636/37. p. 530; 1660/61. p. 298; H. Robinson, *The British Post Office*. Princeton, 1948. Chapters 2, 3 and 4.
60. Calendar State Papers Domestic, 1637/38. p. 55.
61. Calendar State Papers Domestic, 1628/29. p. 422.
62. Calendar State Papers Domestic, 1629/31. p. 21.
63. Calendar State Papers Domestic, 1638/39. p. 262.
64. Calendar State Papers Domestic, 1629/31. p. 131.
65. Calendar State Papers Domestic, 1628/29. p. 487.
66. Calendar State Papers Domestic, 1633/34. p. 396.
67. Calendar Committee Compounding. p. 1804.
68. Calendar State Papers Domestic, 1637/38. p. 78.
69. After 1613/14 Calley's name no longer appears in the livery lists of the Drapers' Society.
70. Rymer. XIX, p. 431.
71. Calendar State Papers Domestic, 1635. p. 433; 1637. p. 467.
72. *Wiltshire Archæological Magazine*. December, 1900.
73. Miss Calley's Papers.

CHAPTER VIII

1. Calendar Committee Compounding. p. 1804.
2. Ibid.
3. Ibid.
4. Ibid.
5. Calendar State Papers Domestic, 1641/43. p. 317.
6. Calendar State Papers Domestic, 1637/38. p. 129.
7. L.C.C. Records. B.R.A. 723/9, 10, 11.
8. Calendar State Papers Domestic, 1638/39. p. 83.

REFERENCES

9. Calendar State Papers Domestic, 1636/37. p. 15; Rymer. XIX, p. 511.
10. Calendar State Papers Domestic, 1636/37. pp. 233, 404; 1637. pp. 62, 140, 225, 433; 1637/38. p. 327.
11. Calendar State Papers Domestic, 1637/38. p. 129.
12. Calendar State Papers Domestic, 1638/39. p. 269.
13. Calendar State Papers Domestic, 1641/43. p. 317.
14. Calendar Committee Compounding. p. 1804.
15. Wyndham. pp. 222–31.
16. Rymer. XX, pp. 240, 241; Rushworth. II, p. 1103.
17. Calendar Committee Compounding. p. 1804; M. Keeler, *The Long Parliament*. Philadelphia, 1954. p. 311.
18. Calendar State Papers Domestic, 1634/35. p. 178.
19. Calendar State Papers Domestic, 1634/35. p. 201.
20. Calendar State Papers Domestic, 1637/38. p. 29.
21. Calendar State Papers Domestic, 1629/31. p. 207.
22. Calendar State Papers Domestic, 1629/31. pp. 270, 287.
23. Calendar State Papers Domestic, Addenda, 1625/49. p. 465.
24. Gloucestershire County Records Office, D213/9/3.
25. Calendar State Papers Domestic, 1638/39. p. 68.
26. Calendar State Papers Domestic, 1639/40. p. 12.
27. Calendar State Papers Domestic, 1638/39. p. 20.
28. Calendar State Papers Domestic, 1639/40. p. 373.
29. Calendar State Papers Domestic, 1639/40. p. 397.
30. Calendar State Papers Domestic, 1640/41. p. 195.
31. Calendar State Papers Domestic, 1640/41. p. 256.
32. Calendar State Papers Domestic, 1627/28. p. 498.
33. Calendar State Papers Domestic, 1639/40. p. 12.
34. H.M.C. Portland MSS. II, p. 131.
35. Calendar State Papers Domestic, 1636/37. p. 369.
36. Calendar State Papers Domestic, 1637/38. p. 129.
37. State Papers Spain, 40/178.
38. H.M.C. Cowper MSS. II, p. 161.
39. Calendar State Papers Domestic, 1637/38. p. 556.
40. Calendar State Papers Domestic, 1637/38. p. 376.
41. Calendar State Papers Domestic, 1628/29. p. 169.
42. Calendar State Papers Domestic, 1631/32. p. 12.
43. Calendar State Papers Domestic, 1634/35. p. 133.
44. Calendar State Papers Domestic, 1633/34. p. 242.
45. Calendar State Papers Domestic, 1634/35. p. 604.
46. Calendar State Papers Domestic, 1635. pp. 315, 509.
47. Calendar State Papers Domestic, 1636/37. p. 86.
48. Calendar State Papers Domestic, 1637. p. 465.
49. Calendar State Papers Domestic, 1637. p. 435.

50. Calendar State Papers Domestic, 1627/28. p. 525.
51. Calendar State Papers Domestic, Addenda, 1625/49. p. 465.
52. Calendar State Papers Domestic, 1637/38. p. 129; 1639/40. p. 108.
53. Calendar State Papers Domestic, 1627/28. p. 496; 1629/31. pp. 257, 300.
54. Calendar State Papers Domestic, 1628–41 *passim; Wiltshire Archæological Magazine.* December, 1900; Miss Calley's Papers.
55. Gardiner. VIII, p. 238.
56. Albion. p. 210.
57. Albion. p. 208.
58. Albion. p. 209.
59. Albion. p. 201; British Museum Additional MSS. 15,390.
60. Knowler. II, p. 128.
61. Ibid.

CHAPTER IX

1. Knowler. II, p. 134.
2. Scudamore Papers. C115/N8/8810, letter of Sir John Finet; G. A. Raikes, *History of the Honourable Artillery Company.* London, 1878. I, pp. 90, 94.
3. Knowler. II, p. 350.
4. Calendar State Papers Domestic, 1639. p. 49.
5. Calendar State Papers Domestic, 1639. p. 113.
6. Ibid.
7. Calendar State Papers Domestic, 1639. p. 195.
8. Calendar State Papers Domestic, 1639. p. 325.
9. Calendar State Papers Domestic, 1639. p. 384.
10. Strafford MSS. Vols. XIII, XIV, XV, XVI, XVII, XVIII.
11. *Salmacida Spolia.* London, 1639/40.
12. *Dictionary of National Biography.*
13. Calendar State Papers Domestic, 1640/41. p. 256.
14. H.M.C. Middleton MSS. p. 193.
15. Calendar State Papers Domestic, 1640. p. 54.
16. Calendar State Papers Domestic, 1640. p. 246.
17. Calendar State Papers Domestic, 1640. p. 75.
18. Calendar State Papers Domestic, 1640. p. 231.
19. Calendar State Papers Domestic, 1640. p. 646.
20. H.M.C. Middleton MSS. p. 193; Cowper MSS. II, p. 260.
21. Calendar State Papers Domestic, 1640/41. p. 248.
22. Calendar State Papers Domestic, 1640/41. p. 126.

REFERENCES

23. Rushworth. III, p. 1310; *Rome's Masterpiece*. London, 1643.
24. Calendar State Papers Domestic, 1640/41. pp. 83, 108, 144.
25. Calendar State Papers Domestic, 1640/41. p. 139.
26. Keeler, *The Long Parliament*. p. 311; W. R. Williams, *Parliamentary History of the County of Worcester*, Hereford, 1897. pp. 121–23.
27. *Victoria History of the Counties of England. Worcester*. London, 1907. I, p. 306.

CHAPTER X

1. Clarendon. I, p. 295.
2. Calendar State Papers Domestic, 1640/41. pp. 254, 256, 279, 414, 424.
3. *An Exact Collection*. London, 1643.
4. Calendar State Papers Domestic, 1640/41. p. 503.
5. *Verney Papers: Notes on the Proceedings of the Long Parliament*, ed. Bruce. London, 1845. pp. 57, 58.
6. R. Cox, *Hibernia Anglicana*. London, 1689. II, p 71; Appendix XLIX. p. 210; Calendar State Papers Ireland, 1633/47. p. 331.
7. *Journals of the House of Commons*, 2nd August 1641.
8. *Nicholas Papers*. pp. 40, 45.
9. Ibid.
10. T. Carte, *James, Duke of Ormonde*. London, 1735. II, p. 256.
11. G. Brodie, *History of the British Empire from the accession of Charles I to the Restoration*. Edinburgh, 1822. III, pp. 203–10; M. Hickson, *Ireland in the Seventeenth Century*. London, 1884. I, p. 167; Gardiner. X, pp. 68, 69.
12. Gardiner. X, p. 92.
13. *The Mystery of Iniquity yet working in the Kingdom of England Scotland and Ireland for the Destruction of Religion truly Protestant*. London, 1643. British Museum. E176/25, p. 38.
14. *Tanner Letters*, ed. McNeill. Dublin, 1943. p. 132; *Journals of Sir Simonds d'Ewes*, ed. Coates. Yale, 1942. p. 352.
15. Calendar State Papers Domestic, 1641/43. p. 256.
16. Calendar Committee Compounding. p. 1804.
17. D. Townshend, *Life and Letters of Endymion Porter*. London, 1897. p. 201.
18. Calendar State Papers Domestic, 1641/43. p. 256.

CHAPTER XI

1. Calendar State Papers Venice, 1642/3. p. 5.
2. Commons *Journals*, Feb. 15th, 1642; H.M.C. *XII Report.* p. 305.
3. Commons *Journals*, April 18th, 1642.
4. H.M.C. Portland MSS. I, p. 39.
5. Calendar State Papers Domestic, 1641/43. p. 315.
6. Commons *Journals*, May 6th, 1642.
7. Clarendon. III, p. 71.
8. Calendar State Papers Domestic, 1641/43. p. 333.
9. *Exceeding Joyful News from Derby*. London, 1642. British Museum. E118/13.
10. Calendar State Papers Domestic, 1641/43. p. 399; Clarendon. III, p. 240.
11. *Army Lists of the Roundheads and Cavaliers*, ed. Peacock. London, 1863.
12. Clarendon. III, pp. 272–98; T. Carte, *Collection of Original Letters and Papers, 1641–1660.* London, 1739. I, p. 10; Bulstrode, *Memoirs and Reflections upon the Reign and Government of King Charles I and King Charles II.* London, 1721. pp. 76–86; Ellis, *Original Letters.* London, 1846. III, p. 315; P. Warwick, *Memoirs of the Reign of Charles I.* London, 1701. p. 229; Aubrey, pp. 128, 129.
13. Rushworth. VI, pp. 42–48; E. Walker, *Discourses upon Several Occasions.* London, 1705. pp. 130, 131; Clarendon. V, p. 183.
14. Calendar State Papers Venice, 1642/43. pp. 128, 155.
15. Margaret, Duchess of Newcastle, *Life of William Cavendish, Duke of Newcastle*, ed. Firth. London, 1886. p. 165.
16. E. Warburton, *Memoirs of Prince Rupert and the Cavaliers.* London, 1849. Abstract of correspondence; H.M.C. *IX Report.* Part II. p. 435.
17. Ibid.
18. Ibid.
19. Rushworth. III, p. 632.
20. Commons *Journals*, Oct. 10th, Nov. 29th, Dec. 2nd, 1644; H.M.C. Portland MSS. I, pp. 192–96; Calendar State Papers Domestic, 1644/45. p. 23.
21. Bulstrode. pp. 134, 137.
22. Bulstrode. pp. 136–39.
23. *Life and Times of Anthony Wood*, ed. Clark. Oxford, 1891. I, pp. 52–67.

24. Anthony Wood. I, p. 72.
25. Anthony Wood. I, pp. 72, 80.
26. J. Spalding, *History of the Troubles in Scotland*. Aberdeen, 1792. I, p. 140; *Letters of Queen Henrietta Maria*, ed. Green. London, 1857. p. 166; *Memoirs of Madame de Motteville*. Paris, 1869. I, p. 273.
27. H.M.C. Portland MSS. I, p. 98.
28. Commons *Journals*, March, 1643.
29. Aubrey. pp. 181–87.
30. Aubrey. pp. 23, 54, 56, 129; Foreword, p. xxxix.
31. Warwick. I, p. 235.
32. Aubrey. p. 13.
33. Ibid.
34. Walpole. II, p. 252.
35. Aubrey. Foreword, p. xxxviii.
36. Calendar Committee Compounding. p. 1804.
37. Calendar State Papers Domestic, 1652/53. p. 167.
38. Townshend. p. 209.
39. *Letters of Queen Henrietta Maria*. pp. 243–47.
40. Rushworth. III, pp. 559–74.
41. M. Napier, *Memoirs of the Marquis of Montrose*. Edinburgh, 1856. II, p. 391.
42. Calendar Clarendon State Papers. I, p. 297; Gardiner, *English Historical Review*. II, pp. 687–708.
43. Walker. p. 126.
44. Bulstrode. p. 127.
45. Rushworth. VI, p. 131; Calendar State Papers Domestic, 1645/47. p. 87.

CHAPTER XII

1. A. Strickland, *Lives of the Queens of England*. London, 1845. VIII, p. 114.
2. Strickland. p. 124.
3. Nicholas Papers. pp. 70–73.
4. Ibid.
5. H.M.C. Portland MSS. II, p. 135.
6. Nicholas. pp. 70–73.
7. Ibid.
8. Ibid.
9. Ibid.
10. Bulstrode. pp. 140–47.
11. Clarendon. V, p. 158.

12. Bulstrode. p. 148; Clarendon. V, p. 281.
13. Calendar Committee Compounding. pp. 1097, 1098; Commons *Journals*. IV, pp. 486, 522.
14. Commons *Journals*. IV, pp. 501, 523.
15. Nicholas. pp. 70–73.
16. Ibid.
17. Howell. II, pp. 504, 535, 536.
18. H.M.C. *III Report*. Appendix. p. 291.
19. Nicholas. pp. 70–73.
20. Ibid.
21. British Museum. Additional MSS. 15,858. II, folio 114.
22. British Museum. Additional MSS. 15,858. II, folio 115.
23. Calendar Committee Compounding. p. 48.
24. Calendar Committee Compounding. p. 1804; Commons *Journals*. V, pp. 434, 475.
25. Newcastle. p. 97.
26. Newcastle. p. 98; J. W. Stoye, *English Travellers Abroad*. London, 1952. p. 309.
27. Calendar Clarendon State Papers. p. 434.
28. Newcastle. pp. 98, 99.
29. Calendar Committee Compounding. p. 1804.
30. Ibid.
31. *Diary of John Evelyn*, ed. de Beer. Oxford, 1955. II, pp. 554–5.
32. Fonblanque. p. 82.

EPILOGUE

1. Calendar Committee Compounding. p. 1805.
2. Miss Hamilton's Papers.
3. Calendar Committee Compounding. p. 1805.
4. L.C.C. Records. BRA/723/12.
5. Calendar State Papers Domestic, 1651/52. pp. 416, 422, 489, 495.
6. Calendar State Papers Domestic, 1650. p. 436.
7. Middlesex Sessions Rolls. III, pp. 210, 211.
8. Calendar State Papers Domestic, 1652/53. pp. 350, 476.
9. Calendar State Papers Domestic, 1654. p. 274.
10. Middlesex Sessions Rolls. III, p. 237; Calendar State Papers Domestic, 1655/56. p. 96; H.M.C. *IX Report*. Appendix II. p. 123.
11. Middlesex Sessions Rolls. III, p. 233.
12. Calendar State Papers Domestic, 1660/61. p. 73.
13. Calendar State Papers Domestic, 1661/62. p. 236.

REFERENCES

14. Calendar State Papers Domestic, 1664/65. p. 396.
15. Calendar State Papers Domestic, 1661/62. p. 577.
16. Calendar State Papers Domestic, 1660/61. pp. 84, 183.
17. Calendar State Papers Domestic, 1664/65. p. 396.
18. J. Cartwright, *Madame*. London, 1894. p. 215.
19. Calendar State Papers Domestic, 1665/66. p. 121.
20. Calendar State Papers Domestic, 1671/72. p. 84; 1673/75. p. 101; 1675/76. p. 175; 1677/78. p. 289; 1679/80. p. 97.
21. Calendar State Papers Domestic, 1663/64. p. 164; 1671/72. p. 583.
22. A. H. Nethercot, *Sir William D'avenant*. Chicago, 1938. pp. 357, 358, 378.
23. Pepys's *Diary*, 20th October, 1662.
24. Pepys's *Diary*, 29th July, 1667.
25. *Dictionary of National Biography*.
26. P.R.O. L.R.2, 124.
27. *Catalogue of King Charles I's Capital Collection*. Printed by W. Bathoe. London, 1757; P.R.O. L.R.2, 124.
28. Vertue. IV, p. 167, 168, 170.
29. H.M.C. *XV Report*. Appendix, Pt. VII. p. 183.
30. Vertue. I, p. 97; III, p. 99.
31. Vertue. V, p. 86.
32. *Catalogue of the Buckingham House Picture Sale, February 24/25, 1763*. Rijksbureau voor Kunsthistorische en Ikonografische Documentatie, The Hague.
33. Walpole. II, p. 225.
34. Newcastle. p. 97.

INDEX

337   M

INDEX

INDEX

INDEX

170, 195, 222, 227–29, 231,
233, 253, 287;
courtship and marriage, 39, 41–42;
children, 48–49, 68, 73, 76, 79,
86, 91–92, 103, 106, 109,
119–22, 124, 127–28, 134–35,
146, 154, 157, 183, 186, 188,
190, 215–217, 222–23, 227–
31, 243, 247–50, 256, 260–2,
269–70, 272, 274–75, 279–81,
283–84, 286, 290, 294, 303–
309, 312;
sisters-in-law, 43;
papers and letters, 11, 41–42,
46–50, 57–58, 67–68, 78–79,
84–86, 89, 91–92, 99–100,
102–04, 106, 108–09, 111,
119–22, 127–8, 141, 154,
160–1, 192–93, 216, 243, 245,
253, 262–63, 265–66, 268–
71, 283, 292–4, 296–99;
interest in arts, 50–3, 97–98, 121,
125, 137–41, 149–53, 158,
169–74, 178–86, 190, 224,
270, 284, 309, 311;
in Spain, 20–8, 30–1, 65–72,
81–113, 158–61;
in Brussels, 188–90, 297–301;
in Paris, 291–97;
Member of Parliament, 254, 283
commercial activities, 196, 199–
213, 218, 224–25, 265;
finances, 38–39, 156–57, 220–
225, 265, 287, 297, 302–03;
grants and patents, 214–18, 220,
287;
death, 303–04
Porter, George (son of Endymion),
48–50, 68, 79, 86, 92, 106,
109, 127, 227, 230–2, 247–48,
253, 256–57, 260–1, 274–75,
279–81, 294, 305–08
Porter, Giles (grandfather of Endymion), 18–20, 22–24, 26–28,
129
wife and children of, 18–19
Porter, Giles (brother of Endymion),
19, 233, 286

Porter, James (son of Endymion),
227, 229, 286, 307, 309
Porter, Marie (daughter of Endymion), 227, 229, 270, 283–84
Porter, Nicholas (uncle of Endymion), 17–20, 31, 39
Porter, Olive (wife of Endymion) and
relatives, 19, 26, 41–44, 46–
50, 57, 67–68, 72–73, 76, 78,
84–86, 89, 98–100, 102–04,
106, 108–09, 111, 119–24,
127–28, 133, 141, 146, 154,
156–57, 159–61, 166, 171–72,
176, 186, 211–12, 218–19,
220, 222–24, 226–27, 229,
233–37, 242–45, 248, 250,
252–53, 269–71, 274–75,
282–84, 286–88, 290, 292,
295, 297, 300, 302–03, 305–
308, 311–12
Porter, Philip (son of Endymion),
227–30, 286, 305–06
Porter, Richard, 17
Charity established by, 17, 19
Porter, Captain Thomas (brother of
Endymion), 19–20, 24, 66–68,
147, 156, 158, 160, 189, 217,
232, 236
Porter, Thomas (son of Endymion),
227, 229, 231, 270, 286, 306–
307, 308–09
Porter, Sir William, 17
Porter de Figueroy, Luis, 18–19
Portsmouth, 146–47, 159, 279
Pym, John, 246, 255–60, 267–69,
274

Rainsborough, Captain, 232
Raleigh, Carew, 37
Raleigh, Sir Walter, 37
Raphael Cartoons, 98, 311
Richelieu, Cardinal, 188, 191, 193
Roe, Sir Thomas, 149, 176–78,
181–82, 189
Roman Catholic Church and Pope,
19, 25–26, 60–3, 66, 69, 71,
81, 87–88, 93–95, 104, 107–

342

INDEX